Advance Praise for
The Chicken Who Saved Us:
The Remarkable Story of Andrew and Frightful

"Emotions are raw and the anxiety is palpable, yet this remarkable story is told with such wit and grace, punctuated by her son, Andrew's hilariously quirky commentary that it makes it impossible to put down. As a physician, I rarely have the opportunity to see the toll that complex medical challenges take on individuals and on relationships. Kristin provides a beautiful reminder of the strength gathered from unique animal companions and tender mercies offered by human friends and strangers alike."
~ Troy R. Torgerson, MD PhD, Pediatric Immunology/ Rheumatology, University of Washington and Seattle Children's Hospital

"A testament to the power of love and the power of family, Adams' provocative tale of her son's medical journey is told with grace, humor and most of all, compassion. She captivates and endears us with witty banter between her autistic son and backyard chicken. But her true gift is in her ability to have faith in the unseen, while transforming the medical world into a place where magic occurs."
~ Corbin Lewars, Author of *Creating a Life*

"A great lesson that our animals teach: To accept others and ourselves right where we are. Readers will be captivated by this tender and brave story of a young autistic boy whose only friend is a chicken named Frightful. Their achingly honest conversations will invite you into their world where superheroes come alive and miracles happen. It is not always dogs, cats, or horses that can touch and enrich the human soul. A backyard chicken can do it, too."
~ Christi Dudzik, MC, LMHC Owner, Healing Paws Inc., Animal Assisted Therapy

T0163778

"If you've ever received news that made you question how you'd endure, or spent days pacing the halls of a hospital, you will want to read Kristin Adams' *The Chicken Who Saved Us*. Adams' story shows us that love can triumph over any curve ball life hurls our way."
~ **Theo Pauline Nestor,** Author of *Writing Is My Drink: A Writer's Story of Finding her Voice (And a Guide to How You Can Too).*

"An honest, raw, and candid look at a family's resilience in a time when there seemed to be no answers. Adams cleverly brings us inside her world as she enlists the aid of a chicken to help her navigate the medical system on her son's behalf. This is a beacon of hope for readers who find themselves in some of life's most difficult situations."
~ **Andrea Duffield MBA MA CCC-SLP B.Sc.Ed,** President, MOSAIC Rehabilitation, Inc.

"I wish every parent could read this book, and not just parents of children with communication and behavioral differences. Having worked with children with autism and other developmental conditions, I often see parents having to come to terms with the fact that the 'playbook' of raising a child may be completely different than what they had expected. Letting go of how you thought it would play out can be extremely challenging for a parent, but ultimately accepting and embracing the path, wherever it may lead, can sometimes be the critical step towards that happiness. "
~ **Gary Stobbe, MD**, Clinical Associate Professor, University of Washington Director, Adult Transition Program, Seattle Children's Autism Center

"This quietly urgent and utterly human telling of a story about faith, family, and a beloved pet chicken named Frightful, keeps us rooting for Andrew, compelling us to turn the pages to find the ending we all hope for and rejoice at the power that resides in even the most fragile among us. "
~ **Donna Miscolta**, Author *Hola and Goodbye: Una familia in stories*

THE CHICKEN WHO SAVED US

THE REMARKABLE STORY OF ANDREW AND FRIGHTFUL

KRISTIN JARVIS ADAMS

Behler™
PUBLICATIONS
USA

Behler Publications

The Chicken Who Saved Us – The Remarkable Story of Andrew and
Frightful
A Behler Publications Book

Copyright © 2017 by Kristin Jarvis Adams
Cover design by Yvonne Parks - www.pearcreative.ca
Front cover photography by Heidi King

Some names have been changed to protect their privacy.

Library of Congress Cataloging-in-Publication Data

Names: Adams, Kristin Jarvis, author.
Title: The chicken who saved us : the remarkable story of Andrew and
   Frightful / by Kristin Jarvis Adams.
Description: [Burlington, Iowa] : Behler Publications, [2017]
Identifiers: LCCN 2016041080 (print) | LCCN 2016044156 (ebook) | ISBN
   9781941887004 (paperback) | ISBN 9781941887011 (e-book)
Subjects: LCSH: Autistic children--Washington (State)--Seattle--Biography. |
   Chickens--Washington (State)--Seattle. | Human-animal
   relationships--Washington (State)--Seattle. | Trisomy--Patients--United
   States--Biography. | Chronic pain--United States--Case studies. | Adams,
   Kristin Jarvis. | Adams, Kristin Jarvis--Family. | Mothers of autistic
   children--Washington (State)--Seattle--Biography. | Mothers and
   sons--Washington (State)--Seattle. | BISAC: BIOGRAPHY & AUTOBIOGRAPHY /
   Personal Memoirs. | FAMILY & RELATIONSHIPS / Children with Special Needs.
Classification: LCC RJ506.A9 A3345 2017 (print) | LCC RJ506.A9 (ebook) | DDC
   616.85/8820092 [B] --dc23
LC record available at https://lccn.loc.gov/2016041080

FIRST PRINTING

ISBN 13: 9781941887004
e-book ISBN 9781941887011

Published by Behler Publications, LLC, USA
www.behlerpublications.com

Manufactured in the United States of America

For my three heroes,
Jon, Andrew and Hannah

An animal's eyes have the power
to speak a great language.
-Martin Buber

A Note From The Author

The biggest challenge while writing this memoir was to choose the right combination of events to bring my story to life. Although it was sometimes difficult to remember the details of each moment in the midst of traumatic situations, what you hold in your hands is the story as I experienced it.

All conversations quoted here occurred, though sometimes have been combined or moved in time. And yes, I witnessed a chicken 'speak' to my son and did my best to translate her words.

For reasons of privacy and respect, the names and details of a few minor characters have been changed. Medical information shared in the book is correct to the best of my knowledge and understanding. And finally, I have done my best to show my deep respect for each character in the book, especially my son and daughter who, in my opinion, are the real heroes of the story.

~ Kristin Jarvis Adams

Table of Contents

Foreword

There is so much to ponder in this beautiful story of human challenge and triumph, so much that is real, honest, and moving. It should be on the bookshelf of every physician that cares for children with serious health problems and every parent facing the unknowns of raising a child with such issues.

The Chicken Who Saved Us is the remarkable story of a family struggling through the challenges of life threatening and chronic illness with wonderful strength, humor, compassion and honesty. In these pages, you will meet Andrew, a young man with autism and a rare genetic disorder so mysterious that other similar cases haven't been reported. You will meet his best friend Frightful, and fall in love with his sister Hannah, who saves his life by donating her own bone marrow.

This amazing story of faith — the kind of faith full of human doubt, fear, and hope — helps us all navigate through the terrors of dealing with serious illness. It is the story of a woman who shares her innermost thoughts, dreams, fantasies, frustrations, and failings in such an honest and real way that I was moved to tears, or was left shouting out loud with laughter.

I have been a pediatrician for forty-eight years and thought I understood it all. I've sat in conferences giving terrible news to shocked and exhausted families. I've seen moms and dads cry as I gave them news that their child had autism, or was brain injured at birth, or had a rare genetic disease that we knew little about and had no treatment. I thought I could empathize. I thought I could imagine how they felt, how they might cope, how they would find the strength to endure. But until reading about this incredible family and the amazing people who walked alongside them, I don't think I truly understood what their lives were really like.

I think about Kristin's description of the mothers in neighboring rooms with their hair askew, in rumpled sweats and no makeup, with lost and exhausted looks on their faces—a scene I've witnessed numerous times, but never really saw. I think about watching a family leave the ICU after the passing of their child, not fully seeing how it impacted all the other nearby families. I think about the touching scene of the priest from Hannah's school blessing the IV bag full of her bone marrow before it was infused into Andrew's frail body before blessing the stuffed chicken that was Andrew's stand-in for his best friend, a chicken named Frightful.

Thank you, Kristin Jarvis Adams, for sharing your heart with us, your readers. I, for one, have gained so much from being on this journey with you.

Charles Cowan, MD
Emeritus Clinical Professor, Department of Pediatrics
UW School of Medicine
Emeritus Medical Director
Seattle Children's Autism Center

Prologue

Sue walked into a scene right out of a nightmare. Vomit covered the walls, soaked the bed, and was dripping onto the floor as fast as the IV pump could push formula through the feeding tube. I was shouting, Andrew was gagging, and the dogs were fighting in the hallway.

"Please stay down, Andrew!" I begged, pushing my sixteen-year-old son back onto the bed. Having thrown up with such force, the bottom end of the feeding tube had come out of his stomach and now hung from his mouth. The other end was still threaded through his nose and taped to his face where it attached to the pump. I detached that end from the pump and went about trying to peel the tape off his face. He jerked, grabbing for my hand.

"Please," I asked softly this time, tucking him in between two dry towels and aiming the fan directly at his hot skin. He had taken all his clothes off in an attempt to get cool—an escape from the fever that burned in him day and night. His usual lean body had become anorexic, bony, and dry, and his skin sagged on wasting muscles.

Sue stood in the corner while I picked at the tape again.

Andrew exploded off the bed. "I have to get up now! I'm gonna be sick!"

Sue reached for him and led him to the bathroom where he lay on the cold tile, naked. Deep guttural moans ricocheted off the bathroom walls, ripping me to my core. We'd been doing this for months, for years actually, and it was only getting worse. I wondered how much a person could take before they said, "That's it, I quit!"

Andrew screamed again and I heard a splash on the tile.

Sue waved an arm in my direction. "I can handle this. I want you to leave, take the dogs for a walk, and don't come back for a while."

I obeyed without protest, barreling out the door with two jacked up dogs at my heels. I would get as far from the house as I could, far enough away that even if I had bionic ears, there would be no way I could hear the sounds of pain coming from my home. I clipped a leash to each dog and took off at a dead run, down the block and to the next, until I couldn't breathe and my own pain felt like ecstasy.

An hour later I came back, tear-streaked and sweaty, ready to walk back into my life. I didn't know what to expect when I opened the door, but I didn't expect this.

Sue was sitting quietly on a low-slung IKEA chair next to Andrew, the rumble of laundry in the next room was music to my fried brain. Andrew was passed out on the downstairs playroom floor on a makeshift bed. Figuring it was the only place in the house cool enough to survive the July heat, Jon and I had fashioned a bed out of sofa cushions and sleeping bags, topped with an old foam bunk-bed mattress, which we shoved next to a north-facing window. I noticed Andrew's feeding tube had been removed and his face was washed. Sue was praying, or what I took to be praying, because her eyes were closed and her lips moved as if she were having a secret conversation. She told me once she prayed for Andrew, prayed for mercy, grace, and healing for this boy she'd grown to love. Conversing with God wasn't new to her, but this level of misery was, and it pained her in a way that broke her heart.

Andrew stirred and opened one eye.

"Should we read a new book now, Andrew?" Sue asked, leaning forward to pull a thin cotton blanket over his legs.

Andrew didn't respond, but she could see his eyes were open now, unblinking, staring out the window. She sat quietly, and waited.

The day Sue arrived as our respite care provider, Andrew's pain had been so intense that he could barely speak above a whisper. When she asked what he liked to do, he'd replied, "I like hero stories."

So she began to tell him made-up stories using characters from old Judy Blume books she found in Andrew's closet. But her stories weren't regular stories. These stories included superheroes Andrew had fashioned in his own mind. These stories transported him to an imaginary world where he could escape the nightmare that had become his life. And Sue was the one who took him there, to the only place he felt safe.

After a moment, Andrew raised a quivering hand in which he clutched a mini SEGA action figure named Shadow.

"Okay. Let's put Shadow in this book instead," Sue said.

She settled back into her chair and opened Judy Blume's *Super Fudge*, to the place where Fudge was teaching his mynah bird, Uncle Feather, to talk.

"This reminds me a little of you and Frightful, right, Andrew?" she asked.

Andrew nodded, then sighed and kicked the blanket off his legs. Moments later he began the slow grind of pedaling his feet up and down the mattress against the pain.

Sue placed a hand across his thin, wiry legs. "Be still, my friend. What are Shadow and Fudge doing? Describe it to me."

Andrew remained still, but made no effort to talk. Outside, a brood of hens scratched at Jon's newly planted flowerbeds, sending showers of fresh mulch across the walkway. A small, bronze and black colored hen hopped up on a broken flowerpot that had been pushed against the window.

"Tick. Tick."

I am here.

Andrew groaned and rubbed at his chapped and swollen face. At sixteen, he was tall—nearly five foot ten—but he weighed little more than one hundred pounds. For months, sudden fevers, pain, and nausea had become constant companions that we battled with a combination of anti-emetics, narcotics, Advil, and Tylenol. During the night, another fever had fingered its way up his body, leaving his skin dry and splotchy and bathing his cheeks and lips in a deep crimson. Even his usual shimmery red hair seemed faded and dull, plastered to his face in salty clumps.

"Tick. Tick. Tap."

Look at me.

Frightful, the bronze-colored hen, pressed her body next to the window and turned her head to the side, regarding Andrew with one yellow raptor-eye. Although she was a petite hen, she queened over the others, puffing her feathers to appear larger, while throwing back her head in a loud *squawk!* if any hen dared to challenge her. She reminded me of the red-tailed hawks we frequently saw circling the tops of the evergreens in our yard, and she had an attitude to match. A low rumble came from Frightful's chest as she rocked from foot to foot before mashing her chest to the windowpane.

"Tap-tap-tap...KACK!!"

Look at me...NOW!

Andrew turned to face the window. With a slender white finger, he circled the chicken's gold, caramel, and black feathers, tracing the areas where the little hen had left a trail of chicken snot in her attempt to get his attention. He pressed the dirty pane with the pad of his pointer finger, saying, "I hear you, Frightful."

The chicken backed off, shook violently, and settled her feathers back into place. She made an elaborate show of easing her body down on top of the broken flower pot where she perched, while never breaking eye contact with her best friend.

"I'm here, Frightful," Andrew repeated again before falling back into sleep.

While Sue read her newly formed story starring Fudge and Shadow, I crept down the hallway into Jon's office and crawled under the desk. A litany of horrors tackled me as I thought about what was happening to our lives. Would we survive? How many blows could a person take before they curled up and died? I wondered. Although Sue came for a few hours each day to provide me respite, the truth was I was almost always too scared to leave the house. Fear had pinned me to the floor.

Sue's gentle voice broke into my thoughts.

"I'm leaving now, Andrew. I'll see you in the morning. Think about what we should read next. Maybe some Harry Potter?"

I listened as she gathered her things, dreading the hours I would be alone with Andrew until Jon came home from work. When I heard her footsteps in the hallway, I ventured out of my cave only to knock my head on the corner of Jon's desk. I waited for her to leave before taking her spot in the chair next to Andrew, where I stared at my son for a long time, feeling terrified and helpless. Flipping through a stack of books on the windowsill, I wondered how Sue did it. What magic did she have that drew Andrew back from wherever he was? She even seemed to take away his pain, or at least make him forget about it for a little while.

I thought about all the specialists Jon and I had taken him to over the years, and still we had no answers. Our son was desperately ill. Besides Sue, his only friend on this earth was a chicken named Frightful. As I sat there for what felt like eternity, Frightful continued her flowerpot vigil. She occasionally flicked a beady bird-eye in my direction as if to say, "*DO something!*"

Crawling onto the floor, I squeezed next to Andrew's frail body on the little twin bed — my desperate attempt to protect him from the darkness creeping into the room. He was dead still, his breath barely a whisper on my bare arm. A sudden wave of anxiety assaulted me, penetrating deep into my bones, making me feel as if my whole body was freezing over. I squeezed Andrew hard in terror.

Frightful shrieked and flew at the window.

"Kuh-kuh-kuh-kuh-KACK!!"

Do SOMETHING!!

Startled, I reached for the phone in my pocket and dialed Jon at work. "You have to come home. NOW!"

Chapter 1

My son was kicked out of preschool because he kicked a visiting clown in the balls. His teacher called me at work and suggested we find another school that would better suit his needs. It would have been really funny except for the fact that this wasn't the first time we'd been asked to find a more suitable place for our son.

"He's non-compliant," his teacher said over the phone after sharing all the gory details about my child taking down a clown with one swift kick. "Andrew won't sit in circle-time with the other students, and he's always wandering around the room. He covers his ears when I try to talk to him and...well, I just can't have that."

"What do you expect a three-year-old boy to do? Maybe he doesn't like clowns?" I asked. I was secretly impressed with Andrew—I hated clowns, too.

I heard an exaggerated exhale on the other end of the line. "You need to get him right now. And by the way, I think he might be coming down with something."

At the time, I was working as an art director in a rapidly exploding dot.com company in downtown Seattle. It was fast-paced and I loved it, although I was putting in long hours each week. Without asking to leave, I waved my keys at my boss and skipped down the stairs, hoping to beat the rush hour traffic across Lake Washington. When I arrived at the school, Andrew stood rigid in the foyer with his coat zipped and his backpack at his feet. He clutched his plastic dinosaur, T-Rex, to his chest like he expected someone to wrestle him for it.

His teacher waited for me to be within earshot before saying, "Here's your balloon, Andrew. It's a puppy."

She handed him a pale blue twisty balloon of a wiener dog. Andrew dropped it on the floor and tore across the parking lot to our van. I said a curt goodbye and followed him, wanting to get out of there just as badly as he did. When I strapped him in the car seat, I noticed his lip had a tiny blister on it that wasn't there in the morning.

"Does it hurt?" I asked.

He shook his head.

During the twenty-minute drive home, I studied Andrew in the rearview mirror. He was staring out the window, wide-eyed and unblinking, while rubbing a thumb across the bumpy hide of the plastic dinosaur. I noticed his usual shimmery red hair was stuck in sweaty points around the edge of his face and that his cheeks had taken on a deep shade of pink. Maybe he *was* getting sick? Was that why he was so upset by the clown? I couldn't figure him out. He was so different from his baby sister Hannah, who at three months was already cooing and babbling with us like she had too many things to say and not enough time to say them. Andrew wasn't talking yet. But Jon and I had become so adept at reading his body language and gestures that it didn't seem to be a problem.

"Sorry about the clown, buddy," I said into the rearview mirror. "We don't have to go back."

Andrew raised T-Rex up to his face and pecked its oversized head at the back of my seat. I smiled back, knowing both he and T-Rex agreed.

We drove the rest of the way in silence while I thought about the difference between my job as a designer and my job as a mother. Mothering required just as much creative energy as my art director position, but ten times as much emotional energy. Being a mom meant that nothing was ever perfect, nothing was ever complete. There were no rewards for a job well done, no kudos wrapped up in a fat paycheck from a happy client. No, this new job of mine was most positively imperfect.

So I tried to be the perfect parent, enrolling Andrew in the Mommy & Me socialization classes that were popular in the mid-nineties: Baby Gymboree, KinderMusic, and special readings at the library. Unfortunately for me, the giant colorful parachute in the gym terrified him, the music hurt his ears, and although he loved stories, the library was too crowded. Jon and I were living in the era of Beanie Babies, Playmobil, Pokemon, and Barney the Dinosaur. A time when our home was a rubble of Legos and Little Tykes construction equipment, yet all Andrew wanted was a velveteen bear named Ben, and a green plastic T-Rex dinosaur.

During this time I made frequent trips to the pediatrician, where my growing list of questions was never quite answered. Questions like: Is it normal for babies to get sick all the time? Shouldn't he be walking by now? Why doesn't he talk yet? He won't look at me. Am I doing something wrong? Through all this, I became a germophobe, one of those psycho overprotective mothers who never let their children out of their sight without a packet of antibacterial wipes. I had become the kind of parent I loathed. I wondered, *was that person still me?*

Turning up the hill towards our home on the east side of Seattle, more memories with Andrew passed through my mind. There were sweet memories of lazy summer afternoons at Puget Sound, dragging long ropes of kelp across the sand, shrieks of laughter and gap-toothed smiles from a three-year-old scrambling down the beach after gulls, and Sunday drives to the mountains just to stomp our feet in the snow.

I also remembered Andrew in the pediatrician's office — fevered, frustrated, and angry. I pictured the doctor moving his stiff limbs one by one, like a doll. I listened as he chattered, cooed, and tickled Andrew. I watched as Andrew stared, unblinking at a fixed object across the room. Through all this, a seed of doubt was planted in the back of my mind. I wondered if I had done something wrong.

"Did you know we were asked to find another preschool?" I told the pediatrician one afternoon during a well-baby check.

"I'm really sorry," he said with a genuine look of concern.

Tears pricked at the back of my eyes. He was a kind man and had always been honest when answering my questions, even when he was just as puzzled as I was.

"You're doing a great job, you know. But I think it's clear we both have some questions."

His comment made me uneasy. After three years of questioning, I wasn't sure I wanted the answers anymore. It's absurd, I know, but I'd found something comforting, something reassuring even, in remaining naive.

In the end, the pediatrician scribbled a name and phone number on a slip of paper. "I'd like Andrew to visit this neurologist. I think he can provide some answers."

That night, I asked Jon what he thought of the doctor's observations—his concerns about Andrew's lack of responsiveness, stiff joints, and delayed speech. He shrugged and reached out to draw me in an embrace while reminding me that Andrew was only three.

"And don't forget," he said. "Andrew *does* smile and laugh, and he *does* talk to us—just not with words yet."

Two months later, I walked into the neurologist's office, took one look at him, and considered backing out the door. He was a short, rectangular man with thick, heavy-lidded eyes that made him look like he hadn't slept in years, and his oversized ears refused to be hidden by an overgrown haircut. His mouth had forgotten how to smile, and by the expression on his face, it was clear he was painfully bored with his job.

He motioned for us to sit, so I placed Andrew on the exam table and waited. He said nothing to me, nor did he engage with

Andrew, yet I noticed he was keenly aware of the way my son sat on the examination table—straight backed, with arms and legs rigidly poking out in front of him.

The neurologist paced the room while tapping on his watch face. Every so often he would stop, glance at the time, then pace again. I could only imagine what Andrew was thinking. Did he sense the doctor's disinterest like I did?

"Aren't you going to examine him?" I asked after we'd been sitting there for fifteen minutes.

He responded by asking me a few questions about my health history, my pregnancy, and the delivery while continuing to watch Andrew. During the hour-long appointment, he never directly touched him, and at no time did Andrew look at or acknowledge the doctor's presence.

"Ok. We're finished now," he said at the end of our allotted time.

"But what do you think?" I asked, desperate for a quick and easy answer.

He was halfway out the door before he said, "I'll have my secretary send you my notes in a few weeks."

I was shocked, and sure he had made all sorts of wrongful assumptions about my lack of parenting skills. Without a word, I pulled T-Rex from my purse and tucked him under Andrew's arm before snuggling him to my hip and walking through the door.

That neurologist visit was weeks ago, and now, here I was driving home in the middle of the day after my son had been kicked out of preschool—the last in a series of concerning things that I couldn't explain or fix. I wondered if maybe I *was* doing a terrible job at this mothering thing.

As I pulled in the driveway, I glanced back at Andrew in his car seat. He waved T-Rex at me this time, and I smiled. "Hey Andrew! Clowns suck, don't they?" I said.

His eyes widened and he let out a giggle before dropping T-Rex to the floor.

Chapter 2

After the clown incident, Jon and I decided to keep Andrew home for a while. Between two grandmothers and a neighbor, we had four days a week covered and I was able to convince my boss that I could work from home on the fifth day.

We also applied for, and joined, a twenty-six week parenting class for 'spirited children' at the University of Washington. I figured it would teach us everything we needed to know about raising a kid like Andrew. I was in serious need of an ego boost after becoming keenly aware of how different Andrew was from his peers. All the young mothers I knew used T. Berry Brazelton's book, *Touchpoints,* as a biblical reference on child rearing. I devoured it and quickly realized we had failed all of the touch points.

On the first day of class we were separated into two groups: Parent Training and Child Play. Andrew was lured into a room with a colorful mat full of non-noisemaking toys, six kids, and a bowl of goldfish crackers. Jon and I were led to a small conference room with six pairs of curious, eager, and uncomfortable parents. I sat next to another young mom with a yellow pad and pen in my lap, ready to absorb and master the information that would solve all my problems. Jon was only marginally on board with my harebrained idea, so when he sat next to another irritated dad, they quickly struck up a conversation on the likelihood of the Seattle Mariners making it to the World Series.

"Listen to what your child is saying," the instructor said as she began the first class.

The mother next to me rolled her eyes and slumped down into her chair. "Yeah, but he doesn't talk, so that won't do me much good."

I snorted, agreeing with her. Andrew didn't talk either. I was doing my best to be the perfect mom, but the truth was, I was terrified and more than a little frustrated. There were so many things I didn't understand. When I asked him to look me in the eye, he would turn red in the face and look away. When I wanted to hold his hand, he'd twist his fingers and slide out from my embrace. When I encouraged him to join other kids in play, he buried his head underneath my jacket, or simply walked away. I wanted him to be normal. I wanted him to fit in, and I was sure I was doing something wrong.

As the weeks progressed, I learned about the other preschoolers in our parenting class. One was a musician, his little hands tapping out a sophisticated rhythm on upturned pans from the kitchen set. His parents said he played at their piano every day, but they didn't know why. Another boy wore a construction paper hat and carried a plastic airplane above his head. He ran around the room flapping his free hand so he could fly. His parents said his grandpa was a pilot. My son wore a cape every day. I never thought much about it.

One morning, halfway through our twenty-six-week class, Andrew and I walked to the mailbox while six-month-old Hannah napped. Andrew trotted ahead of me with his superhero cape billowing behind him while towing a red plastic wagon filled with his worldly treasures. On top of the jumble of treasures lay Ben, a little blue bear with embroidered eyes, pink velveteen cheeks, and a felt smiley-faced mouth. He was loved flat. Flat from being laid on, chewed on, rubbed, and hugged until his fabric frayed and the stuffing leaked out. Ben's shell went with us everywhere, to all the scary places like the grocery store, the park, and the pediatrician's office. Under Ben was T-Rex, a pirate named Joe, a giant sixteen-piece dinosaur puzzle, and a little red plastic lawn mower, for which I had a passing enmity.

The weekend before, after a tug-of-war that ended in tears and shrieks of frustration, I had given up and allowed Andrew to bring the mower to my parent's house for lunch. My mother had thought his idea brilliant, and had set it a place at the table. When we left, she invited the lawn mower to dine again. All hail Mom.

When we reached the mailbox, I playfully scooped Andrew under my right arm, sausage-style. "You do it like this," I said, showing him how to pull the mail out and slide it into his arms.

He clenched his hands into a ball and screwed his eyes shut against my lighthearted play. Pieces of junk mail and a single fat envelope fell to the ground, scattering at our feet. I saw the letter was from the neurologist, and my heart lurched. I wasn't sure I wanted to read it just yet, so I stuffed it in the wagon and we walked back home.

Hannah was still napping an hour later when I pulled a batch of cookies from the oven. I spied T-Rex's head grazing the edge of the kitchen counter, his plastic neck bouncing awkwardly towards the sink. T-Rex stopped to gaze at chocolate chip cookies cooling on a rack—a painted lizard-eye studying the good eats.

"Wanna cookie?" I asked Andrew.

T-Rex nodded. I noticed he was missing the rest of his body—scaly plastic legs, a distended belly and an oversized tail. I suspected it was buried in a sea of toys at the far side of the room.

I lifted a warm cookie with a spatula. "How about this one?"

Andrew nodded, dropping the lizard's head and reaching his hands out in a *yes please*.

"You like it?" I asked as he bit into the warm cookie.

Andrew trotted out the front door without uttering a word. When Hannah and I caught up with him later, he was in the front yard picking the neighbor's raspberries that draped over our side of the fence. I sat Hannah down in my lap and watched him shove berries in his mouth, one after the other, without pausing to chew. For some reason, I couldn't shake the feeling of anxiety that always plagued me, even on relatively calm days like today.

Andrew started to cough.

"That's enough berries, Andrew," I said as he rammed two more into his mouth.

As I led him away from the fence, he exploded in a fit of anger, shoving me with his red-stained hands before beginning to howl. I stood in my front yard feeling helpless, having no way of knowing what really set him off. I wanted to tell him that everything was okay, and that I understood. But I didn't, not really. I didn't know why I couldn't make him happy, and I didn't know why he kept getting sick.

Out of desperation and exhaustion, I called my friend Diana. Diana was a speech pathologist and had been noticing his lack of speech, although she never directly said anything to me. Instead, I felt her eyes on him every time we were together.

"He's just so angry," I admitted to her after witnessing Andrew chuck his lunch off the side of his high chair for the third time. "I don't know what's wrong. Would you please come over?"

When I opened the door twenty minutes later, I was greeted by her infectious grin. "I have an idea," she said, walking straight into my kitchen.

Andrew was bellowing in his high chair, covered in soggy Cheerios. T-Rex lay on the floor in a sticky milk-bath.

"You have any peanut butter?" she asked absently.

I pointed to the bread drawer. Diana came back with a jar of creamy Jif and stood in front of Andrew. He wailed in protest just as she reached into his mouth with a finger full of peanut butter. The crying stopped. Eyes wide in shock, he snorted, then tried pushing the sticky paste from the roof of his mouth with his tongue.

"Laahh, lah, maah ma, paah pa." Diana exaggerated the sounds just inches from his face. He frowned, looking from Diana, to me, and back again. Intrigued, he poked a wet finger at Diana's mouth. Diana ran to my freezer and foraged for another treat.

She held up popsicles for each of them. "Andrew! Do you like grape?"

Andrew took the popsicle and they both began again. Diana twirled the cold popsicle inside her mouth.

"Mmm...mmm. Isn't this pop yummy?"

Andrew stared hard at Diana's mouth as she formed the words.

"Mmmm...BOP," he said around the cold popsicle and peanut-buttery goo.

"YES!!! Pop!" Diana jumped up, shouting.

I was flabbergasted. I covered my mouth as a huge silly grin spread across my face. Scooping Andrew out of the high chair, I smothered his face in sloppy kisses while dancing around my kitchen island.

"Holy cow! You're brilliant!!" I squealed to both my friend and son.

I could tell by the way his face lit up, with a spark in his eye, that something fundamental had connected in his mind. He simply got it. For the first time, he realized what to do with his tongue, and now an entirely new world was open to him.

That evening when Jon came home from work, Hannah and I were watching Andrew put together his dinosaur puzzle on the playroom floor.

Jon joined us, sliding Andrew onto his lap.

"Da!" Andrew said while casually pointing a finger at Jon.

Jon's eyes widened, "That's right, Andrew! I'm Dad!" He caught my huge smile from across the room. *Oh my God, is this real?* he mouthed.

I nodded and smiled back, thinking how long we had waited for just this moment. Three and a half years of worry evaporated as I sat there with my husband and our two kids. I could do this. Life had thrown us a few curve balls, but nothing we couldn't handle.

Before bed, I emptied Andrew's wagon in search of Pirate Joe. The forgotten letter from the neurologist fell onto the floor, bringing back a strange feeling of foreboding. Unfolding the thick pages with something akin to dread, I read these words: *dyspraxia, tactile hypersensitivity, high muscle tone, rigidity, no eye contact. Most likely autistic.*

I reread the letter, word for word, as I allowed the truth to sink in. Waves of shock, fear, grief, disappointment, and even something like relief washed over me in a span of only a few minutes. At that time, what I knew about autism was Dustin Hoffman's portrayal of an autistic savant in the movie *Rain Man*. My son was not Rain Man. But he was mine, and he did seem to think he had superpowers. After all, he could talk to dinosaurs and leap major milestones in a single day.

Chapter 3

Two Septembers later, I sat idling in my red Toyota minivan in the empty grade school parking lot. No one knew I was inside, staring at a single sheet of paper that would define my son's academic life. For eighteen months, I had been wrestling with, and finally accepting, the idea that Andrew needed to be in a special education program in order to learn. I scanned the paper for the label the neurologist had attached to my son: Asperger Syndrome/High Functioning Autism. An inky blue diagnostic code scrawled across the top of the form allowed the public school system to access federal funding for their special education department.

Tucking the paper in my purse, I switched off the car, knowing that I would have to play their game, even if I didn't like it. I pulled down the car visor and caught a glimpse of my pale and anxious reflection. It immediately brought to mind my mother's familiar words: "Put a smile on your face, a sparkle in your eyes, and for goodness sake, put on some lipstick. You look washed out."

I grimaced at the thought and went rummaging through the bottom of my purse in search of something to make me appear more presentable. I wound my hair into a knot, strangling it with a rubber band, then quickly smeared a layer of coral lip gloss onto my pale lips.

"Are you ready?" I spoke into the rear view mirror to two-year-old Hannah.

Hannah kicked the back of my seat with a repetitive *tap, tap, tap,* and a wet thumb grazed her lips before being plugged back into her mouth. I dropped my keys and crawled into the back, huddling next to her car seat. She turned to me, eyeball to eyeball, her nose smashed to mine.

"Good Mommy," she said, planting wet gooey kisses on my cheeks.

I unhooked the straps and drew her onto my lap, stroking her fine blond hair, squeezing her soft body to mine—something Andrew would never allow. Minutes later, Hannah and I were walking together across the parking lot to her brother's new school, her ladybug rubber boots splatting in the puddles along the sidewalk.

"Like this, Mommy!" Hannah hollered, stomping both feet into the deepest puddle.

A spray of mud soaked the side of my jeans and dripped down the sleeve of my coat. Hannah's pleased grin reached up to me as I decided whether or not to be angry.

"Do it!" she urged, pulling at my arm.

I stomped in the puddle. A split second later, we were both covered in splotches of mud. A loud squeal of delight ripped through the air as Hannah broke free and ran down the sidewalk. I reached her as she stopped in front of the office.

The door to the administration office had a construction paper sign on it that read: Welcome New Kindergarteners! School would not begin for two weeks yet, but the office staff was busy. The secretary at the front desk greeted me with an overly sweet smile, then a look of concern as she saw the streaks of mud on our faces. I dropped the neurologist's letter in to her overflowing in-box, leaving before she could ask any questions.

The first day of school set the standard for what would quickly become our daily routine. Andrew began his negotiations the moment he woke:

What's for breakfast?

Cheerios.

Where's T-Rex?
In bed where you left him.
Where's Ben?
Same place.
Which pair of pants am I gonna wear?
Your dinosaur pants.

It was always the dinosaur pants with the label cut out. And they were always on backwards. Andrew's teacher wanted him to sit in a reading circle, knees touching the other students, hands folded in his lap. But that was never going to happen; we had learned that in preschool. Each morning Andrew moved his two-foot square carpet to the far side of the room, sat on it cross-legged with T-Rex next to him — but not touching.

Me? I liked school. A lot. I liked having those few precious hours free from the rigid confines of Andrew's world. And I was just getting into the swing of running my own part-time design business with a steady clientele. After lunch, when the school bus rumbled up the street, I would anxiously wait for a red-haired boy to scramble up the steps and burst through the door. I dreamed of Andrew telling me he had made a new friend and asking me if he could invite the friend to play. But it never happened. It was Hannah who filled in that gap without ever meaning to. She was his one-man fan club.

One rainy November afternoon, as I was proofing brochure copy for a client, I caught sight of Hannah with her nose pressed to the living room window — her breath leaving fog circles on the glass. She raced to the door after spotting the school bus deposit Andrew down the street.

"Hellooo, brother!" she squealed while yanking open the door.

Andrew quickly handed her a green balloon, saying, "Balloons scratch my brain."

A sudden memory of my three-year-old dropping a twisty balloon of a wiener dog and tearing across a parking lot came to mind. Now, three years later, I figured out why he kicked the clown at preschool.

Pulling off his backpack, Hannah took Andrew by the arm and led him to the kitchen where I was preparing lunch.

"It's macaroni and cheeeeeeese and orange carrots and applesauce and gummy bears," she announced, pulling a hand from her pocket to show us both the gummies she had stored in there. Her continued babbling and silliness told me she was ready for a nap as soon as I could get her to finish lunch.

While the kids sat happily in front of their gourmet lunch, one of my clients called in a panic. They begged me to edit some artwork and email a revised draft to them in forty-five minutes for a newly scheduled conference call. I agreed to do it, knowing full well I would need every one of those minutes to complete the work. Part of that time would be spent battling the dial-up modem that took forever to transfer complicated graphic files.

I added goldfish crackers to both kids' plates, turned Barney on the TV, and ran upstairs to the studio. Within minutes, I heard two sets of feet bounding up the stairs and they both burst into the room.

"I want to play with the Play-Doh, Mama," Hannah said, reaching into the bottom drawer of my file cabinet. I watched as Andrew gathered colored pencils, markers, and paper I kept in my office for such occasions, then quarantined them to a table at the back of the room with their art supplies. Five minutes later, a fight broke out. A quick glance at the clock showed I had less than thirty minutes left.

Negotiations went poorly, so I quickly resorted to bribery. With little hands full of M&M's, the dispute was settled. Eventually, I heard kind voices in the background and an offering to share. The TV clicked on in my bedroom down the hall and the sound of cartoons floated into the studio. All was well.

With only three minutes left, I entrusted my file to the static-y screech of the modem cramming my artwork into small byte-sized pieces. Sensing that the room was too quiet, I got up to check on the kids.

"We're making art for you!" Andrew said, looking up.

He had removed the cutting board from my drafting table and placed it on the carpet in front of the TV. Paper and painting supplies were laid out for both Hannah and himself. Paper cups filled with poster paints were lined up like soldiers in front of each workstation. Four empty paint bottles were piled up against the base of my bed, with most of the thick poster paint splattered on my white bed skirt.

Hannah had obviously become bored with her paper and found the carpet a better medium with which to work. Broad, blue, yellow and green paint strokes arched across the carpet. My heart skipped a beat.

"This is just like you do, Mama," she said without breaking her concentration.

I did exactly what my parenting lessons said *not* to do: I completely freaked out.

"What were you thinking?!!" I shouted at my three-year-old.

Stunned, she stared at me.

"Why would you do this?!" I yelled some more, grabbing at a tipped-over paint bottle.

Her lower lip quivered. Her mouth opened and then closed before she scrambled for her brushes and took off at a full run.

"I will wash them for you!" she shouted.

Blobs of sticky poster paint streaked its way down the hallway carpet. Andrew made a bee-line for the door.

"Stop!" I yelled at them both.

Andrew froze in place, his brushes rolling from his hands, diving at angles into the carpet. I picked him up by the armpits and dropped him on the floor of his room before slamming the door. Seeing what happened to her brother, Hannah dropped everything and bolted to her room.

I just stood there, wild with frustration, my feet firmly planted on a rainbow-colored carpet. Why was this so hard? I was trying to do everything right. I loved my job as much as I loved being a mother. I was contributing to the family with my small business, and I was staying at home to raise my kids. Isn't that what I was supposed to do?

Hannah's little voice floated through the door, "We're sorry, Mommy." And then silence.

I spent the next ninety minutes trying to clean the carpet and failed. Two hours later, the carpet cleaner was at our house and I was left with a bill for three hundred and fifty dollars.

Only then did I brave a call to Jon at work. I described in detail what had happened, adding in all the gory details and admonitions, wondering out loud why the kids just couldn't wait.

"And I can still see some of the paint!" I whined.

For a moment the line was quiet.

"Maybe we should have them paint the walls to match?" he said, laughter in his voice.

I wasn't amused. I wanted to be mad at somebody other than myself, and he wasn't helping matters. Slumping down against the wall, I had a better view of my Technicolor carpet. Maybe it was just a little bit funny? After all, I wasn't much older than Hannah when I started secretly painting on every blank surface I could find in my grandmother's basement. Maybe Hannah would choose to be an artist like me someday?

Dinner that night was a quiet affair. Afterwards, I slunk up to my room, flipped open a book and tried to read, but too many questions swirled through my mind, making it impossible to concentrate. How did my friends make it look so easy? Karen next door had seven kids, all in different sports. Two of her middle schoolers were also in the local theatre productions. Did she ever sleep? When did she have time to get pregnant anyway?

The truth was, my work defined me. I enjoyed it, knew where I fit in, and knew how to speak the language. I was afraid to give up that feeling of belonging. But it was clear I couldn't keep up. My children needed all of me, not the back of a mom who was always facing away from them, engrained in work that seemed so much more important. Something needed to change.

After dinner, my mood improved a little. Andrew and T-Rex ventured across the soggy carpet into my room where I was hiding. I noticed he was flushed, but his sweet smile told me he was in a good mood.

"We were quiet," he explained to me, "and we painted pictures for your studio. I told Hannah you would be proud."

My autistic son, who only knew how to speak the truth as he saw it, was telling me something I was ashamed to hear. That maybe I needed to take a break and stop splitting myself in so many different directions. I pulled him onto my lap, hugging him as much as he would allow.

"Mommy's going to take a break from working. It's kind of like a vacation. Do you understand?" I asked.

Andrew nodded, wide-eyed and solemn. "Then we can do art together." He touched my mouth with T-Rex's head—an involuntary kiss—before sliding off my lap and padding back to his room.

Jon crawled into bed much later that night, tugging and yanking the comforter in a loud, wordless statement of frustration. I played possum, lying as still as possible, eyes squeezed tightly shut. Jon bounced around a little more, smacked the feather pillow into shape, and eventually flung the sheets off and went in search of water. I still played possum. The next time he slipped into bed, he moved right up to the back of my head, hovered there a few long seconds before speaking into my right ear.

"I know you're not sleeping, so you can quit faking it."

I rolled onto my back, blocking his probing eyeballs with a hand.

"You don't have to say it, I know I screwed up. This working full-time and trying to be a supermom thing isn't working out too well, but if I could just get the kids to cooperate..."

He clamped a hand over my mouth and ran the other through his hair, making the long pieces stand up like a deranged artist-serial-killer. It kinda turned me on, the deranged part. I tugged at his hair, pushing it up on both sides into a Mohawk.

"Would you please quit trying to fix everything? Can't you just *be*? Life is more fun that way," he said, biting at the tip of my nose.

Jon's way of loving me is easy and fluid. He gives me all the space I need to be myself—happy and whole—space I rarely take. A tender and strong man, he cares for me in a way I rejected at first. It was too strange to have someone wrap me up in such a comfortable cocoon of care without strings attached.

"But the carpet..." I said.

"Who cares! Maybe this new mixed-media-pastel-carpet thing you have going will become a new trend."

I bit his fingers and pulled away before laughing.

"Seriously though, you might want to rethink about how much you're working right now," he said, brushing stray hairs from my face and tucking them behind my ear. "It seems to stress you out as much as the kids."

I rolled on to my back and addressed the ceiling, "I feel like everyone else can juggle work and kids. I just wish I could, too."

"It's not forever. Maybe just scale it back a bit?"

It was enticing. I was always running ragged and often had little patience for the kids. I turned towards Jon and slung a leg over his, seeking out the warm spot at the back of his knee to place my cold toes.

He leaned in and kissed me. "You'll always be my crazy-Type-A-nutball-artist. That's what I love best about you." Then he rolled over and yanked the remaining covers to his side of the bed.

We woke to a blood-curdling scream in the middle of the night. I was the first responder, levitating out of bed and streaking into the hallway to find out which room it was coming from. Andrew sat up in his bed—his hair gleaming like a burning bush, his entire body covered in sweat. He squeezed a hand over his belly.

"It hurts all over," he moaned when I reached his bed.

I could tell by looking at him that his fever had spiked again. Jon knew the routine by now and was already halfway down the stairs to find Tylenol. I stripped him of his wet clothes and turned on the closet light. Even in the weak beam, I could see his lips were swollen and I knew without a doubt that tiny ulcers lined the inside of his mouth. His body looked so frail, unlike the little boy that sat on my lap just hours before and told me he wanted to make me proud.

Within a couple hours, Jon and I were able to get the fever down to a tolerable level—just long enough for the pediatric clinic to open in the morning. When I brought him in, the receptionist must have heard us coming around the corner because she called out for us to go down the hall into Room Three—the soundproof one in the back.

"I swear it's not the flu," I said to the pediatrician as I set my whimpering son down on the bench. "Would you please take another look?"

"He's in school now, right? Is there something going around?"

"No."

I was afraid he would try to blame his frequent illnesses on school. I was sure it wasn't school, but if I remembered correctly, it was the third one since he began Kindergarten in September.

"It seems like he gets sick like this every month. It's always the same," I said, more to myself than the pediatrician.

For the next few minutes, he tended to Andrew. With gentle and slow movements and a soft voice, he lulled my nearly six-year-old into a trancelike state. *Why couldn't I do that?* I thought.

Sitting quietly on the stool in the corner, I watched as he peered into Andrew's eyes and ears, pausing to listen to his heartbeat and his breathing. I held my breath, waiting for a revelation. When one didn't come, I started getting twitchy.

"Something weird is going on. Look in his mouth!" I blurted out.

He peeled back Andrew's lip, revealing a row of blisters, some having already popped, forming lesions that looked like red-ringed cancer sores.

"Maybe he has herpes?" he suggested.

"How in the world would he get herpes?' I asked, clearly annoyed.

"Let's test him to rule it out. And in the meantime, I think we just have a case of bad luck. Andrew might be one of those kids that catches every virus that comes by. I wouldn't worry about it."

I walked away from his office feeling a little like I did when we saw the neurologist—shocked, confused, and with an ever-growing list of questions. It seemed like every time I visited a doctor's office, I was talked out of my anxieties, like a hysterical, overprotective mother. Even if it was just a nasty virus, I couldn't shake the feeling that something was being overlooked.

Weeks later, when Andrew was well, I asked him what his belly felt like that night. He drew two fingers across abdomen in the shape of an X. "There were knives slicing me open," he said.

I knew he wasn't talking about a virus.

Chapter 4

I took a year-long hiatus from work before easing back into my design business, but this time I used my graphic design skills as an interior designer. I started by providing clients with custom sewing for their homes, then quickly found myself in the middle of small remodel projects—a place where I could still keep my hands on all aspects of a design job. I thrived in my new role, but again, my home life was beginning to fray around the edges. In the end, Jon and I made a compromise: I would scale back my client base even more, and he would step in as needed, coming home from work a little early, or taking the kids for long weekend outings so I could work. It worked beautifully, until we began to frequent the emergency room with Andrew's escalating fevers.

Hannah found me in my studio one afternoon, straddling six yards of upholstery fabric while coaxing it inch by inch through my sewing machine.

"Andrew needs you, Mama," she called from the doorway.

"For what?"

I knew better than to question her, but I was eager to finish my project. I focused on long gathering threads, trimming them to the edge of the seam.

"He's feeling slow," she spoke in my ear.

Hannah reached for my hand, tugging me down the back stairs and out into the yard where they were playing. Although she was only in Kindergarten, her radar was highly tuned to her brother, and despite my continual protests, she had assumed the role of her brother's keeper.

Andrew was sitting in a half-made fort in the back yard, pulling a sword fern crown onto his head when I arrived. Rust-colored pollen spores sprinkled his nose and covered his jacket.

"What's up?" I asked.

He pulled a light saber from the back of his shorts and pointed it at Hannah.

"Hannah! Why do you always run to Mom?"

I looked at my daughter.

"Andrew is sick," she said, shrugging her shoulders.

"Am not!"

Andrew poked the light saber at her face. Hannah grabbed it and ran. Usually, Andrew would have taken off after her, but this time, he just stood there, watching her leave.

"I feel funny," he admitted.

"Funny how?"

"Just woozy."

I knew what that meant. We'd been doing this over and over for months now. Andrew would be perfectly fine, then within an hour, or even less, he would begin to experience phantom pain. First, it was a pinprick in his mouth, like he had eaten something sharp that poked his skin. Within an hour, he would become weak as the fever rushed through his body. And then came the pain — the real pain that twisted in his gut, leaving him doubled over and breathless. I knew from experience that by the time Jon got home from work, Andrew would have tiny sores in his mouth and we would be well into one of his five, six, or seven-day fever episodes.

I called my client to say my sewing wouldn't be delivered for another week and sat Andrew in the downstairs playroom with a Gatorade and two Tylenol. The plan was to get him to drink as much fluid and electrolytes as we could before the fever burned it out of him. Hannah sat next to her brother playing a game of tease-the-cat with a laser pen. Charlie, our obese orange tabby cat lurched at the red dot while occasionally bumping into walls — another distraction that would buy us some time.

Somehow, Hannah had known this insidious monster was coming again. To this day, I don't know how she knew what was happening inside her brother before the rest of us were even aware. The only thing I knew for sure was the monster visited on a regular basis. At one point, I began a dedicated calendar and notebook just for Andrew's fevers. What I discovered was the fevers came precisely every twenty-eight days—like a menstrual cycle—and they always peaked at 105 degrees. I also noted that the pattern never varied. It always started with a twinge in the mouth, followed by fever, pain, and nausea. During the worst episodes, when the pain became unbearable, we were admitted to the hospital.

That night we did avoid it, but on the next month and the month after that, we stayed for days while they hydrated Andrew and gave him his first taste of IV narcotics. During one visit, when we were asked to recount his health history yet again, I told the emergency room doctor about my discovery. He told me it was most likely a coincidence. It felt like a slap to the face, and I retreated with a burning sense of anger.

Between episodes, when Andrew sprang from bed looking like any other healthy third-grade boy, we left the house in search of adventure. One Sunday morning, Jon announced we were going on a family drive. A collective groan came from the breakfast table—we all knew this meant hours in the car running errands.

"The only stop is the feed store to pick up some grass seed," Jon told us on the way to town. "Then you kids can choose where we go."

His announcement did little to quiet the grumbling.

As soon as Jon put the car in park, both kids scrambled out the back seat, following a crowd into DeYoung's Feed Store for their annual Chick Fest.

"There are bins and bins of peeping colorful fluff balls!" Hannah shouted to the entire store.

"What are they called, Dad?" Andrew asked, looking through the chicken wire into the box.

A kind-faced man walked over to us, wearing a green apron with a sticker that said, "Hi! My name is Tony."

"These are baby chickens, about two days old. People call them 'chicks' when they are little babies."

Hannah wriggled out of Jon's grasp and started hopping up and down. Andrew stood mesmerized. Even with the pressing crowd, the buzz of heat lamps and noisy cheeps coming from hundreds of birds, he stayed positively still, breathless in anticipation. Of what, I didn't know.

I nudged Jon. "Look."

Andrew was pointing to a bin of chicks on the far side of the room. "What are those? The ones with the black stripes around their eyes?" he asked Tony.

"Those are Araucanas. They lay the most beautiful blue eggs."

Andrew stared at a photo of a full-grown hen clipped to the top of the bin. "I would like one of those."

I moved towards Andrew just as Jon reached out an arm, blocking my path. "Wait," he said with his eyes.

Tony and Andrew leaned into the bin, Andrew pointing and gesturing. He emerged a moment later, both hands cupped like a bowl around a tiny chick. Then he walked straight over to us, announcing, "She is my new friend. I'd like to bring her home with me."

I pressed a hand to my mouth, astonished he'd spoken so clearly. Although he chatted and conversed as much as most eight-year-olds, he rarely spoke to us directly. More often, his gaze was fixed on the far side of the room, his words a riddle for us to solve.

Hannah went ballistic in Jon's arms. "I want one, too!"

I gave Jon the let's-get-out-of-here-quick signal, and when he didn't respond, I left to wait in the car.

Twenty minutes later, Jon arrived with both kids and a flimsy peeping box the size of a Happy Meal. Tony trailed behind, pushing a wooden cart overflowing with all of the necessary accoutrements needed to sustain life for baby chicks.

I glared at Jon, who shrugged. "What was I supposed to do?"

"We got six tiny peepers!!" Hannah shouted as soon as we pulled away.

Andrew was silent in the back seat, grinning, with the box clutched in his arms. I stared straight ahead, wondering why we were adding more things to be taken care of. Two kids, two dogs, a cat, and now a half dozen chickens? My plate was already overloaded with responsibilities, and I had no idea what it would take to raise a small brood of hens.

"What did that cost?" I asked Jon, referring to the trunk load of equipment.

"The peepers were only ninety-nine cents each," he said, grinning at the road.

I snorted, choking on my laughter.

That night, the kids and I huddled on Jon's workbench in the garage staring into a cardboard box full of peepers. The lamp's orangey glow illuminated Andrew and Hannah's round, happy faces — my springtime pumpkins. Our little corner was a cozy place to be on a late spring evening and I was enjoying myself, despite my lingering irritation at Jon's purchase. I couldn't imagine where we would put six full-grown hens.

"What are you going to name them?" I asked.

"Mine is called Buttercup, because she is yellow," Hannah chirped.

Her nose was pressed to the mesh lid Jon had rigged up to fit across the top — a wise suggestion from Tony, since it was clear they were close to fluttering out.

"Well, hello there, Buttercup!" I said.

Hannah smiled and scrambled into my lap smelling of freshly washed hair and strawberries. How could I be angry about Jon's purchase? I knew most parents would pay anything to see their kids this blissfully happy.

"What about you, Andrew?"

He reached his hand into the box, pulling out the splotchy black and brown chick. "She is Frightful," he said.

I stared at him, unclear what he meant. From past experience, I knew there was something more to this odd choice of name. I wanted him to tell me more.

"*Who* is frightful?" I asked, careful to keep my tone neutral.

"She's the falcon!" Hannah piped in, "...from Grandpa's book." She slid off my lap and disappeared into the house.

"Why do you call her Frightful?" I asked Andrew again.

He ran a finger across a fragile, three-toed foot, whispering something to the opening between his palms. His gesture was as intimate as a kiss.

"Because she told me that was her name."

This was turning into another one of our circular conversations that left me confused and a little anxious. I tried another tact. "Are you scared, Andrew?"

A pink hue colored his cheeks and he raised the tiny chick to my face, blocking his own from view.

"Her name is Frightful. She will be brave for me," he replied.

Hannah zoomed back into the garage, waving a tattered paperback book.

"This is it! Grandpa's book about the falcon!"

I took it from her and studied the cover: *My Side of the Mountain*, by Jean Craighead George. Sure enough, it pictured a falcon perched in a tree behind a young boy. Its feathers looked a little like the picture of a full-grown Araucana hen, but I still didn't understand the reason for the deep connection he already felt for the chick.

I showed the book to Andrew. "Is this why you named your chick Frightful?"

"Frightful will save me," he replied.

From what!? I wanted to scream. What are you trying to tell me? What don't I understand? I felt a trickle of sweat run down my neck as the anxiety of years of confusion overcame me in that single moment.

"It's a good story, Mama," Hannah said, sensing my angst.

Through a blur of tears, I concentrated on the book, scanning the blurb on the back cover. Bits and pieces of the story filtered through my mind, snippets I caught while Jon's father read the story in our living room. I recalled a boy rescuing a baby falcon who fell from her nest, naming her Frightful, and teaching her to hunt. I remembered the falcon becoming his best friend, keeping watch over him, protecting him from harm. I also remembered the boy was alone, lost in the mountains, feeling like no one in the world understood him. Did Andrew feel this way? Was he living in a place so lonely...so frightful...that he felt the world couldn't possibly understand?

Andrew touched the end of the chick's beak with a finger. Then he peeped. She peeped back and jumped out of his hand, landing on the workbench. Maybe *she* knew the answer? I stared at my son, confused and heartbroken, wishing I could draw him in to my arms and tell him everything would be okay. But I wasn't sure it would be.

Both kids scrambled to get ready for school the next morning, eager to hold the chicks before the bus rounded the corner. After they left, I cleaned the box, scooping wet shavings from the water dish.

"Why did you choose him?" I asked the mottled chick.

Frightful walked around on my hand, ignoring my question.

"I know you chose him just as much as he chose you. Was it because you knew he needed you?"

She refused to answer—not even a peep. I felt foolish talking to a bird. What did I think it would say? Was I secretly hoping for answers to an eight-year-long list of questions? Her featherless wings stretched and flapped as she dive-bombed toward the cardboard box, landing right in the middle of a sleeping pile of yellow fluff. Under the heat lamp, her black and brown puff was a cool spot in a ring of golden fire. Frightful tucked her black beak under a naked wing and slept. There was something about the scene that made me pause. She was different, like Andrew was different, but something else tugged at the back of my mind, something I couldn't quite grasp. It was clear she had somehow performed a mind-meld on my autistic son, but what I didn't know was that she had crawled into his heart and set up camp. And now she was speaking to his soul.

Chapter 5

Summer arrived in a burst of wild green and vivid blue and I felt like I could breathe for the first time in months. Every time I walked outside, I wanted to strip naked, drop to the ground, and let the Seattle sunshine infuse vitamin D into my bones. During the months of July and August, I refused to schedule the kids with the usual camps and clubs, opting instead to let them guide their days. They ran me just as ragged as if I were hauling them to and from scheduled activities, but with much less scheduled stress.

The low rumble of Jon's lawn mower drew me in to the yard one Saturday afternoon. I found Jon on the far side of our half-acre lawn near the chicken coop, happily following a self-propelled mower across a perfectly striped turf. A sprinkler's bowing wave polka-dotted the tip of the outdoor pen where a half dozen hens were busy making shallow bowls in the soil. A sunny dirt bath.

"Have you seen Andrew?" I hollered over the drone of the mower.

He shook his head no before making a sharp turn around the edge of the rose garden and heading in the opposite direction. I took my time walking back to the house, stopping to enjoy Jon's newly planted shade garden. Gardening had become Jon's way of cleaning up our brokenness, his way of fixing our shattered dreams. He trimmed, pruned, planted, and raked until each plant and piece of earth was in its proper place. He never told me this, but I saw his disappointment, his look of helplessness and frustration when his son wouldn't catch a ball, but instead dodged it or ran away crying. I realized while looking at the perfect roses, exotic hosta, and pure white hellebore that we had never really talked about our grief.

My way of coping with those feelings was my new fever calendar — an intricate diary of sorts pertaining to all the quirky and weird things I noticed about Andrew. For the last few months, I'd been able to track Andrew's fevers, allowing me to make plans during the times we predicted he would be well. This gave me the right amount of control I craved in my life.

Behind me, the distinct click of a latch, followed by a bang, told me that someone had entered the henhouse. Hannah disappeared into the back of the shed, rustled around and finally emerged with a dirty bucket, a rake, and hand trowel. The hens walked around her feet, striking up a conversation as they made their way into the yard. Frightful quickly left the brood, took a right hand turn and circled around the back of the house, calling for Andrew to play with a long trill, followed by two short, staccato chirps. To this day, I have never heard another chicken make that sound.

"Krrillll...Chirp. CHIRP!"

Where are you, Andrew?

A streak of black and gold whizzed past my feet and rounded the corner by the garage.

"Chick-chick-chick-a-DEE!" Andrew answered from somewhere across the yard.

I heard some more chirping and squawking amongst a loud, "hold still!" before it was quiet again. I wouldn't be seeing them for a while, so I sat on the porch to soak up the sunshine.

Moments later, Hannah wandered across the lawn, dragging a garden hose. "Come play, Mama!" she said.

I sat next to her as she filled her grimy bucket with water, scooping rocky soil into the bottom using Jon's garden trowel. I sensed where this was leading, but before I could protest, she plunged her open palm into the bucket, showering both of us in tiny chocolate drops of mud. I bit my lip. A loud peal of laughter ripped through the air as she ran across the grass in search of her brother. A while later she came back with another bucket and some more garden tools. She frowned slightly as a honey bee landed on the bucket rim.

"No brother," she said.

"What do you mean?" I asked, picking at dried splatters of mud on my bare legs.

"Can't find him."

I left her to her gardening and went in search of Andrew. I found him wrapped in one of his superhero capes, sitting on a crumbling cedar stump at the edge of the woods, half hidden behind lacy huckleberry branches. He didn't notice me walking towards him. His relaxed conversation floated on the late summer breeze, unassuming, as if he were simply asking for a glass of milk.

"I think my body is trying to kill me," he said to the little hen in his hands. "I don't know why it would do that."

I stood rooted to the ground as waves of terror shuddered down my spine. Why would he say that? What was *that* supposed to mean? Could I have heard him wrong? I watched him carefully stretch the bird's fragile wings, revealing new amber and black pinfeathers. Then he lifted her juvenile body up to his face, stared into her beady bird-eyes, and touched the tip of his nose to her beak.

"But you make me feel better, Frightful. Plus your feathers are silky. Like the flour in Mom's bins that she doesn't know I like to play with."

Frightful turned her head to the side, gazing at him, eyeball to eyeball.

"Do you understand?" Andrew asked.

"Crawww-cruk-cruk."

Yes. I'm here for you.

She answered him like a mother hen would her chicks, in a low quiet voice. Andrew tucked the little bird into his shirt and stared out onto the lawn. Chirping protests came from somewhere near his belly and he patted the little lump, saying, "It's okay. I'm here, too."

The chirping stopped.

I remained motionless, my breath caught somewhere between inhale and exhale, still not sure I'd heard him correctly. It was clear, however, that he was telling Frightful his secrets, secrets he had never shared with me, at least in a way that I could understand. Did he really believe the chicken understood him? Or even stranger yet, did they actually understand one another? From my vantage point, it looked like they had an instinctual relationship I couldn't comprehend. Jon had even commented a few nights before that it seemed like they spoke some secret language—a language that we could never access, but had clearly opened a window into Andrew's mind.

Andrew hopped down from the stump, bounding across the side lawn calling, "Chi-KENS! Back-ACK!"

Five cheeping raptors scrabbled around his ankles, running past him into the front yard. Andrew chased after them, his Darth Vader cape licking at his heels, causing me to stare at his retreating figure in disbelief. He looked fine to me. His loping gait was a little awkward, his skinny arms and legs those of a geeky little boy who had yet to show the promise of the man he would become. I was sure I had heard him wrong. It wouldn't be the first time I was confused and baffled by something he said.

Even so, I crept over to the stump, wishing those terrifying words would somehow be forgotten, leave my mind and float away. Because the truth was, the day Andrew was born, I had known my life had somehow taken a sharp left hand turn. My world wasn't black and white anymore. I was swimming in a sea of grey, and now I was drowning in confusion, trying to decipher just how this child of mine saw the world. After hearing him say those words, I feared his world was nothing but pain.

T-Rex stood on the stump, abandoned, covered in splintery bark and lime-colored moss. T-Rex had been Andrew's first friend, the first creature he talked to. But Frightful was entirely different. She talked back. She had a way of making my little boy's body soften and his eyes focus. She drew the words from his mouth in a smooth, even flow, revealing a part of him we had never seen before. When speaking to Frightful, Andrew came up with extraordinary insights, things most eight-year-olds would never be able to put to words. Now I was left guessing what he meant when he told his chicken his body was trying to kill him.

From my hiding spot in the woods, I could see him playing with the chickens on the front slope of lawn—five little birds climbing into his lap, hoping for a bit of the cracked corn in his pockets. Frightful sat on his shoulder, pecking at bits of grass in his hair.

"Fright-feee!" Andrew called, and the chicken called back with a series of chirps.

She hopped around his shoulder and stepped into his waiting hand. Andrew walked to the raised planter box next to the driveway with Frightful tucked safely in the crook of his elbow. A few mature tail feathers poked out the back in various directions, making her look like a toilet brush. I watched as the remaining hens chatted and chirped their way across the lawn, followed by Hannah, then our dog Sawyer, who carried a mud-drenched ball that had come out of Hannah's gardening bucket. I watched my two children from a distance—brother and sister, friends, companions. One was tall and lean, rigid and mysterious, with a riotous bush of flaming hair and ice blue eyes. The other was petite, soft, bubbly, an engaging little girl with blond curls and eyes that varied between olive and a deep shade of grey. Two children who Jon and I believed couldn't possibly have come from the same gene pool.

Hannah's chattering floated through the air—a negotiation to hold the little bird.

"No, Hannah. She likes me best," Andrew grumped, clearly irritated she would ask such a question.

I emptied a mud-filled bucket and walked towards them, sensing an argument on the way. Hannah shrugged, crouched low and poked a stick at something in the dirt below the planter. I slowed my step, turning my face to the pale sun and fragile blue sky. I felt the first twinge of angst at the thought of the school year to come. I wasn't ready to see my little tribe of special needs moms quite yet. I wanted to stay in my current state of denial, a place where the word 'autism' was never uttered, a place where all people were quirky and strange in their own unique way.

I handed Hannah the empty bucket and leaned against the planter next to Andrew. Hannah began scooping dirt onto my shoes, patting the mounds into little cakes. Frightful's slim body was nestled in the narrow space between Andrew's crossed legs, pecking at a fistful of weeds he had crammed into a paper cup.

"Eat your greens, Chick-a-dee. They're good for you."

The little bird tilted her head as if he had just told her something interesting. He held a single blade of grass to her beak. "Go on. It's good."

She stood, turned her head to the side, regarding him patiently, not blinking.

I ruffled Andrew's hair. "Maybe you could eat a few of those greens yourself," I said, noting that he needed a haircut before school started. Third grade, I was told, was going to be an academic nightmare, made especially so for Andrew and any other child with special needs.

"Not interested," he said, crouching down to avoid my touch.

"How about I cut your hair this time? I won't use the clippers. Only scissors."

"Still not interested."

I noticed his body had gone from soft and relaxed, to the familiar rigid posture, as if he were ready to bolt at any second. I moved a few inches away from him, giving him his personal space.

"You could use a haircut, Frightful," he said, pulling a puff of baby fuzz from a wing.

He started to hum, a hint of a smile tipping the edge of his lips. Frightful stood motionless, still gazing into his face, beak forward, eyes looking left and right. Andrew stared back in wordless communication. I watched this exchange between my son and his chicken, wondering what it was she said to him to make him respond in such a profound way. It left me aching with envy — craving that type of intimacy from him.

Andrew turned his body towards me, keeping his eyes fixed on Frightful. "She is my lady friend. She knows me," he said.

I knew it was the truth. And I also knew exactly what he was telling me. She was the one who kept his secrets.

"I know she does, sweetheart. I'm glad you found each other." I reached out to touch my son, but sensing him pull away, I smoothed my hand across Frightful's back instead.

Hannah finished making dirt mountains out of my feet and wandered off. I stood next to Andrew, thinking about his conversation in the woods, feeling like I had swallowed a boulder. I started to ask him what he meant when he said he thought his body was trying to kill him. But when I looked at him, I saw he was smiling, content, caressing the chicken in his lap, chatting about all the adventures he had planned for the two of them. I stopped, certain I had heard him wrong.

As memories often do, the details of that summer day on the lawn were swallowed up by my everyday life. In early November, I was pacing Andrew's room once again, waiting for the thermometer to beep. T-Rex glared at me from the windowsill with his oversized head, and all I wanted to do was swipe the toothy grin off his nubbly face. One look at Andrew's face that morning told me there were new ulcers on the inside of his lips in addition to the inferno ravaging his body. Andrew had already missed fifteen days of third grade, and the school work, as I'd feared, was a nightmare. My fragile hold on control was unraveling quickly.

In addition, Andrew had tried to bring Frightful to school in a paper grocery sack, resulting in a phone call from the front desk reminding me that livestock was not allowed in a public school. I reminded them that chickens were poultry, not livestock. That didn't go over well. After much negotiating, Andrew finally agreed to bring T-Rex instead, claiming he was a Jurassic chicken anyway. That incident alone guaranteed my relationship with his teacher would be uneasy at best. Between chickens, dinosaurs, and sporadic attendance, he wasn't making any progress, so I tried working with him at home.

One evening, I sat with Andrew at the kitchen counter, determined he would learn to count.

"If you just put your finger in front of each M&M, then you can eat it after we count the number," I said, offering up a form of bribery that was common around our home.

Andrew looked at me—not really *at* me—more like his eyes darted towards my face before landing somewhere on my shoulder. T-Rex stood on the counter across from Andrew, his green toothy head turned to the side, eyeballing me with his yellow painted lizard-eyes.

I avoided the raptor's pointed gaze.

"Can we try it?"

"I like the orange ones," Andrew replied.

I took his pointer finger in my hand, guiding it to each piece of candy. "One, two, three, four," he said, echoing my whispered words.

"Good! Now you try it," I said, willing him to repeat the words we had just recited together.

He studied the candy carefully, moving his finger up and down the line. His answer came a long ten seconds later. "Six."

"No! You *just* said it a minute ago. How many pieces of candy?!" I jabbed my finger at each one, frustration oozing into my words. He stared back at me, a blank look on his face.

I swiped the M&M's back into an empty bag and tossed it onto the counter. Andrew patted my face with a sticky palm, saying, "T-Rex doesn't like candy, anyway."

My frustration evaporated as he continued to pat my face and gaze into my eyes—something he rarely did.

I pressed his warm hand to my cheek. "Counting is hard, buddy, isn't it?"

He nodded. I reached for the colorful candies, spilling them onto the counter.

"Let's eat them all for that dinosaur of yours."

Once Andrew was back at school, I redoubled my efforts to help him fit in. Lacking any other place to use my talents, I joined the elusive tribe of 'parents of special needs kids.' We were the ones who volunteered for every class party to quietly orchestrate our child's behavior so they wouldn't stand out among their peers. We hung around the fringes of school, offering help to those poor teachers who just didn't get it. We thought we were somehow superior to regular parents—we just knew more.

Without divulging the secret diagnosis attached to our child, we circled one another with knowing smiles and encouraging comments.

"Tommy has really made progress," I heard from a parent commenting on the child who always rolled out of his chair and wandered around the room.

"Yes. And Jackson has stopped picking his nose," Tommy's mom snapped back.

Colored Skittles littered a tray in the corner where Andrew sat. His scowl said: *Get. Me. Outta. Here.* I knew exactly how he felt; I didn't like being lumped in with the special education crowd, either. I secretly wanted to be a part of the Parking Lot Club—the group of parents who stood outside the school chatting about their kids' soccer teams, ballet lessons, and birthday parties. There was still a part of me that thought I could force it to happen for Andrew if I worked just a little harder at making him fit in.

At home, our days flowed smoothly, as long as we followed our prescribed routine. After Jon left for work each morning, Andrew and Frightful would sit on the front porch, deep in conversation. Hannah was never included, but she didn't seem bothered by it. Instead, she insisted on selecting and laying out her brother's clothes for school. Each morning, she created an unstuffed scarecrow on the floor, starting with his shoes, a sock crammed in each toe, underwear, then pants and T-shirt, inside out, with no tags. Both kids assumed this was the natural order of things, but I knew it was quite different from most sibling relationships. No matter how hard I tried to stop the two of them from relating to one another in this way, it never worked.

One evening, after finishing a new logo for a client, I told Jon about the Parking Lot moms. "I don't really fit in with the other parents at school," I lamented.

"You don't need them," he said. "You have your work, your clients, and our whole family lives in the area." When he saw the look on my face, he added, "What I meant was, it really doesn't matter what any of them think."

But it *did* matter to me. I *wanted* to fit in with the cool crowd. And most of all, I needed somebody besides Jon, who could understand all the anxious feelings that were building up inside me. Later that night, when I heard the cluck of a chicken come from somewhere downstairs and the admonishment of Hannah parenting her older brother, I decided to form a club of my own.

Chapter 6

We called ourselves the Breakfast Club. We were a new tribe of special needs moms hand-plucked from several local elementary schools. I started with Tommy's mom, sensing from our many encounters that she was a kindred spirit, and the two of us branched out from there. It was a clandestine recruitment, as we were actually watching other kids to see if we thought they might be lumped in the same category as our own. Then we would find out who the moms were and perform a one-way interview unbeknownst to them. We ended up with a group of six fantastic women, each full of keen advice and a listening ear.

We sat around our coffee tables, sharing stories with one another, hoping to glean bits and pieces of wisdom each time we met. We set the ground rules right away: No Bitching — about husbands, school, other people, or other people's kids. But it was very hard to do, since we were a bunch of freaked-out moms who were trying to figure out how to navigate the unfamiliar world of special needs parenting. We all desperately wanted to feel included, valued, somehow compensated for the gaping wound our child's label had inflicted on our hearts. In the end, when we established who we really were, we became a powerful little posse of truth-tellers.

On one such Tuesday morning, I dared to drop my pretense of perfection and admit that all was not right in my world. "My son talks to a chicken," I said, forking the remnants of an omelet.

Nobody blinked. Their kids did all sorts of unusual things, and my telling them that Andrew spoke to his chicken was not that special.

"I mean, that's the *only* thing he talks to. And, well, during the summer I thought I heard him tell the chicken his body was trying to kill him." Embarrassed, I quickly added, "But I think I heard him wrong."

This morsel of truth got a few raised eyebrows. Tommy's mom, who was sitting next to me, choked on her egg, spraying tiny bits of yellow across the table.

"Sorry," she said, wiping at the table. "Why in the world would he say that?"

I told the group about Andrew's repeated fevers, the specialists we had seen and even the modern-day woo-woo healer we consulted. When I described his gaping ulcers and his sudden pain and nausea, the breakfast became unappetizing.

"Autism is a piece of cake compared to this," I said, only half joking.

From the stunned looks on their faces, I realized it was the first time I had described Andrew's illness to someone who was not a doctor. I'd been carrying around a terrible fear that to speak about it would somehow make it even more real. And then where would I be? Trapped inside my panicked, powerless self?

"How long has this been happening?" one of the women asked.

"Since he was in preschool. At least that was the first time I noticed the ulcers."

I remembered the day I drove him home after he kicked the clown. I had asked him about the blister on his lip and he hadn't even noticed it was there. Thinking it unimportant, I didn't mention it to Jon, and truthfully, I hadn't thought of it again until that moment.

Only days after meeting with my breakfast group, Jon and I carried a limp, fevered, nine-year-old Andrew into the Immunology clinic at Seattle Children's Hospital. By this point, Andrew had seen more specialists than I could remember, and we were on a first-name basis with much of the staff at Children's. We had been waiting six weeks for this appointment with Dr. Torgerson, and I was hoping this Immunologist would finally have some answers rather than more questions. I secretly wanted him to be a genie, to grant me my single wish—to take away Andrew's pain and transform him into something new.

Dr. Torgerson was a kind looking man with gold-rimmed glasses and bow tie. He didn't look like a genie. I noticed a picture of his family tucked into the backside of his name badge—three young kids pig-piled on his lap, his wife's arms wrapped around his shoulders. He introduced himself to Andrew, touching him gently on the shoulder.

Andrew reached out, gripping his arm. "I think my body is trying to kill me."

A familiar feeling of terror washed over me. Dr. Torgerson's face registered surprise for a brief moment before quickly being replaced by a look of compassion. Andrew's body relaxed—a softening of the muscles in his face, a look of gratitude. *This man understands me*, his eyes said when he turned to Jon and me.

Dr. Torgerson sat down next to Andrew. "Have you told anyone this before?"

"Frightful knows."

I groaned, sucking in a breath that sounded like I was choking. Dr. Torgerson glanced at me, my face now frozen with the realization that Andrew had known something was desperately wrong all along.

"I think I may have heard something like that before," I squeaked.

Jon's eyes were on me, probing, his gaze scratching at the side of my head.

The room went still as the memory assaulted me: Young Frightful folded in Andrew's arms, all pinfeathers and fluff. I could still hear his voice, like it had somehow been captured by the leaves of the huckleberry and was just being played back now. *I think my body is trying to kill me.* No. It wasn't real. I had heard him wrong.

I exhaled, the spell broken. Dr. Torgerson turned to Andrew, handling his fevered body with great care, delicately probing his ulcerated mouth, gently moving his aching limbs, studying his hands, fingers, and the soles of his feet. With closed eyes, he ran his fingers up and down along Andrew's spine. I had no idea what he was looking for, but I trusted him. He was the first physician to be so reverent of my son's condition.

"I really don't know what to make of this, but I'm very interested in your case," he said, turning back to us. "I would like to help if I can. In fact, I have a colleague at the National Institutes of Health in Maryland who may be able to help us."

He scratched the name and number on a piece of paper and handed it to us. I couldn't imagine what Dr. Torgerson was looking for, but I hoped the NIH guy was a genie.

Jon and I nodded our consent and instantly found ourselves buried in a flurry of paperwork in which we agreed to obscure blood tests and to provide a sample of Andrew's DNA. Ten minutes later, we were politely escorted from the office.

"We'll be in touch," the receptionist called out as we left.

Jon and I exchanged a look of bewilderment. "What just happened in there?" he asked with Andrew curled tightly in his arms.

"I think they just kicked us to the curb again," I said through frustrated tears.

Andrew turned his head to Jon. "I liked him."

I stroked our son's sweaty head, smoothing the tangled hair around his hot face. It was a shimmery shade of red, the same golden-red mane that caused people to stop me on the street while he rode in a stroller as a little boy.

"He's the best one, Mom. I know it."

Andrew said it with such conviction that I groped for Jon's eyes over the top of his head. Right as the elevator door chimed, Jon nodded to me, a signal that he agreed.

Two weeks later, Jon, Andrew, and T-Rex traveled to the NIH in Bethesda, Maryland on a quest for answers. Andrew became a part of a human genome research project and was asked to supply blood, skin, and hair samples. He was photographed, charted, swabbed, biopsied, and examined, then sent home with a thick packet of information and a code number. They were told we would receive a phone call if they discovered anything noteworthy. When the two disembarked at SeaTac airport, I anxiously waited for some indication that there had been a breakthrough. Jon's face told me it had been a difficult trip, but Andrew told me it was fantastic.

"They have HUGE machines at that place! T-Rex and I had our picture taken a zillion times, and they would have taken Frightful's, too, if they allowed poultry on the airplane, except they don't, apparently."

Jon rolled his eyes at Andrew's description of the week, then reached for my hand. "One step closer...to something," he whispered in my ear.

I hugged him tight, a confirmation that, indeed, it seemed like we were making progress.

We heard nothing for months. Then, one Tuesday morning during Breakfast Club, I received a call from Dr. Torgerson's office, asking us to come in at the end of the week. My posse of women-warriors told me that it was an excellent sign—they must have discovered something to help Andrew.

Two minutes into the appointment, Dr. Torgerson opened Andrew's bloated medical file, and I started to panic. Considering my experience with the neurologist, I was terrified of what we might hear.

"We discovered something interesting," Dr. Torgerson began. "It seems that Andrew has a gene mutation called Trisomy 8 Mosaicism (T8M)."

Jon and I sat in stunned silence. "So, what does this mean?" Jon queried.

I sat on the small bench next to him, mute, digesting this unexpected news. I did not like the word, 'interesting.'

Dr. Torgerson leaned forward in his chair. "Well, I call it a genetic misprint. It means that some of Andrew's cells have three number eight chromosomes, and some of them have the normal two chromosomes."

When we looked at him in confusion, he began drawing on a white board, giving us a rudimentary lesson in genetics.

After several minutes of watching red X's and blue Y's tangle together with lines and arrows, Jon interrupted. "Is this what's making him so sick?"

Dr. Torgerson sat back in his chair, the whiteboard forgotten. "I don't really know. There are very few of these people living because Trisomy 8 Mosaicism rarely results in a viable pregnancy."

A litany of unwanted thoughts tackled me, familiar thoughts from when the autism word was dropped in my lap. What if I had not conceived that night? If the odds of having a child with T8M were so staggering, wouldn't my child be normal if I had just waited to have sex another time? I should never have had sex. *I will never have sex again.* Did I consume caffeine, drink any alcohol, eat too much fish, absorb too much mercury during those first few weeks of pregnancy? Did I do something wrong? Could this be my fault? The questions flooded my mind, and I was overcome with remorse over something of which I had no control.

I glanced at Jon, noticing his jaw set in concentration, his eyes unreadable. There was nowhere safe to land my gaze, so I hyper-focused on the colored dots speckling the floor tiles. They looked like a frustrated child had mashed crayons all over them. I wanted some crayons.

Dr. Torgerson shuffled through a stack of papers. "It seems that T8M manifests in a variety of ways." He pulled out a cluster of graphs, turning to a dog-eared page in the middle. "It doesn't seem to have a specific profile of symptoms such as a more common genetic condition like Down Syndrome. From what I have found, there are only fifty-two documented cases of T8M in the world—none with a set of symptoms like your son's."

A wave of heat rushed up the back of my neck, making me feel sick. Could it be possible that we had been hurdled into another storm? Wasn't autism enough?

I thought about my autism tribe. I had found my place in that tribe. My little group of educated over-achiever mothers had been hand-picked to be the perfect support system. We navigated the public schools with the ferocity of a mama bear protecting her cubs. We grieved together, encouraged one another, admitted to the truths of our lives, and celebrated each other's triumphs. But *this*? Fifty-two documented cases? *In the world?* There was no tribe. No familiars I could lean on who could say, "I know what you are going through."

Jon and I were on our own.

"I can see I'm losing you," Dr. Torgerson said, addressing me.

"I'm okay. Go on," I said absently, envisioning myself anywhere else on the planet.

Per Dr. Torgerson's suggestion, Andrew began taking several off-label medications that subdued his monthly episodes. Once Dr. Torgerson was convinced that Andrew was stable, he encouraged us to get away. So when Diana, the speech pathologist who had taught Andrew to talk, invited us to her family cabin on Lake Michigan, we jumped at the offer. It would be our first vacation together as a family.

We arrived in Traverse City, Michigan at dusk and were astounded at the relaxed manner of the tiny airport. No high-powered radar or x-ray machines, no random luggage checks, or the fear that our children might say something that would necessitate a strip search.

When Jon inquired about the rental car, the young man at the desk handed him the keys and gestured toward the door. "It's the silver one," he said.

So much for shuttle busses and long walks through layers of parking lots. Revived at the prospect of reaching our destination, both kids began bouncing around the back seat, clicking the seat belts off and back on, while Andrew spewed random facts about the legendary pirates of Lake Michigan.

As we headed towards Northport, we began to wonder what the next week would hold. Would we all get along in the small cabin? Would our friends tire of us? Would Andrew be well?

We passed acres upon acres of cherry groves, the trees showing their heavy burden of fruit even in the darkening sky. Our first glimpse of Lake Michigan confirmed what we had been told—it looked like a great ocean. Only the dunes, grass, and lake algae gave it away as we peeked into the hidden coves and inlets common in the area. And the wildness! Even the quaint little towns had not tamed the dense wildness of the land.

Turning down a well-used gravel drive, we got our first glimpse of Diana and Tim's cabin. It immediately reminded us of our favorite childhood summer camp. No baths, spas, luxurious beds, or that convenient distraction we think we need: television. Our friends, delighted to share their adventure with us, reverently showed us around the small cabin, explaining the history of each modest piece of furniture collected by their family over the last three generations. At the sight of our bunk beds, any hopes of romance over the next week flew out the window, joining the thunderclouds and bugs that mysteriously appeared since our arrival. By evening, every square inch of light that escaped our little home attracted the bugs, some nearly as big as a golf ball. In the unspoken exchange couples know, Jon told me he was ready to pack and leave.

In the morning, I awoke to the purposeful stride of my daughter as she checked on us in our bunks. Rolled in her pink blanket, Hannah assured herself that we were where she had left us the night before. She padded to the front room. Later, I found Hannah, Andrew, and Cory flipping through a stack of Calvin & Hobbes comic books. Not long after, I heard the bang, bang, bang of the screen door as the three kids stole away to the beach.

Following the children with mugs of steaming coffee in our hands, Diana and I carefully made our own way down the path. Not fifty yards from the cabin, the trees opened up to a sight I hope remains embedded in my children's memories for life. The water was a transparent blue, reflecting a peerless blue sky flecked with wisps of clouds. The vanilla dunes were already warm from the morning sun, and we relished how the breeze had chased away the Amazon bugs that visited us the night before.

"We're looking for pirate gold!" the boys shouted as we walked down the beach towards them.

"...and we must be getting close!" called out Andrew.

Just then, Hannah's blond ponytails popped out of a hole. Covered entirely in sand, she grinned at us opening up little hands filled with flat round stones. "I have treasures, too!"

Hannah's treasures were sprinkled in the soft white sand. In the water, they seemed to float to the surface. As I leaned over to study one, Diana laughed, noting the familiar stooped posture of everyone who discovers the treasures of Lake Michigan for the first time: Petoskey stones. I had thumbed through a book about them in the cabin that morning. A caption under a colorful picture said the little pieces of fossilized coral were three hundred million years old. I turned one of the legendary stones over and over in my hand.

"They're called, 'Sunbeams of Promise,'" Diana whispered from behind.

I studied the smooth stone in my palm, gleaming with life centuries ago, and the promise of new life yet to come. I slipped it in my pocket. A promise to keep.

The moment we arrived home, Andrew ran out to the hen house. Frightful pressed herself to the gate, dancing from foot to foot, waiting. He scooped her into his arms and sat in the doorway, smoothing her feathers with both hands while she hummed deep in her chest, a sound not unlike a kitten purring.

"Coo-coor-coo-rrrr."

I missed you, Andrew.

"I missed you too, Frightful," he answered back, running his hands along the tips of her tail feathers.

"Krrillll...Chirp. CHIRP!"

Where were you?

"I went to a ginormous lake and dug for Pirate Joe's hidden treasure. Hannah even brought some home with her. It's called Petoskey Gold."

Frightful nestled deeper into his lap and resumed her song, presumably satisfied with his answer, but mostly glad that her friend was home.

I kept my Petoskey stone with me for years, either in a pocket, on my dresser, or more often in the bottom of my purse with a jumble of gum wrappers, pens, and lip gloss. When my fingers brushed against the smooth stone, I remembered that perfect week—the shared memories with our friends, and the reuniting of Andrew and Frightful. It had been a week that I tried, and even sometimes forgot about, the fear that lived in the back of my mind.

Chapter 7

By the next spring, our flock of six chickens began laying eggs every day, causing an egg-glut in the neighborhood. To ease the burden on our small refrigerator, I packed our extra eggs in large squares of colorful cloth and tied the top with yarn from Hannah's craft bin. Our friends and neighbors received these tasty gifts frequently, whether they wanted them or not.

True to the picture at DeYoung's Feed Store, Frightful matured into a blaze of golds and reds, with deep bronze feathers outlined in black. Her eggs were the color of a summer sky. She and Andrew had a strict routine that varied only on the days he was in bed with fever. It started with an early morning chat on the porch, followed by a walk around the yard. In the afternoons, Frightful had superhero practice which included a series of maneuvers Andrew put her through, ranging from balancing on his shoulder, to sitting on his head, clinging to a stick, or riding a bike while stuffed into his jacket, zipped up to her beak.

But the most extraordinary thing was their conversation—a mesmerizing combination of gestures, vocalizations, and humming you wouldn't think possible between two different species. While it was true we could distinguish a variety of sounds that came from the coop, there was something about the way Frightful communicated with Andrew that was very different from the usual barnyard banter. We were all used to the morning cackle that sounded like, *wra-wra-wra...WRA!* as each of the hens announced the arrival of an egg, or the *cluck-cluck-cluck!* as they scored a patch of tasty bugs in the yard. But when she was with Andrew, Frightful's sounds became almost musical—a soft cooing, a trill, and even a purr that made her love clear.

"Andrew is singing and clucking again," Hannah said one afternoon, "…in the playroom. And it's annoying."

"Then you should ask him to stop," I said while hemming a curtain panel for a client.

"He's talking to Frightful."

Annoyed, I walked downstairs to verify Hannah's story.

"We don't live in a barn, Andrew!" I said.

Andrew was playing X-Box with a controller in each hand, one for him and one for the chicken. Frightful clutched his leg. I'd seen that look in her eyes before. I could almost hear her scolding me. *"What's your problem?"*

"Andrew, Frightful is a barnyard animal. Why do you think Dad built her a condo in the back yard?"

I was irritated that I kept finding the chicken in our house, and definitely wasn't keen on the occasional plop of chicken poop on the floor.

"This looks like a barn to me!" Andrew said, waving a free arm around the room.

Frightful climbed up on his shoulder and stared at me. I had to admit, with two dogs, a cat, Legos, stuffed animals, books, and Barbies clogging the floor, it did look a little like a whacko barn. I brushed a stack of comic books out of my way and sat on the floor next to him. Andrew continued to hum and click his tongue while playing *Sonic the Hedgehog*, and Frightful responded with a series of chirps and cooing that could not be mistaken for anything other than a love song.

"Tell me about your game," I asked.

"I'm teaching Frightful to play. It's about a hedgehog named Sonic, but I like the one called Shadow. He's the best."

"Why is Shadow the best?"

"Just 'cuz," he said.

It was obvious he was done with the conversation, so I sat next to him, silently, watching Shadow the Hedgehog gobble up gold coins on the screen, the soundtrack eerily reminiscent of a Vegas slot machine.

"See! I'm getting more energy. More superpowers," Andrew said, bouncing in the chair.

Frightful grabbed onto a tuft of hair with her beak for balance while keeping one lizard-eye on me. I noticed Andrew's ears were turning a deep shade of crimson, the pink having already begun to finger its way to his cheeks. *Was it happening again?* It hadn't even been a month! A fresh wave of anxiety speared my gut, leaving me hopeless, and fearing I may never get my life back. I closed my eyes and prayed it would go away, this unseen monster that plagued my son. I prayed that when I opened my eyes, the fire would have left his body. I cracked open an eye, then went in search of Ibuprofen, pain meds, and a glass of water.

This time, the ulcers were deeper, more painful, and more aggressive, spreading to his tonsils and down his throat. It left him curled on the floor in agony as the feeling of burning sharp sticks poked at his flesh. The fever blew in with such force that by the next morning, we were in the hospital.

A month later, it happened again. Dr. Torgerson, having exhausted his arsenal of trial medications, sent us to Rheumatology, where they tried a variety of biologic drugs. Andrew was subjected to monthly, then weekly, then finally, daily injections of immunosuppressants in hopes of calming the raging inflammation in his body. Sometimes it helped.

But there were days when he would not leave his bed and we feared we were losing him to some dark place in the back of his mind—a place beyond autism's grip. Days when the only living soul he would speak to was Frightful, the chicken who was supposed to live in our back yard, but who had moved into our home and become a part of our family.

There were other times when it seemed like our nightmare was just some sort of temporary insanity we had conjured up. Andrew and Hannah would behave like other teenage siblings who quarreled, plotted, and bickered, and were generally doing their best to figure out how to grow up.

During one of those times, on a whim, when Andrew was thirteen and Hannah ten, we took them to France and Switzerland. Our friends and family told us we were crazy and reckless, that Andrew shouldn't travel. That something could happen. We told them we believed that children must see the world, but the truth was we felt compelled to go. We feared if we didn't go right then, we might not have another chance. So we plunged into our savings and left. For two weeks, we hiked in the Alps and fed cows the white petals of edelweiss. We visited the Normandy beaches and marveled at the remnants of the mighty Romans in the south of France. And when the fever tried to break through, we threw prednisone at it and kept going.

Even when we returned home, there were months when we were able to manage the fevers with an emergency dose of prednisone. But then the days came when his body threw the prednisone back at us with even higher fevers, more inflammation, and more pain, and there was nothing left to do but ride the tsunami. During those months, we were carried out to sea, tossed and mangled, and hurtled back to shore a little less confident, a little more wary. At times, I was able to go with the ebb and flow, and at others I railed against the beast. *Why? Why Andrew? Why us?* I would cry out to the gods of my nightmares. And then the daylight would come, pushing the blackness away to the far reaches of my mind, and I would seize the sunshine, harness it really, and ride it all the way to the next fever.

Chapter 8

A barrage of automated phone calls began clogging our voicemail each day at precisely 10:15 a.m. I stopped answering the phone around ten, knowing it was the high school office reporting that Andrew hadn't shown up for school. No matter how many times I called the front desk, inevitably, one of his teachers would report him absent or tardy, kicking the automated system into gear.

I was standing in the foyer of the high school one afternoon with a grumpy and impatient line of students and parents behind me. "He's still sick. And no, I don't know when he'll be back," I told the secretary.

"What kind of bug does he have?" she asked.

I started to answer, then finished with, "It's too hard to explain."

A week later, I received a threatening letter from the school district, stating that Andrew had missed seventeen days of his freshman year and it was only October. They were holding us, as his parents, responsible for his lack of education and would not guarantee a passing grade.

For the rest of the afternoon, I was plagued with thoughts of hostile replies to the school district. When I went in search of Andrew before dinner, I found him engrossed in a drawing of a hostile takeover by the Allied forces. After our visit to Normandy, he had taken a huge interest in World War II, and was now an expert in all things pertaining to D-Day. Both grandmothers fueled this interest by purchasing every single book and movie about the Allied forces and the D-Day invasions they could get their hands on. Anything that would make him happy or put a smile on his face was worth every penny they spent. It kept his mind occupied during the times he was ill, but it did nothing to calm my nerves. We had made little progress since joining the rheumatology team, and I was becoming increasingly alarmed by his escalating pain and fevers.

"What does the pain feel like?" I asked him more than once.

Searing pain from the gaping ulcers in his mouth I could imagine, but the phantom pain that roved through his body was a mystery. Nobody could get him to describe what it felt like. But one day, I saw him show Frightful.

"It's twisty," he said to the bird in his lap. He raised both hands, fisted, in front of him. "Like this, Frightful." He cracked both fists together, rotating one forward and one back. Then he sliced two fingers in an X across his belly. "Do you see? There are sharp knives in my belly that are twisty. Sometimes my bones hurt, too, like they were crushed," he said.

Frightful stood, turned to face his clenched fists, and pecked at something on the cuff of his sleeve.

"You understand, don't you, Frightful?"

Frightful answered with a low rumbling in her chest, followed by a familiar warbling coo—a song to soothe his soul. I murmured my silent thanks to Frightful for being there to draw my son's pain out into the open.

When I saw Andrew make the sign of cracking-fists one other time in the throes of a scorching fever, it prompted me to call the hospital nurse line. "It's twisting knife-like pain," I said. "I heard him say his bones felt crushed. What does that mean?"

The nurse had little to offer beyond forwarding my message to the doctor. My anger at the lack of answers drove me to become a bitchy pain-in-the-ass parent who refused to be ignored. So I called the nurse line every day, using his hand motions as a way to describe his misery, verbally documenting the amount of drugs I gave him to alleviate the pain, and begging for more doses of prednisone to throw at the inflammation clearly beginning to take over his entire body.

When that didn't help, I changed tactics radically. I cried out to the God of my childhood, the one who promised to never leave me, and the one I assumed would make my life easy if I just followed the rules. I realized it had been a while since I chatted with God, and I wasn't sure where to start, so I dove in with what I thought was a legitimate complaint:

"Why is this happening to me, God? I'm doing everything you asked of me. You said you would make our paths straight, but mine definitely has too many switchbacks in it, and I think I'm gonna barf! Can't you fix it?"

When I didn't receive an immediate answer, I attempted bargaining, mixed with pleading, followed by begging for mercy in exchange for anything He wanted from me. In the end, I was left to the rudimentary prayers I had learned in Sunday school—prayers that made me feel safe.

My first introduction to God was in the basement of a local church. There, I met a bearded man with a flowing white robe, who was flat and lived on a felt board. There were other important characters on the felt board, too, like Jesus, Moses, Mary, and King David, and something called the Holy Spirit, really a silver bird that looked like it was dive-bombing the earth.

"These three are actually one," my Sunday school teacher told us.

She had moved the grey-bearded God figure next to a sandal-clad Jesus and the shimmery bird. I remember trying to wrap my head around what she just said. All I could think was, "A kamikaze bird is an animal, you dummy. I don't think you got the story right." But as young children often do, I took her words as gospel and began my relationship with this mysterious bearded man.

In those school years, God became a one-dimensional man with whom I could hold a one-way conversation. He was also an idea — a perfect set of convictions that I put in a box and tied with a bow. I had no doubts in my beliefs, and knew God would forgive me at my best and at my worst. I also learned about acceptable behavior: Swearing was bad, lying was worse. You must love everyone, even if you knew they were wrong and going to hell. Never sit on a boy's lap, mini-skirts were begging for trouble, kissing was okay but wandering hands were not. God was watching. Surely I would be eligible to walk through the gates of heaven if I could just follow those rules?

In college, my world exploded as I bumped up against people who had a different God-shaped box. I became lost. I wasn't sure what I believed, and God became a little more confusing. So I kept Him in my own box where he fit best, a place where I could easily define the Trinity, wrap my arms around it, and understand it.

And that's where God stayed until my son was born and my carefully crafted box was blown to shreds.

The day Andrew was born, I cried out to God, *Please help me!* and I trusted He would hear my cry.

Here I was, once again, calling out for His help, yet I wasn't certain he had heard me.

If you are there, God, please make my son well, I begged. I waited for some divine feeling to come over me, assuring me my prayer would be answered. When it didn't come, I became even more desperate. So one night as I chased sleep in vain, I decided I needed help from someone with a direct line to the Almighty. I left Jon in bed and crept into my studio, where I sent a desperate email to a church we attended only a few times.

"HELP!!" it read.

Within minutes, Becki, the care pastor, called. I had seen her in the pulpit only once, but knew she was somehow different from other clergy. She engaged the congregation in a way that made us feel like she was a dear friend we had known forever. She made the Gospel relevant, speaking the truth as she saw it. I left church that day feeling like she had spoken directly to my heart.

"I have all the time you need," Becki said.

Between bouts of tears, I told her our family's story, the one we so carefully kept under wraps. I told her I couldn't reconcile my childhood God with what was happening in my life. I had spent years trying to live a blameless life, hoping it would somehow spare me troubles in the future. But here I was now, with a desperately ill autistic child who preferred to speak to a chicken rather than me, and a daughter who thought it was her job to keep him safe. Becki was quiet on the other end of the line, leaving me to wonder if I had done the right thing by calling.

"I don't think I can do it anymore. Where is God in all of this, anyway?" I cried out of desperation. I couldn't imagine a way out or a time I would ever feel at peace. I was living in a dark tunnel of despair, searching for a tiny speck of light that I hoped was there.

"I don't believe God has ever left you," she told me. "But He never promised a trouble-free life."

"I'm not sure what I believe," I admitted after a few minutes.

"What would you think of a visit?" she asked, changing the subject entirely.

"Now?" I was intimidated by her offer. I had never had a pastor over to my house.

It was near midnight when Becki slipped through our front door wearing her pajamas and fleece sweatshirt. The house was asleep, my dog Finn and I were the only ones to greet her. I knew it was only a matter of time until Andrew would be up again needing pain medication.

"You need to let people help you," Becki said as we made our way to the kitchen.

I plunked down wide-eyed and numb on a kitchen barstool, my reflection in the window a ghostly white. Two shadowy reflections stared back at me, and somehow I knew the stranger next to me was supposed to be there.

"I don't even know what to ask for. People don't know how bad it really is," I said with a deep, shuddering sigh.

I told her what our days were like—how I experienced a constant feeling of anticipation, even loathing, of the fever that would strike our home every month. I described the mouth ulcers that appeared out of nowhere, bringing with them a searing pain so intense that my son refused to allow anything to pass his lips. Then there was the roving, jabbing pain that couldn't be pinned down, which often landed in his legs or his chest or deep in his belly.

"But the nights are the worst," I said. "His pain somehow magnifies and we all hear his cries coming from the bathroom. Sometimes I even feel his pain in my own body. Do you think that's possible?"

Becki reached out to take my hand and something ruptured, something primal and out of my control. A keening escaped from my lips and I looked up, wondering who had made the sound. Snot and salty tears streaked my kitchen table, and a growing mound of wadded toilet paper formed a snowy white mountain in front of me.

We moved to the living room. Becki was on the floor, barefoot, looking up at me. Finn draped himself across my legs, his golden retriever body anchoring me to the couch, protecting me from the grief he sensed in the room. I studied Becki through narrowed eyes, wondering about this stranger I had let into our home. What did she think of my story? Did she think I was crazy?

"I do think it's possible to feel another's pain. But I wonder if a mother can feel it on a deeper level than we might imagine? It's a mystery," she said to the ceiling. "But regardless, this all sucks so bad."

I smiled through my tears at her unexpected comment.

"Can I share your story with a few people who I think can help?" she asked, turning to me.

I nodded, yes.

She held my gaze. "You will have people now. People who can hold you, your family, and your story."

Becki left my home as quietly as she had come, but somehow in that short time, she had created a tiny opening in my black tunnel and had let in the smallest glimmer of light.

The next morning, Jon asked me what I was doing up so late, if I was watching TV.

"No. Not exactly."

He pulled toast from the toaster and stuck a coffee pod in his Krups coffee maker. "Oh. I heard voices and I just assumed."

"I called the church down the street. One of the pastors came over to visit," I said as casually as I could.

His face fell. "Why?"

"Because I can't do it anymore. *We* can't do it anymore!"

He scowled and tossed his coffee into the sink. "I think we're doing just fine. Why didn't you talk to me first?"

I felt the cold chill of being reprimanded. Like I was a kid who had deliberately disobeyed their parents. I knew Jon wasn't thrilled about others knowing what went on in our home. Even our own parents didn't know how dire the situation was.

"What about Hannah?" I asked. "She needs more of us, and I have nothing left to give."

Hannah had been shuffled between home, grandparents, and neighbors for months and she had started to withdraw in a way that concerned me. Her contagious laugh had all but disappeared, and more often than not, I saw a slight frown crease her pretty features, making her appear angry and unapproachable. Although Jon and I could see her struggle, neither of us had emotional energy left to draw her out of her cave. The truth was, tiny micro-fissures had formed in our marriage and we were using what little energy we had to keep it glued together.

"She seems okay to me," he said, with a little less conviction.

But it was clear to me we needed help, and Becki had promised to get back to me right away. In fact, I had slept with my phone for the first time that night, determined not to miss her call.

Andrew moseyed into the kitchen and sat down at the counter, looking first to Jon, then me. "I heard you talking, too," he said, reaching for the cereal.

My heart gave a little leap. How much had he heard? Had I told Becki something that could be misunderstood?

After school, Andrew hung out in the chicken coop, refusing to come into the house. He dumped his backpack on the floor and, as usual, I checked his binder for any notes from his special education teacher. I found a stack of drawings—his familiar pictures of dinosaurs—bloodthirsty raptors chasing docile herbivores. There were a few new drawings with schematic plans of D-Day invasions he had traced out of books, but the one that took my breath away was the drawing of a boy with wings and a cape, and what I am certain was a chicken on a cloud labeled: *Heaven*.

I burst into tears. I didn't know what this meant. Did he mean that being with Frightful was heavenly? Or did he think that he was dying and going to heaven soon? I was terrified that maybe he was right, and I couldn't bear to think that thought.

I walked out to the chicken coop with his drawing in my hand, fully intending to ask him about it. When I reached the door, I heard Andrew talking in that reserved tone to his chicken.

"Frightful, you are my only friend."

"Krrillll...Chirp. CHIRP!"

You are mine.

"You know me best."

"Crawww-cruk-cruk."

I'm here for you.

"I can tell you anything."

"Tooka-tooka-took."

I will keep your secrets.

"Please don't leave me, Frightful."

For the second time, my son's words sucked the very breath from my lungs. I was drowning, reaching for the surface of my world, with no air in sight. I walked back to the house, clearly shaken, with the drawing crumpled in my hands.

Chapter 9

"The medicine Frightful takes doesn't make her better," Andrew told me one gloomy October afternoon.

Frightful was shoved in the front of his sweatshirt with both scaly feet poking out beneath the hem.

"What do you mean?"

"It's not working."

I knew he wasn't talking about Frightful. He was talking about his weekly infusions of methyl prednisone and the fact that he was only getting a few days of marginal relief at a time. The first time he had transferred his feelings to something else was with Ben, his little velveteen bear. Then came T-Rex, who took the brunt of his pent-up childhood frustrations. I suppose it allowed him to avoid feeling the full impact of emotions he couldn't really explain.

"What does Frightful think we should do?" I asked.

He shrugged his shoulders and patted the bird that let out a squawk. "I dunno."

"Well, I don't know either!"

A million conflicting emotions clashed in my mind. I was out of ideas and it seemed that no matter how hard I pushed for answers, the doctors just threw their hands up in the air and repeated the same thing: "We don't know what to do."

It made me crazy, this feeling of helplessness. I had no power to change things, so I channeled my frustration into a maniacal cleaning of the house, starting with Hannah's closet. I stripped hangers and shelves, and tossed toys and shoes on to the carpet. Drawers were dumped, walls were cleaned, and I disinfected every surface I could reach. I was headfirst in the back corner of Hannah's closet scraping something sticky off the wall when it occurred to me: "Maybe...being a superhero is the only option," I said.

I emerged from Hannah's closet holding a Batman cape I found wrapped around one of her American Girl dolls. "All you really need is one cool trick or talent...or just a plain old cape," I said, more to myself than my audience of two.

Both kids gawked at me from the hallway, a little fearful of my frenetic activity and my recent announcement.

The glossy black cape I held in my hand was Andrew's first in a collection of capes he'd acquired over the years. He became animated the moment he tied it around his neck, taking on the persona of the hero he envisioned himself to be. When he added the Batman mask to hide his eyes from a prying world, he became invincible. Nothing could hold him back, not even the shadowy veil of autism. Those were the times I felt he was the most real, my little boy whom I loved with every fiber of my being.

I dove back in the closet, pushing a set of rollerblades into the room.

"What are you talking about, Mom? And why are you shredding my room?" Hannah huffed.

I said it again, slowly this time, as I let the truth settle over me. Was this what Andrew craved all along? Power? There was power behind a mask; there was power cloaked in a cape. And I was determined to seize it, too.

I sat back on my heels, considering my answer, something the kids would understand.

"I think we have to harness our own power. It's like recognizing something inside us that makes us special, or unique. I think it's something that's bigger than us."

I was still grasping at the concept, not quite able to put it to words. But on some level, I suspected Andrew had figured it out a long time ago. From the time he was very young, he was convinced he could defy gravity, fly like a bird, or climb walls with his fingertips.

He also wanted to be an excavator.

"You mean you would like to *drive* an excavator?" I had asked.

"Nope. Be one."

"But humans can't be construction equipment," I said.

"They can if they want. And besides, excavators are super strong. Huge teeth. Like T-Rex."

I remember shaking my head, exasperated by his logic. For years, I spent an extraordinary amount of time trying to make my little boy conform to all the norms I thought were important. Yet by doing so, I had been deaf to the murmurings of his heart. What he was really trying to tell me was: *I want to be strong. I want to be powerful. I want people to hear me roar. And most of all, I want to be special.*

He *was* special. The day Andrew pulled a peeping fluffball from a bin of a hundred chicks, we knew something extraordinary had occurred. He found his voice. From that moment on, we were able to join him in his complex and fascinating world.

We began telling others our son was bilingual — he spoke English and Chicken. "The Chicken Whisperer" we called him. He would call, "Chi-KENS Back-ACK!!" out his second-floor bedroom window and the hen house would go wild. Six feathered dinosaur beasts with impossibly skinny legs went nutso until he ran across the yard to let them out of the coop. Then they would follow him around like he was a god, so I guess that was another one of his super-talents.

Finishing my purging of Hannah's room, I crossed the hall and began rummaging through Andrew's closet.

"Are you assembling your superpowers, Mom?" Andrew asked, following me into the room.

"Yes, I guess I am," I replied.

Buried beneath a landfill of Legos, I found a light saber and a pair of vinyl Spiderman boots. Andrew grappled for the boots. "That's where they went! I've been looking for them." He scrunched his too-large feet into the kid-sized Halloween costume. "Do I look like Spiderman?" he asked.

"A little," I shrugged and started pulling more things from his closet.

On top of a cardboard box lay Ben, forever smiling at me with his worn velveteen face. I rubbed a thumb across the knotted-thread nose, remembering Andrew doing the same thing. "Take good care of him," I spoke to the flat little shell of a body before placing him back in his hiding spot.

In the wreckage of Andrew's room I came across a pair of pants with fat, crinkly pockets. I emptied them of a few coins, a rumpled dollar bill, a note from his special education teacher, and a black and red action figure of a goofy looking creature with an oversized star-shaped head and wide, probing eyes. I turned it over in my hand, wondering what it was, then suddenly remembered it was the Shadow, the little hedgehog. I set it on his nightstand.

Hannah stood in the hall, dress-up clothes spilling from her arms to the floor, making a colorful heap at her feet. "Do you want us to make you into a superhero?" she asked.

"Oh! I've got just the weapon!" Andrew added, pulling the light-saber from the back of his closet.

For the next hour, my children transformed me into their version of a 'Supermom.' Listening to them plan the best way to create the perfect costume, I couldn't help but wonder if this was who they thought I was, or if this was what they needed me to be. When they finished, I was wearing a discarded ballet tutu, motorcycle chest pads, Batman's cape, a tiara and wig. In one hand, I carried Cinderella's princess wand; in the other, a light saber. With the final addition of Batman's mask, my costume was complete.

"Do you feel different?" Andrew asked eagerly.

Hannah stood in the hallway, snickering at the seriousness of her brother's question. *Did I feel different?* I didn't know what I was supposed to feel like.

"You have powers now!" Andrew added, pleased at my newly created look.

Staring at the stranger in the mirror, I tried to grasp what he meant. I peered at myself through the mask, searching out the only thing that was truly me—my eyes. What did they say about me? Were they scared? Lonely? Overwhelmed? I smiled, and they changed, giving me permission to feel...different. Both kids gazed at me expectantly...and something inside me changed. A giggle escaped my lips and I threw my head back and roared, lunging at them with both sword and wand. Andrew and Hannah screeched with laughter and took off down the stairs, with me in hot pursuit. In that instant, I remembered how it felt to fling my arms and voice into the air. Wild. Powerful. Free. Without a care in the world.

It was short-lived. Two days later, Andrew was struck with another fever. This time it held him in its grip for nearly two weeks.

"The space between episodes seems to be getting shorter," I told my mom on the phone one afternoon.

"Are they more frequent, or are they just running together?" she asked.

In my head, I calculated the date of his last fever. "Maybe they're running together. There's less time during the month that he's well. And he's not bouncing back like he used to."

From the corner of my eye, I caught sight of Andrew dragging the chicken tractor across our front slope of lawn. I moved to the window to get a closer look.

"Actually, today is the first time in days he's been out of bed," I said, wondering what in the world he was up to.

The ulcers in his mouth still swelled his lips, his eyes were ringed with the bluish tint of illness, but apparently the pain had diminished enough for him to schlep the heavy moveable coop across Jon's perfectly groomed turf.

When Jon had banned the chickens from roaming the yard after they had dismantled the garden during a particularly nasty rainstorm, Andrew's solution was to build the portable coop. It was fashioned from leftover chicken wire, two by fours, and wheels from his old wagon. On the front of their contraption was a half-moon of rope used to drag the square box across the lawn to a fresh patch of grass. This allowed the chickens to access only certain parts of the yard and surrounding woods.

"Oh, Mom, you won't believe what Andrew is doing now!" I told her with a snort.

Andrew trudged through a giant puddle at the edge of the lawn, pulling at the coop with both arms. Frightful rode on top, queen-like, in a Tupperware throne. Bits of cracked corn popped out of the bowl as she pecked, sprinkling the perimeter of the pen. The other hens, trapped in the tractor, squawked in protest as grain showered the wet grass out of their reach.

"Really? Does Frightful just stay in the bowl?" she asked.

"She'll do anything Andrew tells her to do. I suspect she would stand there all day if he wanted her to," I replied, still laughing.

"I just love that boy. He's going to do remarkable things, you know."

I knew she loved him deeply, but I had a hard time imagining what those remarkable things would be. Watching him play with Frightful that day gave me hope, but I couldn't have predicted how much I would need it.

Andrew disappeared, and a moment later I heard his voice find its way through the garage door. "Frightful is hungry!"

"Oh, she is?"

I smiled to myself, knowing this meant he was getting better rapidly. Tomorrow he would go back to school.

"Yep. Hungry."

The door slammed and I heard his impression of Arnold Schwarzenegger's famous *Terminator* line, *I'll be back!* Ten minutes later, Andrew sat on a barstool in our kitchen, picking at the food I put in front of him. The BRAT diet, I called it: Banana, Rice, Applesauce, Toast — the only thing halfway agreeable to his body when he was sick.

He absently studied a spoonful of applesauce as it plopped onto the counter. "I don't feel right," he said.

"What makes you say that?"

He shrugged. "I don't know. I just don't."

I sat down next to him and brushed my fingers through his hair, taking a moment to study his face for clues.

"But you're better than yesterday, aren't you?"

He nodded and tugged my hand away from his face. Why would he say that when I could clearly see he was getting better? I didn't understand what was happening. I never did. The answer always seemed to linger just beyond my fingertips, making it impossible for me to discover the truth. For years, I had been living on a mood rollercoaster, riding the waves of his illness. Today I was hopeful, but just days ago, in the throes of fever and pain, I had been terrified.

Along with Andrew's predictable illness, I had developed a predictable pattern of insomnia. At the first sign of fever, I slept with an ear cocked and one eye open. When I heard Andrew's first groan in the black hours of night, I flung the covers onto Jon and streaked into his room with a pounding heart and a fist in my throat. On those nights, fear and anger warred for supremacy, leaving me no room for sleep.

Frightful became my lifeline to Andrew. We talked about her as if she were in the room.

"How's Frightful?" I would ask after school.

Andrew would pause, considering how the chicken was feeling. "Good. She likes history class."

I wasn't surprised. Andrew had become a history buff, and had since expanded his interests beyond World War II to include World War I, the Revolutionary War, and Vietnam. Our house was inundated with books, maps, and videos of each era. For his sixteenth birthday, Jon glued a giant map of war-era Europe to his wall—his very own war room. Andrew added hand-drawn pictures of Churchill and Roosevelt as superheroes complete with capes. Stalin and Hitler were portrayed in black—leaders of evil empires, forces that would need to be overcome and conquered. I wished I could overcome the evil empire lurking in his body and conquer it once and for all.

The next morning, Andrew left for school with a backpack full of books and a new series of war maps he had sketched for his history class. As I walked him to the bus, a few chunky clouds clotted the horizon, leaving Seattle with an ominous reminder that more rain was on its way. This recent fever had kept him in bed for twelve days, leaving his face drawn and absent of its usual goofy smile. I felt an odd need to hug him tightly that morning, hold him a little longer, shelter him from something I couldn't see.

After the bus groaned its way down the street, I stood in the yard as filtered sunlight poured through the evergreen canopy, leaving slices of emerald and lime across the lawn. Under any other circumstance, it would have been a beautiful scene—the black clouds pushed against a bright blue sky—but somehow, that day, all I saw were the muddy tractor marks across the lawn, and mucky pools of water left by the chickens' search for worms.

I saw T-Rex standing alone on the chicken tractor at the far side of our property. I rescued the rain-soaked dinosaur from his exile and tried to shake off the sense of *déjà vu* that overcame me each month. This month seemed more unsettling, although I couldn't put it into words as to why. Rounding the corner of the garage, I saw Frightful sitting on the front porch in her green wicker chair, waiting for the bus to bring back her friend. I dropped T-Rex and scooped her into my arms.

"What secrets are you keeping?" I asked the bird who was my son's best friend.

She avoided my gaze, pecking instead at something on my sleeve.

"Do you know something I don't know?"

She didn't answer. She stood motionless, gazing across the yard until her wings pressed gently against my hands, pushing them outward. Then she fluttered and jumped down without looking back.

Chapter 10

We withdrew Andrew from high school just two weeks after I was transformed into a superhero.

"We'll be back soon," I told the principal behind a fake smile. "He just needs to concentrate on getting better."

What they didn't know was that neither Jon nor myself thought it would happen any time soon. We were hoping he could start again the next fall and repeat his sophomore year, but we weren't sure if that was possible.

True to her word, Becki had been sending us help in the form of meals and drivers for Hannah to get to and from her after-school activities. But with Andrew home full time, we needed more.

"I can't get Andrew to talk to me," I told Becki during one of her visits to the house.

"What do you mean?" she asked.

"He just won't share how he feels about any of this."

"You said he likes stories," she said. "I've been thinking of sending over a woman to help with some things and read to Andrew. She's great, and I really think he will like her."

"I'm not sure…" I said, not wanting to sound ungrateful.

"Why?"

Truthfully, I didn't want anyone to see what went on in our home. If it was nightmarish to me, it would be horrifying to anyone else.

"I think you are all exhausted and it would be good for Andrew to see a new face. Think about it," she added.

I was curious. I would never have thought to have someone over to read to him.

"Who is this person?" I finally asked.

"I call her, 'Books on Tape' Sue. She's amazing! Let her help you. And trust me, she can handle it." When I didn't answer, she said, "She'll be here tomorrow."

How did she know that I was worried about someone else caring for Andrew? When I called, I thought she would offer more help with Hannah, or even someone to run errands for me, but with that simple line: *Trust me, she can handle it*, she had cut through my anxiety and allowed me to breathe.

The next day, 'Books on Tape' Sue walked into our home and into our chaos. Andrew was in the bathroom, lying on the cold tile floor, clad only in his oversized underwear. His pain and nausea had been so demanding that even the highest dose of narcotics I could safely give him offered little relief.

I was upstairs when I heard a knock at the door, followed by a hesitant, "Hello?"

"Just a minute!" I was mortified Sue was in my home, and was secretly cursing Becki's hare-brained idea.

Sue climbed the stairs and found me wrestling with the cord of an oscillating fan near the sink in hopes of cooling Andrew's scorching body. Sue dropped her purse and crawled onto the floor next to Andrew. "Hi Andrew. I heard you like stories. Can I read to you? We can sit right here."

Andrew flicked an eye in her direction. A long minute later I heard, "I like hero stories. Stories like *The Hunger Games*."

I ran to his room in search of the book. I didn't know why he had chosen such a gruesome tale. He had insisted on it at the library, along with a World War II documentary, *Harry Potter*, Calvin & Hobbes comics, and an assortment of Judy Blume books. None of it made sense to me—the cacophony of young children's books, fantasy and war.

"Who's your favorite hero?" Sue asked.

"Shadow," I heard him reply.

He was talking about that strange black and red hedgehog again. I kept finding the small plastic action figure in his pockets or school bag, even perched on top of the TV.

"Is Shadow that cool black and red guy with the crazy spiky hair? My grandson loves him!" Sue said.

A look of surprise crossed Andrew's face, and for just a second, a hint of a smile. In that moment, I fell in love with Sue. Her easy manner and the way she engaged with Andrew changed everything. Sue quickly became his comrade in adventure. She easily slipped into conversations with my son, something I hadn't been able to do for a long time. Each day she visited, Sue would weave new stories together aloud at Andrew's instruction and the two of them were off into their own world. For weeks they explored the life of a quirky boy named Fudge, in old Judy Blume books, and read and reread tales of young men and maidens warring against evil in order to save the world from fear and destruction. And some days, when he was well enough, they left the books inside, choosing instead to sit on the porch with Frightful.

"Frightful has powers," I heard Andrew tell Sue one afternoon. "She talks."

"Do the other chickens talk?" Sue asked.

"Of course not. They just cluck."

As if on cue, Frightful stood up and clucked. She slipped out of Andrew's grasp and hopped down to the walkway to peck at a string of moisture ants.

"Do you think Frightful will go to heaven?" Andrew asked, twirling a loose feather between his fingers.

Sue looked at her new friend, surprised at the change of topic. "I suppose so. I think God's creatures are special. And I think we agree that Frightful is extra special."

"Good. Then I will always get to see her," he replied.

Later, as Sue shared Andrew's conversation with me, the drawing of the boy with wings came to mind. My heart sank.

Andrew always circled difficult topics, never discussing directly what it was he wanted you to know. Instead, he led you to a conclusion he had already made. This conclusion paralyzed me.

Many days when Sue visited, I hovered around the corner in the hallway, waiting, listening, thanking God for sending us relief in the form of an intensely patient woman with a bewitching voice, who could lure my son into a trancelike state. But one day, things changed. Andrew's fever skyrocketed to an all-time high, the lesions in his mouth became gaping holes, and he stopped eating entirely. During our next trip to the ER, they proposed Nasogastric Intubation (NG) for hydration and feeding.

"You should be able to put some weight back on him without disturbing those ulcers," we were told.

Andrew was stabilized, and then sent home with an NG feeding tube threaded through his nose and down to his stomach. Remembering my son that day, frail and weak, I have no idea why we agreed to bring him home. I think we had just begun to accept his illness and ongoing pain as something we had to live with. It had become our insane version of normal.

In an attempt to cheer him, Hannah pressed Frightful to the downstairs playroom window where Andrew lay on a makeshift bed. Soon after, the chicken took up residence on a broken flowerpot next to the window, and we heard the constant tap-tap-tap of her beak on the pane. When we locked her in the pen, she screeched and squawked, causing Jon to make not-so-veiled threats.

"Wk-wk-wk-wk-wanh! Wk-wk-wk-wk-WAHN!"

I want out! I want OUT!

Frightful poked her beak through holes in the chicken wire in her attempt to escape.

"Don't you think it's a little weird for a chicken to act like that?" Jon cornered me one afternoon.

I glanced out the window at the chickens scratching in the rose garden. "I'd be mad, too, if I was the only one locked up while my friends were out feasting in the garden," I said.

"You know what I mean. Frightful doesn't care about the garden. She just sits in front of the window all day, staring at Andrew."

He was right. She'd been acting unusually odd for the last couple of days. When Hannah went to the coop to collect eggs, she screeched and bolted through the door, running across the yard to her flowerpot. I had tried to nudge her away with a toe and she had lunged at me with a clawed foot.

"She's gone batty!" Hannah cried.

"She's just scared," I told her, wondering if that was really true.

Sue walked into chaos the next afternoon when I was on the verge of collapsing under the sheer horror of each long day. Andrew was screaming and had been vomiting for hours. When I called his doctor, he had tried to convince me to give him more anti-emetics and wait it out. I sometimes wondered if the doctor thought I was exaggerating his symptoms, because on many days when he saw the doctor, Andrew would behave normally, feeling perfectly fine. The next, he would be horrifically ill. It made no sense.

Sue took control, sending me out of the house to get fresh air and perspective. After she left, however, an eerie, almost haunted silence descended over the room and Andrew. Outside, Frightful suddenly stood frozen on the flowerpot in the rain, her wings spread wide like a shield. We made eye contact, the raptor and I. She pierced the air with a screech before throwing herself at the window, imploring me to take action, to help her best friend. Horrified, I reached for the phone in my pocket and dialed Jon at work.

"You have to come home. NOW!"

In a fit of panic, I drug Andrew and the mattress through the door and into the hallway where Frightful couldn't see him. When Jon arrived, the two of us lifted Andrew into the car and left the bird calling for our son in the rain.

Chapter 11

Jon peeled into the circular drive, the tires of his SUV chirping to a halt. For a frozen moment, I sat in the passenger seat, staring through the rain-splattered windshield — a terrifying thought pushing at the back of my mind. While Jon flung open his door and his shoes crisscrossed pavement, I watched water gush from overflowing gutters. The light in the red and white sign flickered like a firefly I had once seen on a hot summer night. Curious, I wondered why they hadn't fixed it.

There was no sound. Then there was: a roaring in my ears, a heartbeat thudding through veins...the sound of fear. My arms and legs moved without allowing time for my brain to catch up. I was out of the car, my hands reaching through the door, dragging my sixteen-year-old son from the back seat. He was taller than me by six inches, but somehow, during the time of no sound, I had developed superhuman powers. My arms easily lifted his skeletal frame, cradling him against my chest. Then I turned and walked straight through the double doors of the Emergency Room.

"My son is dying," I said in a voice I barely recognized.

The woman behind the desk had a paper butterfly pinned to her shirt. I stared at her. She stared back, a polite smile curving at the edges of her mouth. "We'll get him all fixed up. Why don't you take a seat?"

Puzzled, I stared at her lips, thin, painted pink to match the butterfly fluttering about her neck. She spoke again, this time her words a slap across my face. "Take a seat, ma'am. We'll be with you shortly."

Take a seat? Was she kidding?!! At five foot ten, Andrew weighed barely 100 pounds and hadn't been able to eat in nearly two weeks. No matter how much Tylenol and Advil we administered, his 105-degree fever rarely decreased. That night he began vomiting blood. She was crazy if she thought I was going to take a seat.

Consumed with rage, I spun around, scanning the waiting room filled with anxious parents and miserable kids. Ten sets of tired and weary eyes gazed back at me, challenging me to sit down. I was *not* going to sit. I would stand there and stare them all down with laser-vision if I had to, starting with the woman behind the desk, who was now speaking into the phone.

I adjusted Andrew in my arms, preparing to wait her out. He lay limp, his head turtled into the neck of his sweatshirt. I rocked from side to side, singing, "You are my goofball, my only goofball..."

The woman's anxious gaze kept flitting between me and something on her desk as she continued her conversation on the phone. A moment later, the double doors yawned open, spitting out a round woman in dinosaur scrubs pushing a wheelchair. She reached out to take Andrew from my arms and the room began to roar—a deep, guttural roar that made the rage twist in my belly.

"You make me happy when skies are grey..." I sobbed while squeezing Andrew hard against my chest just to hear something, anything that would make me believe he would be okay.

"You're a terrible singer," he croaked.

I continued to sing while Dinosaur Lady peeled Andrew from my grip and set him in the chair. A name-tag was clipped to her shirt—a blue logo of a whale within a whale—with her name below: Martha Reed. Martha grasped me by the arm and looked me directly in the eye. "We'll take good care of him. I promise."

They took off through the double doors, the mouth of the giant whale consuming my heart. My arms were empty, my superpowers vanished, my body turned to stone. "Please don't take my sunshine away," I sang to no one in particular.

I stood frozen in the doorway, allowing my mind to replay the day: Andrew's rising fever, the untreatable pain. Nausea, vomiting, not even an ice cube to the lips for comfort. While Sue sat with Andrew, I poured over my files of notes and diaries I had kept since Andrew entered grade school. I sorted and rearranged each piece of information in an attempt to get a glimpse of the whole picture. It was a puzzle with no borders. Defeated, I'd swiped at my dinner plate, sending it off the edge of the counter in a shower of half eaten spaghetti and soggy bits of salad. I'd returned to glowering at the stack of paperwork again, willing some pattern to reveal itself.

Still churning the day's events over in my mind, I finally walked down the hall of Seattle Children's Hospital, my feet guided by the familiar orange and red salmon etched into the linoleum floor, urging me deeper and deeper into the belly of the whale. Harried voices led me to a large exam room, lights blazed in one corner where an orderly was setting up a tray. I took note of the bed in the center, my son's frail body occupying barely half the space. Someone washed their hands with disinfectant soap, the odor analogous with the countless doctors we had seen over the years who tried their best, but ultimately had no idea how to help. Even Dr. Torgerson felt like a faraway dream, unreachable. We hadn't seen him since we joined the rheumatology team three years before.

From the doorway, I watched as a young doctor hovered over the bed, barking orders at a lone nurse. An IV was inserted, a saline bag hung.

In contrast to Andrew's desiccated body and swollen red cheeks, this man was fresh-faced with a country club haircut and a stylish three-day scruff. Sperry boat shoes poked out beneath cuffed khaki's. No socks. He looked more like a deck hand at the Shilshole Bay Marina than an emergency room doctor at one of the finest research institutions in the country. I hated him instantly.

He began pebbling my son with questions: How do you feel? Where does it hurt? How long have you been sick? You look a little thin. When did you last eat?

Andrew just lay silent.

"Fever, pain, vomiting, ulcers in his mouth throat and gut," I snarled, like a mantra I had come to know month after month of this recurring hell. *Don't these people keep records?*

I walked over to the bed, grabbed one of Andrew's bony hands and squeezed. In his own version of sign language of which I had become the translator, Andrew lifted his other hand, stabbing a forefinger into the area below his belly button in the same way he'd shown Frightful those many years ago.

"His belly pain is unbearable," I said.

"Where exactly?"

"In the middle. It's always the same."

Andrew sliced two fingers across his belly.

"It feels like knives are cutting him open."

The much-too-young doctor on call sat down next to the bed and pulled out a clipboard and pen.

"I know it can feel scary to be in an emergency room, but I'm sure he just has a bad case of the flu. There are lots of viruses going around this spring."

Oh good God! You have no idea! How could he say such a thing? My vision narrowed and, for an instant, I felt I could have murdered the doctor. He had no idea where we had been, how weighty our story had become, what Andrew had endured for the past ten years. Rage bubbled up through my own belly, leaving me with an urge to slice him open with the phantom knives that cut across my son's belly. Frightful understood more about Andrew and his condition than this marina-coiffed doctor ever would.

A nurse sauntered into the room, handing the doctor a thick file of notes with Andrew's name printed on the glossy yellow tab. While he carefully flipped through each page, I glared at his throat, the crease of skin, a recent sunburn, the Adam's apple protruding out a little too far. As we all stood there silently, I watched him passive-aggressively read my son's medical tome while my boy lay suffering between us. Angry tears welled up, spilling down my face and splatting onto the floor, causing the colorful linoleum fish to swim in front of my eyes.

Doctor No Socks started the clinical questions. I held up my hand, palm facing out, as a signal for mercy. "We were in here a few days ago, so why don't you just check the chart."

Despite regaining an outer sense of control, I started to shake from somewhere deep inside—an uncontrollable shivering that took over my entire body, forcing me to clench my jaw to keep my teeth from chattering. Groping for the wall, I guided myself to the floor, squeezing my eyes shut and clamping my hands over my ears to block out the noise—just like Andrew does. It helped. As I sat on the floor in the emergency room for what felt like the hundredth time, my world cracked open.

"Something is happening. It's different this time."

My mind flashed on Frightful throwing herself against the window while letting out an unbearable screech. She'd known it was different this time, too. I felt the young doctor's eyes boring a hole in the side of my head. I heard, or rather felt, the groan of his chair, the catch of his breath, as if he was going to say something but then thought better of it. I cradled my head in my hands, wishing my world was anything but fevers, pain, emergency rooms, and an autistic son who communicated with a chicken named Frightful more eloquently than he ever had with any human. Tonight, I was terrified. I needed Doctor No Socks to understand what I knew in my gut: Something we couldn't see was killing my son.

A scuffling in the hallway told me Jon was back from the parking garage. He was on the phone, his words drifting in through the open door. "Yes. We'll be here a while. No. I don't know. Please pick up Hannah and take her home with you."

With my eyes still closed, I let out a long, slow exhale, realizing I had forgotten to breathe. I pictured Jon's mother Connie, rushing to rescue Hannah from the monsters that lurked in the shadows of our empty home. *Thank you,* I breathed—my silent offering of gratitude to the only person who could comfort our daughter on nights like these.

Jon entered the room, nodded to the doctor, then crouched low to meet my eyes. He took my face in his hands and spoke the same words I'd heard so many times before: *We will get through this.* I nodded in a crazy way that meant I didn't really believe it but hoped to God it was true. Then I fled the room and bolted down the hallway, back through the gaping maw of the whale, and out into the rain.

Chapter 12

A few stray streetlights cast amber pools of light on the far side of the street from where I stood. Dense cloud layers hung over the city, seeming to squeeze the life out of it. I huddled next to the sliding glass doors, teetering on the rough edge of a cement planter box until reality slammed the breath out of me. Life wasn't supposed to be this way. At least not like this. I wasn't supposed to live in a constant state of grief, trauma, and panic, wondering when the next proverbial shoe was going to drop. But this had become my reality. I told myself that with all this newly built character, I was stronger; now that I'd acquired a whopper-load of life experiences under my belt, I'd be tougher. It was all just a big fat lie. I didn't feel wise. I felt scared, vulnerable, and alone. I secretly wondered if I stood in the wrong line when they were handing out lives.

Pulling out my phone, I scanned through my contact list, wondering who I could call in the dead of night. I thought of Becki, but truthfully, I was too embarrassed to call her. We had spoken the day before and I had convinced her that we were doing okay, thanking her again for sending Sue to us. I scanned further. My parents were surely sleeping, and Jon's mom was on the way to our house to get Hannah. I considered my Breakfast Club ladies, but over the years, as our children grew and attended different high schools, we had become involved in our own lives and found new tribes. My thumb stopped on Julie. Yes. Julie was one of my oldest friends, my 3:00 a.m. person. Someone I could call at any time, even when we hadn't spoken for weeks, or even months.

Julie answered the phone on the third ring. A rustling of sheets and a single *click* told me she had sat up in bed and turned on the light.

"I'm sorry to wake you," I croaked into the phone while on the edge of hysterics. I collapsed into the planter box, crushing the newly planted geraniums. Rainwater pooled at my feet, reflecting a mass of red and white jumbled letters. "We're at the emergency room. *Again!*"

"Tell me everything. From the beginning," she said.

And so we talked, me standing in a Seattle downpour, her in the heat of an Arizona night. I told her about my horrible day, how I had felt something sinister come over the room as I lay next to Andrew, and how Frightful had tossed herself against the window in a fit of anxious foreboding. I told her about Sue, what a godsend she was, yet even when Andrew was in her capable hands, I couldn't relax. I told her about the picture Andrew had drawn weeks before, of a boy with wings and a cape and a chicken on a cloud labeled 'Heaven', and how I couldn't get it out of my head. I also admitted to her for the first time that I was terrified my son was going to die.

"I told the lady at the front desk tonight that my son was dying," I said. "What do you think? Am I overreacting?"

She paused for a long time on the other end of the line. "I'm so sorry. I don't know what to say. It breaks my heart." She took a breath before adding, "Please remember that you're not alone."

I wanted to believe her, but right then, I felt more alone than I had ever felt in my life.

"Imagine me sitting next to you right now," Julie said, "and we're chatting in the corner of the living room where we met. Remember?"

I did. We first met as young parents in a bible study at a local church Jon and I were attending. We were a bunch of uptight parents who wanted to believe that God had His hand on the pulse of our lives, but in truth we were all skeptics, hoping to latch onto someone else who was stronger and wiser and more faithful than we were. Julie and I sat in the corner that first day, sharing our stories, oblivious to the rest of the group. We had laughed at the silly antics of our Kindergarten sons and shared in the sudden weight of responsibility we felt for them the moment we became mothers. And somehow, during the course of that night, we found we spoke the same language.

The sweetness of that memory dissolved as Julie's voice broke into my thoughts. "Have you prayed?"

"Yes! Well, I think so. I don't know. What does it matter anyway?"

I splashed my foot in the puddle, causing the reflected letters to shiver into streaks of color. I desperately wished Julie was there with me. She had moved to Arizona years before and, strangely, I still felt the sting of her absence.

"It's worse than ever," I said. "Way worse. I don't know how long this can go on."

Grim thoughts filled my mind, but I refused to speak them aloud, so I just sat there among the crushed flowers, listening to my friend breathe.

"I have your back," she said.

"I know," I replied through a mass of tears.

In the span of twelve months, Jon and I had made fourteen trips to the emergency room with Andrew. We now had our own direct phone line and social worker assigned to us. I guess I should have felt privileged, but I could only feel a gnawing sense of despair at our impossible situation.

"They're replacing his NG tube through his nose right now. It came out this afternoon."

I didn't tell her about the drama that preceded Sue removing it. That was a story I didn't have the energy to tell. I shifted my weight in the planter, triggering the glass doors to open. Andrew's frightened protests tumbled out from the end of the hall, skewering my heart with a fresh wave of pain.

"Does anyone know why he continues to get worse?" Julie knew it was a loaded question.

"No. They have no idea." I turned my face to the sky, catching flecks of rain off the edge of the overhang, cold splatters dampening the front of my sweatshirt. Grabbing a handful of broken geraniums, I crushed them in my hand before tossing the bruised petals to the pavement. "Tonight they discovered he has an inflamed liver, appendix, spleen, bile duct, and part of his lower intestine." I said it like it was a common thing to be chatting about on the phone.

Julie sucked in a deep breath on the other end of the line.

"I honestly don't know what to think. I'm numb," I said.

The phone vibrated in my hand. Pulling it from my ear, I saw my favorite picture of Hannah flash onto the screen, one taken at the beach a few summers before. A picture of a little blond girl clad in a pink and tangerine swimsuit, leaping in the air above a glittery sapphire sea.

"Hannah's calling. I have to go. And thank you for listening."

I clicked over. "Hi, Mom," Hannah said in her sing-song voice, the one she used when trying to cheer me up.

"Hi, sweetheart. You still up?"

I checked my phone for the time. 3:24 a.m.

"The dog gacked on the carpet again. But don't worry. Grandma and I cleaned it up before we left."

Finn had a little problem with doggie-anxiety. When he sensed tension in our home, he didn't know what to do with himself. It usually resulted in him leaving his coveted spot on the heat register to drag himself down the hallway to the area rug in front of the TV where he proceeded to barf on the carpet. Never mind that he had just crossed miles of hardwood floor to get there.

"Me and Grandpa are making waffles in the morning. Do you want me to save you one?"

Rainwater ran down the sides of my face and I wiped it away with the sleeve of my sweatshirt.

"Mom?"

"Yes, honey, I'm here. Why don't you save me a couple for when I get home?"

"I love you, Mom. Brother will get better."

Brother will get better. It was part statement and part question and since I didn't know how to respond, I said, "I love you, too. Very much."

I shucked my wet sweatshirt and tied it around my waist before walking back in to the lobby. I slipped past the woman with the paper butterfly and back into the room, where I found Jon sitting bolt upright, asleep in a chair. The room was full of shadows, the only sound Andrew's drugged breathing and the whir of the narcotic pump.

I pressed my face to the top of Jon's head, breathing in the familiar scent of his spicy shampoo and my favorite lavender soap — a perfect mixture of the two of us.

"You can go now," I whispered into his hair.

He reached up to stroke my face before fishing his keys from his pocket. "Let me sleep a couple hours, close up a few things at work. I'll be back after lunch." And then he was gone.

I stood there, feeling alone, like I had never been here before, although I knew for a fact we had been in this very room the week before. I reached for the doctor's wheeled stool and crab walked it to the edge of Andrew's bed. Andrew reached out a hand, placed it in my open palm, and made his familiar symbol for bird: Pointer finger and thumb pinched together, the remaining three fingers spread out in a fan.

"You miss her, don't you?"

He bent his wrist forward, then back, confirming his answer with a hand-nod. I cupped my other hand over his, sandwiching the thought of Frightful between my two palms.

My skin prickled as a thought pushed its way into my mind. I remembered seeing Andrew and Frightful on the porch only days earlier. But instead of their usual place in the old wicker chair, he lay flat on the wooden steps with her nestled on his chest. His body had been soft, relaxed, melding into the wooden planks. A look of contentment painted his features, even though I knew he was in pain. I thought it a little odd at the time, but hadn't asked him about it.

Andrew slipped his hand from between my palms, tapped his chest twice and laid his hand over his heart.

"Yes. I know she likes to sit right there," I said, reaching out to touch the area above his belly. He winced. "Does she know how you feel? That you've been having a hard time?"

He nodded with his head this time. "Frightful has special powers," he said in a voice barely above a whisper. "She fixes my heart. When it's scared, it flutters and jumps around. When it's sad, it's too heavy." He reached for my hand, placing it on his chest. "She makes it work right. She makes me better."

I let my head fall to the bed, face down in a rumple of starched hospital sheets. How did this child of mine, who so often spoke in a way I didn't understand, make more sense than anyone else? After a while, I felt Andrew's breathing deepen, his body twitch. He was asleep again.

That night, Andrew was admitted to Seattle Children's Hospital for the fifteenth time. He was hydrated and medicated for pain. When the pain went beyond what the medications could mask, I became his voice again, translating his version of sign language to his medical team. This time, they didn't tell me it was the flu. And this time, he didn't come home with us the next day, or the next week. He remained in the hospital for months.

At home, to bring some outward show of control in our lives, Jon thrust himself into gardening. Soon, our lawn was devoid of any weed, moss, or fir cone, and an unnatural shade of green due to the amount of fertilizer he poured on it. I, on the other hand, scoured the Internet like my hair was on fire, anxiety propelling me into the wee hours of the night, hoping for a morsel of information I could grab onto, something that would be a miracle cure. When I failed, I threw myself into my growing stack of notes, sure that some clue would reveal itself.

Hannah was just the opposite. She became quiet, reserved, even stoic at times. "This is for Andrew," she said one day, a shy smile tipping at the edge of her mouth.

She handed me a construction paper envelope full of notes, each with a hand-drawn picture of Frightful in a variety of poses and costumes. One as a soldier with a rifle, others as The Hulk, Superman, Iron Man, and Shadow, each with a determined look on his face—if that was possible for a chicken with a beak for a mouth. "It's for courage," she said. "He can be strong if we're strong, too."

I started to weep. Hot tears pushed through my simmering anger and despair at the unfairness of our life. How could this be happening to us?

I drew her close, squeezing her in a bear hug. "Yes, Hannah. We all need courage. Thanks for reminding me."

That simple gesture stopped my frenetic searching, and served as a stark reminder that I had two remarkable kids who needed not only my love and attention, but my courage, too. It would take courage to summon faith in something I couldn't see. I wasn't at all sure what that meant.

Chapter 13

With Andrew in the hospital for an undetermined amount of time, we became hospital dwellers. We were surrounded by people twenty-four hours a day, yet we felt completely alone. Andrew was now a part of the Complex Care Team—a group of freaky patients with unusual and unexplainable ailments. We were stuffed into rooms with others like us, children who had no diagnosis, people from the land of misfit toys.

Nobody really wanted us, but we were hard to ignore. We tried to ignore one another, but a flimsy curtain was hardly enough of a barrier to escape from another's pain. The fact is, hospital dwellers don't like to share. We don't want to look at you, hear you, or see you. We don't want your pain to somehow attach itself to us, because our own burdens are already impossible to carry.

The day Andrew was admitted for the last time was the same day my design business came to an abrupt halt. It was the day I lost a fraction of myself, the piece that was an artist. Twenty years of building a stable design clientele, and now I had to call my clients to tell them I couldn't finish their jobs. Instead of designing or sewing or working on remodeling projects, I spent my days at the hospital, alternating with Jon, who spent most of the nights. We both saw little of Hannah. It was a lonely life.

As hospital dwellers, we understood we were not to ask others about their child, or why they were there. But when a mother in pajamas with bleary eyes sat next to me in Starbucks in the lobby, I couldn't help but meet her eyes, and I knew she wanted to share her story. We all wanted to share our story. We somehow hoped that when someone else witnessed our abyss, our loneliness would vanish, if only for a brief moment, and we'd feel like we could survive another day, and then possibly another. That day, I sat and listened to a mother describe her love for her daughter who had been battling Leukemia for months. I listened more to her heart than her words, and over the course of an hour, I could see relief tugging at her face, the slight shifting of her shoulders as they relaxed. As we parted, she reached for my hand, thanking me with a genuine smile.

"No, I should be thanking you," I said. "Today, I needed you to tell me about your beautiful daughter. You brought me hope this morning." And I meant it.

That night, Jon stayed home with Hannah, and I took the night shift. I had the misfortune to cross our roommate's surly mother when I asked if she would mind turning off the TV at three o'clock in the morning.

"NO! I will *not* turn it off! I like watching TV," she harped back at me.

I heard a rustling, her son whispering, "Mom, just do it. I'm trying to sleep."

"Hmphh!" There was a grunt, a complaint of springs, a rearranging of her ample body on the skinny fold out chair. A few clicks of the remote and the volume soared.

When I woke after just a couple hours of sleep, I saw Andrew for the first time through the eyes of a stranger. I studied his puffy fevered face, his emaciated body, and the ulcer on his gums that had eroded through to the root of his tooth. A mixture of fear and anger tore through me, propelling me from the room in search of someone from his medical team. I called Jon. An hour later, seven of us were squeezed into the staff lunchroom, five in white coats on one side of the table, Jon and I on the other, sleep deprived and disheveled.

"The medications you are giving him clearly aren't helping," Jon said to a group of steely-eyed doctors.

"Sometimes these anti-inflammatories take several months to show signs of working, so I think we should give the medication a little while longer," the gastroenterologist replied.

He was a small, wrinkled man in his late sixties with papery yellow skin and large nose that easily held up a pair of thick glasses. He didn't make eye contact with either of us. Instead, he studied a finely carved wooden pen, slowly rolling it back and forth between his fingers.

My blood was simmering, leaving me queasy. I wanted to scream, grab his pen and chuck it at the plate glass window.

"But you said he clearly does not have Crohn's Disease, or Inflammatory Bowel Disease. How can we know if we're even heading in the right direction with these medications?"

I could feel my pulse quickening, heat moving up the back of my neck. A small prickle at the base of my head—a hint of a migraine—made it difficult to maintain an amiable look on my face. Somehow, I knew we were looking in the wrong place, that we were losing ground, wasting time, but I had no better ideas.

Jon spoke what I was thinking. "Something isn't right here. What are we missing?"

"We'd like to propose a much more aggressive trial of medications," the current team lead interjected.

I had heard this before. *Would it be anything new?* With each meeting, a new group of doctors, specialists, social workers, and psychiatrists analyzed our situation from their own unique perspective. This meeting was no different.

"We want to blast the inflammation like we use chemotherapy drugs to combat cancer. It should allow us to get on top of things much more quickly," he added.

I took a slow, deep breath in through my nose, held it, and slowly exhaled through my mouth. My yoga teacher said this signals the nervous system to relax. It wasn't working.

"We'd like to double Andrew's daily dose of oral prednisone and add an additional weekly infusion of methyl prednisone. We plan to up his pain meds, add some antibiotics in case we are missing any infectious process, and try an additional anti-emetic to calm his nausea."

I looked at him like he was a lunatic.

He raised a finger, "Oh, and we would like to give him an additional booster dose of the biologic anti-inflammatory to see if there is any response."

Jon and I sat glued to our chairs, the silence louder than if he had not spoken at all. This was crazy talk. It sounded more like an experiment to see how much a person could take before you killed them. The pen in the gastroenterologist's hand suddenly went squiggly, wavy lines worked their way up his arm and neck, filling my vision. There was a hard pinch behind my right eye; moments later, a dull throb rolled through the right side of my head.

I was furious, powerless. It had been more than a decade since we began searching for help. I couldn't fix my child, or even comfort him. I wondered if God had ditched us, moved along to something more interesting, more important, like chasing down the terrorists I read about each day in the news. Slumping down in my chair, I dropped my head to the table, feeling like someone had ripped my backbone right out the top of my body. All that was left were the soft parts of me, bruised and limp and helpless.

"Do you realize this is my child... *and* my heart you are dealing with? How much more can we take?"

Jon reached for my hand under the table and squeezed—a sign that we were in this together, even if it felt like our entire world was shattering.

After a long minute, I squeezed back.

Jon answered for the both of us. "We're willing to try anything."

What we did not know is what "anything" would turn out to be.

The following day was Saturday. Jon was able to relieve me from the hospital so I could go home to close my business. After my last call to a very disappointed client, I tossed my cell phone onto my desk where it promptly slid in to a coffee cup, sloshing a two-day old latte onto a stack of client files. I wasn't happy about abandoning my career, but secretly relieved to stop the unnecessary insanity. With nothing left to do, I sat on the floor among bolts of fabric that had been carefully laid out and measured for cutting. Finn lumbered into the studio, circled twice and laid his furry canine body next to me, resting his head on my lap.

I closed my eyes, thinking of that long ago summer at Lake Michigan. I pictured myself kneeling in the water, sifting through bone-colored sand for Petoskey stones as I had a little chat with God. Or rather, I lectured and God listened. I assumed He would agree to my terms and was willing to leave it in His hands, but now, eight years had gone by and things had become even more dire. God and I were not on speaking terms. I really didn't like Him, or Her, for that matter. God, Jesus, and the Holy Spirit were all pissing me off. Three had become a crowd, and I was looking for a cave to run to so I could lick my wounds and patch up my mangled heart.

Yet still I felt this deep connection with Becki, this desire to know her God, the one who manifested Himself in ways that felt so normal, they were profound. He sent Sue, who calmed Andrew with her soothing voice. In the form of a kind woman, He found me in the grocery store, weeping in the toothpaste aisle because I couldn't decide whether to buy Crest or Colgate. The woman filled my cart with a meal for my family, paid for it, and loaded it into my car. I told her nothing of my circumstances, yet when she left, she said, "You are taken care of tonight. Bless you." Long after she left, I sat in my car, trying to understand what had happened. More and more, I was convinced God had something to do with sending Frightful to heal my son's heart.

When I told Becki how I was feeling one afternoon, she said, "Be mad. You have a right to be. God already knows how you feel, so no need to hide any of it. You certainly aren't the first one to feel that way."

So, I decided to talk honestly to God. I wasn't sure where He was, or if He cared to listen, but I was lost. With my family life crumbling around me, and my career having vanished, I didn't know who I was. I had become a hospital dweller whose name was printed on a badge and stuck to the front of her shirt everyday.

On the days I could eke out a few short hours for myself, I tried to vent by painting, but quickly put the brushes down before touching the canvas. I tried to sew a soft pillow for Andrew to lie on at the hospital, but when the sewing machine gobbled up my bobbin thread, I unplugged it from the wall and walked out of my studio. I even tried decorating sugar cookies with Hannah, but couldn't keep focused long enough for the first batch to come out of the oven. Not only had I lost my artist-mojo, but I had also lost the rest of myself in our medical abyss.

I was lamenting this to a friend one afternoon when she suggested I see a therapist.

"I'm not a therapist kind of girl," I had replied.

"Believe me, she's not your basic therapist." She slid a business card across the table, extracting a promise from me to make a call.

I walked into the office of the art therapist a few weeks later. Leah's office was a menagerie of little gifts given by those who had shared their stories within those sacred walls. Pieces of art were tucked into every corner, treasures crammed the bookshelves, all created by students she had mentored over the decades. On the floor was a giant ball of twine, inside of which were tiny charms and slips of poetry tightly nestled in between the layers of string. Leah said it took her client six years to complete.

After meeting with Leah once, I knew I wanted to see her regularly. Each time I entered her 'studio,' my eye would catch something new, and off we would venture into conversations I never intended to have. It was an artist's dream, a place to unwind, dig deep, and create. Even on the days I left a wastebasket full of tears, I would somehow leave unburdened — my heart and hands having been set free to roam in that safe place.

She had a project in mind for me one afternoon as I shuffled in, weary from tending to Andrew as he endured so much pain. Without a word, she handed me a white pastel board before opening a box of oil pastels resembling fat tubes of lipstick.

"These are Sennilier Pastels. Picasso had them especially made for him in Paris. He wanted them to be as smooth and pliable as women's make-up."

I smiled to myself, remembering from my art history classes how Picasso liked his women — smooth and pliable.

I reverently picked up a luminescent blue that looked like a perfect Parisian sky. The oil, made warm by my hands, smeared onto my fingers — slick, greasy, smooth — nothing like any medium I had used before.

Leah got up to turn on some music, then turned back to me with her kind, soft grey eyes. "I want you to let your hands create something beautiful. Fill the entire space. No mind."

No mind? I tried to grasp what she was asking.

"Let's say... about ten minutes," she said, checking her watch.

Ten minutes? Not a chance. I had to think of something to draw first.

"No mind," she repeated when she saw me struggling to start. "Don't try to think what you should draw," she insisted. "What color grabs your eye?"

"Blue," I said, reaching for the Parisian sky.

"Mmmm..." A soft hum of agreement came from Leah. I glanced up to see a Mona Lisa smile on her face.

Her gentle presence helped me to free up my hands. I pulled the crayon along the length of the board, pushing pigment into the tiny pores. Then I chose another, and another, filling the board with soft oily pigment before using my fingers to smear the colors into shapes. And then we talked. Me with my face down, Leah with her eyes on me. I don't remember what we talked about, but a lifetime went by.

"It looks like you're nearly done," she said, breaking me from my trance. Seeing me pause, she asked, "Do you want more time?"

I shook my head.

"All that in ten minutes," she mused.

I couldn't believe it. *Only ten minutes?* The ecstasy of not having to bring the burden of my thoughts with me had freed me from time. That was the very first time I understood what true meditation must be like.

"What do you think that is?" she asked after we both looked at the image in my lap for several minutes.

I looked at the drawing thoughtfully. "It looks like a mother holding two children, keeping them close. See the curve of the arms?" I pointed to the drawing where vivid colors were broken by a black line fading into a deep violet. "Where the two lines join at the top, makes me think of the head of a mother."

"Yes," she said, "I see it, too." Leah's smile reached her eyes, and back out to her fingertips. "May I show you the image from my vantage point?" she asked.

Carefully taking the drawing from my hands, she held it upside down—the way she saw it.

"It's a heart," I whispered to the woman who was holding my secret. It was *my* heart. Two uneven, rounded swells at the top, culminating in a point at the base. I stared hard at the image.

"It looks like the entire left side is on fire," I gasped, recoiling from the red and gold flames that seemed to come from the left side of the image. The right side was colorful, cool, like watery pools. Like a lake, I thought. *My* lake.

I had frequent dreams about a lake, but it was always shrouded in a heavy, moving mist, until one night just before my appointment with Leah, I saw it clearly.

I was operating a floating coffee shop in the middle of a very deep lake. The lake was its own world, filled with trees and other living plant-like things that grew from the bottom up to the surface. Light penetrated all the way to the bottom of the lake. When the coffee shop closed, I would sit on the edge of the raft with my feet dangling in the water. At night, I would de-pressurize it and go to my home in the deep. The next day I would come back to the surface, my coffee shop restocked with coffee and the typical goodies. People would come from all over to buy my coffee and visit a little. One day at closing time, I had two friends with me. I invited them to de-pressurize with me. We went down the same as usual, but I could feel the ropes getting tighter and tighter until they snapped. We were too heavy. My shop jerked to a halt, and we had to work fast to try and re-pressurize it. I tried everything, but it was too deep now and it wouldn't move. We were desperate for air and pushed off from the roof of my shop towards the surface. It felt like I had to go hundreds of feet. I sucked in a lungful of water right before the surface...

I woke up in a sweat, gasping for air. I remember pulling back the blinds in our hospital room to see the glow of streetlights, a soft apricot darkness. It felt like I had been away for days. Trembling, I stripped off my damp t-shirt and wriggled into my sweater from the day before as I went in search of something hot to drink. I carried that dream around with me all day and the next. It refused to fade like most dreams in the waking hours, when the mind sets itself on sorting the tasks of the day. Something about the lake forced me to pay attention to it. It was the way light passed through it, moving in such a way that it felt alive. When I walked to the parking garage later that night, I caught the scent of it on the breeze.

Here it was again, that same lake.

"Hmmm," Leah said, looking thoughtfully at my pastel image. "Fire is purifying. It cleanses with heat to allow something new to take its place. A forest is renewed and transformed after it has been burned."

I gulped down tears. She read my face with her eyes, a mere ticker tape of my anxieties flashing in front of her.

"Fire is necessary for its survival," she said to the top of my bowed head.

"And what about water?" I asked.

"Water quenches the soul."

I couldn't meet her eyes. I was too afraid to believe her. It was just ten minutes of a coloring lesson. My heart was just fine. I didn't want to be purified. I was working so hard to cling to life as I imagined it, that I couldn't fathom what would happen if I were to let go. Would I be destroyed? And what about the lake in my dream? It had lulled me into its depths and soothed me — then turned on me and tried to drown me. I crossed my arms across my chest, a shield to protect me from those unsettling thoughts.

Leah handed the picture back to me. "This is strikingly beautiful," she said in her gentle voice. "I knew it was inside of you."

Chapter 14

Frightful was perched on the handlebars of Andrew's bicycle when I pulled into the garage. On the way home from visiting Leah, an idea had been running around in my mind, and it was confirmed the moment she tilted her head to the side, and our eyes met.

"What secrets do you keep in that bird-brain of yours?" I asked, slamming the door.

She two-stepped on her perch, sensing my approach.

"You really are a beautiful girl," I said, stroking her back.

A few downy feathers fell off in my hands. It seemed unusual for her to molt in November. Was it possible she felt the stress? Could she sense our worry? Our dogs were responding to the stress in our lives, but I found it hard to believe a chicken could sense the emotion.

Frightful allowed me to scoop her off the bicycle without protest, placing her on the grass next to the rest of the hens. She was constantly underfoot now, determined to make us notice her. She had all but abandoned her usual perch on the green wicker chair, opting for more unusual places like ogling at me from a low branch outside the kitchen window, pacing the dining room deck as we ate dinner, and more recently, taking up residence in the garage as we trudged to and from the hospital.

Andrew had been asking about Frightful nearly every day and we had been placating him with vague answers. I didn't know when he would get to see her again, and I knew that truth would crush him. Instead of a direct answer, I delivered Hannah's hand-drawn pictures and notes from Frightful to the hospital, where he was becoming less and less enthralled by the poor substitute for his friend.

After one brutally long day where it seemed that no matter what we did, Andrew could not get comfortable, I came home to find Hannah squatting in the pen, in the middle of a one-way monologue. "You know Brother will be coming home soon. You have to be patient, Frightful."

She reached out to catch the hen, but Frightful slipped from her grasp, circling the perimeter of the coop.

"Krrillll...Chirp. CHIRP! Bah-bah-bah-GAWK!"

Where are you Andrew? I can't find you!

Frightful jumped onto a cedar branch Jon had slipped through the chicken wire and regarded Hannah with a fixed stare.

"But I said he will come back! Won't he?"

Frightful continued her complaint, punctuated by a loud, insistent *chirp!*, while she paced the branch.

"Why does everybody act so mean all the time? No one even notices I'm here!" Hannah's voice became desperate, rising in pitch, ending in a sob. In that moment, my fourteen-year-old daughter was a child again, her words a heartfelt longing to understand all that scared her. "You have magic in you, Frightful. I've seen it! You can help him. Won't you *please* help him?"

I felt like an intruder, watching my daughter implore a chicken to save her brother. I also knew her desperation for her world to be righted, to be made whole, to feel safe. God must be swayed by the cry of a little girl to save her brother...wouldn't He?

Without disturbing Hannah, I walked back to the house and wandered around until she entered the kitchen. I didn't mention I had seen her in the coop.

"I had an idea on the way home and thought you could help me," I said. "I was thinking we could video Frightful in the chicken coop. Andrew could play it back on the iPad, and then maybe he won't miss her so much." When she didn't respond, I added, "You could be in charge of the whole project and teach the rest of us how to do it."

Hannah concentrated on screwing the lid back on a jar of peanut butter. Then she began slicing an apple.

"What do you think?" I asked.

She tossed the apple, peel, and core into the garbage and glared at me. I eased myself onto a bar stool, knowing I had crossed some unforeseen line.

"You want to talk about it?"

"You're never home! And then when you do come home, all you do is talk about Andrew. Have you ever thought about how I feel?"

I winced. She was right. Hannah had been shuttled between grandparents, neighbors, and unfamiliar people from the church for so long that she had developed a hard shell around her usual bubbly personality. I couldn't blame her. Her brother's condition had become all-consuming, and there was little room left for her.

"I'm sorry, Hannah. I wish I could change things. I really do. I guess I thought this would be something we could do together."

Her face crumpled. "It's just so hard. I don't know what to do."

I led her to the family room where we collapsed on the sofa. Seeing an opportunity to be pet, Charlie wandered over, easing his ample body into her lap. Hannah's hands automatically stroked his ears, and I saw an immediate softening of her face.

"I've got a better idea," she said over the purring feline. "How about FaceTime? We could wire Dad's iPad to the side of the outdoor coop. Then Andrew can see her in real time instead of having to watch her in a video. Maybe he can even talk to her through the speaker? Stranger things have happened."

***

It was true. We were never sure what Andrew might do. When he got an electric bike for his sixteenth birthday, Jon and I hoped it would give him some independence. He liked to ride to the neighborhood market to buy Lay's potato chips in the yellow and red bag. He wouldn't touch any other brand. Soon after he got the bike, I received a phone call from the King County Sheriff.

"Is this Andrew's mom?"

I heard traffic in the background, Andrew's voice, and my heart gave a lurch.

"Is he okay?" I blurted into the phone.

"Yes. Just fine, but I wanted to let you know that I pulled him over."

"For what?! Where was he riding?"

I was becoming more panicked by the second. He didn't have a license, but the bicycle didn't require one in order to ride in the bike lane.

"Well. It seems he's riding with a chicken," he said.

I heard Andrew's frightened protests in the background, saying, "I told you they don't make helmets for chickens!"

Knowing this was heading in a bad direction, I asked to talk to him.

"Do you understand what the officer is saying?" I asked.

"Frightful wanted ice cream," he told me. "What else was I supposed to do?"

I groaned, wanting to wring his neck. At the time, I was infuriated that it never occurred to him how dangerous it was to ride on the street—especially with a chicken. All it would take was her fluttering into traffic, and she'd cause an accident.

Remembering that afternoon, and sharing it with Hannah, made us both laugh. It all seemed so normal, or what we knew to be normal. The warmth of a good laugh spread throughout my body, shedding some of the eternal weight I seemed to carry around all the time. I felt lighter. And wiring up Jon's iPad to the chicken coop so Andrew could talk to his best friend was our brand of normal.

When I arrived at the hospital later that afternoon, Andrew was in the middle of an animated conversation with Sue — something that had to do with Shadow and Katniss Everdeen nuking the Capitol with AK-47 rifles. His fantasies had become more and more aggressive over the last few weeks, and I wondered if that had anything to do with him feeling more and more powerless.

A quick glance at the IV pump told me he had just received a dose of his favorite narcotic. This always brought out his chatty side, a side only Frightful saw at home. I knew it would only last for a short time until his body greedily used up the effects of the liquid pain relief, so I let them talk, slipping unnoticed into the conference room down the hall. It was by far the best room on the floor, boasting a huge picture window and an upholstered window seat that stretched the entire length of the room. I stretched out flat on my back and watched the world outside carry on without me. Displayed on the far wall was an elaborate artist sketch of their new building. I studied it, praying we would be long gone by then.

"Excuse me, are you Andrew's mom?" a familiar voice came from behind.

I was startled to see Dr. Torgerson, the immunologist who discovered Andrew's Trisomy 8 when he was in the third grade. It was thrilling to see him, but at the same time, I held the resentment of being passed along to rheumatology when he had run out of ideas.

"I saw Andrew's name on the chart this morning and wanted to come by to say hello. Things don't look to be going very well," he said.

"They aren't."

"I had no idea he was still sick. May I visit him?"

"Sure," I said, but the crazed thoughts that were zipping through my mind were: *Yes! Yes! Hell yes! Please be the genie I always hoped you were! Grant me my deepest wish and heal my son!*

Dr. Torgerson followed me down the hall to our room where we found Sue, now silent, in the chair next to Andrew. He was in a drugged sleep, moans of pain escaping his blistered lips. His red cheeks were chapped from a continuous fever, and his eyes sunk in to their purplish sockets. Sue reached out to still his bony legs that were in constant motion under the sheets. I watched for Dr. Torgerson's reaction. A widening of his eyes, and a catch of his breath told me everything I needed to know.

That day, Dr. Torgerson stepped back into our lives, taking the lead in a quest for answers. And that same day, I somehow knew it hadn't been mere chance that he walked by and noticed Andrew's name on the wall. It brought to mind Hannah's request for Frightful to use magic, and in that instant, I pretended that she did. While I waited for Dr. Torgerson to review Andrew's chart, I wondered if he remembered the first words Andrew said to him when he was only eight: *I think my body is trying to kill me.* It was obvious now that he had been right all along.

Dr. Torgerson immediately set a team of research analysts to work behind the scenes on our behalf. When he had exhausted all possible tests that could be done in Seattle, Andrew's blood was shipped to labs out of the country. A paper trail was laid throughout the big research hospitals in the region: Had anyone ever had a patient who presented a group of symptoms like this? Does anyone know of a person with Trisomy 8 Mosaicism who suffers from ulcerations, fevers and unstoppable inflammation seeming to come from no known source?

They were met by dead ends.

Some days, the gentle mannered immunologist would slip into our room and talk to Andrew. Mostly, he dropped by at strange hours with his gold-rimmed glasses and signature bow tie, flashing a handful of research studies he'd been analyzing.

"I'm still looking," he'd say. Then, just as quickly, he'd shake my hand and disappear.

During that time, we fell into the habit of using FaceTime to connect with Frightful. True to Hannah's plan, we successfully wired Jon's iPad to the side of the chicken coop where Frightful liked to dust herself. The first time we tried it, I set my iPad in the bed next to Andrew and listened for the electronic 'vrruuumm' of the line making a connection.

"Fright-FEE!!" he called out when he saw her.

The chicken stood up. Clucked. Andrew caressed the screen with his finger. I was overcome with tears and turned away, pretending to look for something in my purse

"I want out of this place," he said, talking to her.

Frightful paced back and forth in the pen. She clearly recognized Andrew's voice, but was unsure where the voice was coming from.

"It's scary in here, Frightful. But Sue comes and I tell her about our stories," he told his friend. "I want to go home."

"Crawww-cruk-cruk. Crawww."

I am here. Waiting.

Frightful settled on a patch of newly overturned dirt and started scratching, spraying a cloud of dirt on the camera lens. Hannah's finger appeared from the side, wiping at the lens. A second later, her face loomed into view, an impish grin spread across her face. She stuck a thumb under each arm and flapped her elbows while dancing around the coop. "Bock-bock! Bockety-bock! I am the queen of the roost!" she sang.

The chickens scattered in noisy protest.

"Stop that, you noob!" Andrew said, clapping a hand over his eyes. "You're not a chicken!"

"Well, neither are you!" she said, sticking out her tongue.

I smiled through my tears as I watched my children play in the most unusual way. It was remarkable that under such dire circumstances we had once again found a way to create our own version of normal.

From then on, the iPad stayed in Andrew's bed. While he slept, we played recordings of Sue reading Judy Blume's *Fudge*, into which she had inserted Frightful as a superhero who saved the precocious boy from all manner of disasters. When Andrew was awake, he talked to Frightful, and Frightful kept listening. We filmed Frightful in the laying box as Hannah's small hand reached underneath a bloom of feathers to remove the day's eggs. We filmed Frightful in the yard scratching for bugs, and sitting on the green wicker chair waiting for her friend to come home.

Hannah's brilliant idea turned out to be the perfect solution for two best friends, a boy and a chicken, who missed each other terribly.

Meanwhile, Dr. Torgerson broadened his search to include the east coast and eventually back again to the National Institutes of Health, where we first made contact with the doctor who was studying T8M. He found a small non-profit group in the UK by the name of *Unique* that had some valuable information about this genetic misprint, but nothing that described the constellation of symptoms Andrew was experiencing.

Andrew's story traversed several continents before finding its way to a little known physician in Japan, who had published an article about a young male patient with Trisomy 8 Mosaicism. Like Andrew, this young man had been gravely ill with similar inflammatory symptoms. The physician proposed that cytokines (proteins that modulate the inflammatory response) were responsible for these unusual symptoms. He had also discovered something peculiar about his patient's cells that led Dr. Torgerson in a new direction.

Suspecting cytokines were also playing a role in Andrew's illness, Dr. Torgerson ordered another round of tests. A bone marrow biopsy showed that Andrew's marrow had mutated to nearly 100 percent Trisomy 8 cells. It was clear these mutated cells had wreaked havoc to the point that his body was beginning to shut down.

Several days later, the cytokine test results arrived. Dr. Torgerson came flying into the room with a fist full of papers. "I want you to look at these!" he said, quaking with the thrill of discovery. "See this chart here?"

"Yes, but I don't know what I am looking at," I replied.

"This is a list of lymphokines, interleukins, and chemokines we looked at in this study," he said excitedly.

He was pointing to what looked like a series of Greek letters, equations, and dashes. Noticing I was unusually quiet, he glanced up at me and motioned me to join him on the bench. "I know this is overwhelming, but we may have discovered something significant. On all variations of cytokines tested, Andrew's numbers were far beyond the normal range."

I squinted at the paper, trying to decipher the chart. In many instances, it looked like they were hundreds of times higher than normal.

"But what does that mean?"

"In essence," he said, "Each time Andrew's body goes through an episode of illness, his immune system rightfully sends out 'killer cells' to attack the foreign ones the body perceives are there—except, there *are no* foreign cells to attack."

He went on to explain that the most unusual thing about Andrew's body was that the particular cells his body produced did not die off like a normal cell. Instead, they lingered in the body, creating a firestorm of inflammation in all of his soft tissues, eventually affecting his bone marrow. "I know there is some link to the T8M that creates this cellular confusion, but I don't know why," he said.

Dr. Torgerson was quiet, presumably allowing me to digest this information. After a moment, he surprised me by taking my hand and saying, "I believe a bone marrow transplant may be the only option for your son."

Silence yawned between the two of us. I felt empty, relieved, and weirdly comforted. Finally, I had my promise of a new life, or at least a tangible twinge of hope. I held onto it like a lifeline, thinking if we could just get through it, we might all survive. I nodded my okay, knowing in my gut, like Andrew had the first time we met, that this brilliant man told me the truth.

Chapter 15

With a simple nod of the head in Dr. Torgerson's direction, we entered a time called Discovery. It was the time to look into every possible aspect of Andrew's medical condition to determine whether or not he was even a candidate for transplant. Due to his unique genetic condition, they suspected it would be difficult to find a good marrow match. The first place they planned to look was his closest family member — his sister. If she was not a match, they would post a global search, hoping there would be someone, anyone, who would have a close enough genetic makeup to be an acceptable candidate.

"Chances could be slim," we were told.

We agreed to take 'slim' over the agony of nothing.

It seemed fitting to me that Andrew's sister could be the person to save his life. Since the first days Hannah could walk, she designated herself as Andrew's caretaker. She would carefully set out his clothing in the morning for school and make sure to point out whether or not his shoes were on the correct feet. She corralled him, followed him, encouraged him, and learned about every subject he was interested in. She did all of this just so she could relate to him and spend time with him. She was his biggest cheerleader. I would often ask their pediatrician what I could do to redirect her and remind her that he was not her responsibility, but any suggestion failed.

I named her Hannah Grace, and the name fit her perfectly. When there was no room to show Hannah the love I had for her, I gave her new names to quell the feeling that I was not a good enough mother.

When our family's future became uncertain, she came to me and said, "I don't really like growing up. I want to stay your little girl. Can I do that for a while?"

And because she was growing up too fast and I didn't know how to stop it, she became Teeny, and then Tiny, and for one crazy day, Tortellini. When she was told she might be the savior — a donor of the marrow that could save her brother's life — my emerging young teen slunk back into the little girl she remembered as being safe.

"Will my brother live?" Teeny spoke to me in the darkness.

"I don't know," I whispered softly back.

Three days later, Hannah agreed to be tested as a possible match. Three more weeks passed with no word. There were nights we were certain we would lose Andrew, but then he would wake up, his fever having subsided, and back would come our quirky and mysterious son who communed with chickens.

When I asked Becki what I could do to keep from drowning in uncertainty, she replied, "Just be with Andrew. Enjoy him today. We can't pretend to know what's coming."

On another occasion when she called to check in, I was sitting on the front steps of the hospital under a cold, wet sky, feeling like the rain and the wind were the only ones who understood my grief. I told her I wondered if there was something wrong with me because I felt an aching in my depths that never left.

"This whole situation sucks. Let it suck," she said. "You gain nothing but wasted energy by trying to pretend. Lean in, and let it be what it is. Then trust yourself to do what you need to survive this."

I tried to trust. Trust the doctors, trust my gut, trust that Andrew was strong enough to survive. But I wasn't sure if I was ready to trust God. My vision of God was blowing up in front of my very own eyes. I didn't even know what trusting meant.

"Is God trustworthy?" I asked her one night when she visited the hospital.

"Trustworthy...yes. Here with you...yes. Easily understood...not so much. I don't believe the terrible things that happen to us are the way God wants it. When things go bad, I usually cry out to God. I beg Him to fix it so I can breathe again — at least for a few minutes," she replied.

Each time I spoke with Becki, I had to marinate in her words for a while before I could internalize the truth in them. Our conversations sparked in me a desire to capture all the feelings that were threatening to overcome me. I began to write. I wrote on napkins, scraps of paper, and receipts. I snagged brochures from the hospital lobby and began drawing images, sketching around the emotions that spilled from me in a torrent of grief, gratitude, and wonder. I copied scripture to remind me that I was not alone. Sometimes I wrote a prayer as simple as a thank you; other times I wrote poems and love notes that I slipped into Jon and Hannah's pockets, stuck to the mirror, or placed in a coffee cup — something they would find in the morning when they dressed. It was my way of reminding us that we would survive.

As I walked in the house late one evening, Hannah wandered into the kitchen with Charlie's front half held between her hands. His huge back end was swinging at her knees — a feline pendulum. "Grandma Cherry left you a note on the fridge," she said, slowly dropping the cat onto one of the bar stools.

My mother had been picking Hannah up from school every day and staying with her until Jon or I could relieve her. Her round handwriting, a hybrid of printing and cursive, stated, "Foodie in fridge! Soup and salad! Yummy bread!! Dessert on counter!!!"

Hannah scooped a huge spoonful of apple pie into her mouth as I reached for a *Veranda* design magazine with dog-eared pages and yellow sticky notes with arrows all over them.

"Oh, and she left you that, too," she said around a mouthful of hot pie.

A Starbucks gift card slipped from the inside cover. "For a treat!" it read.

I sat next to Charlie in a daze. It was all so thoughtful, but sometimes I just wanted her to sit down and talk to me and listen to what my week had been like. I wanted her to hold my hand, tell me I was a good mom, reassure me that I was doing all the right things. But that had never been her thing. Talking softly is not her love language.

My mom lives her life in exclamation points. Her energy is palpable. As far back as I can remember, she has always served on educational boards, city planning commissions, as president of the PTA, and myriad local fundraisers for the community. She is a natural magnet for people, drawing them into her circle while making them feel comfortable sharing all sorts of tidbits of personal information. So when someone in her family is ill or in pain, she does what she does best: She takes action. My mom's care comes to me as soup in the fridge, a loaf of crusty bread from the Macrina Bakery in Seattle, and hot gooey apple pie. It smelled like home and everything wonderful I remembered about growing up. "Life is short," she would say. "Better start with dessert first." And I did.

A few days later, my mom spent the afternoon with Andrew while Jon and I met with his medical team. Andrew continued to get weaker, and it was clear they were struggling with where to start. Dr. Torgerson had petitioned our insurance company for a transplant in hopes of eradicating the T8M in his marrow, but since nothing like it had been attempted before, they were dragging their feet. After the meeting, Jon left for work and I walked back into the room to find my mom in her usual spot, snapping a fresh piece of Trident peppermint gum and flipping through a current issue of *Vogue* magazine.

"Hi, Kris! Andrew and I have been visiting, talking about deep fryers. He found one he wants."

Andrew held up his iPad. A full-sized picture of a commercial deep fryer with the convenient price tag of $3,200.00 was slapped across the front in a red banner. I looked over at my mom with an oh-yeah-sure look. She tilted her head in my direction and smiled.

"You're going to buy him that?" I challenged.

"If he wants." She tore a page from the magazine and kept flipping.

"Yeah. And I want a big one that can fry ten baskets of fries at a time," Andrew said.

Never mind that he had been unable to eat anything for the last eight months, and anything deep-fried sounded like a basket of rotgut to me.

"Looks like you're having a good day," I said, sitting on the side of his bed.

"I will need a chef hat, too," Andrew mused. "So I can be a deep-fry chef."

My mom had always encouraged Andrew to dream big. Nothing was set in stone; nothing was impossible. She taught me that, too, but for some reason, I had begun to put a filter on that. My dreams had been knocked around one too many times and I was feeling a little bruised at the moment.

Andrew dropped the iPad on the bed and disappeared into the sheets. I knew the pain medication was wearing thin; the color in his puffy cheeks was deepening. I checked the notes on the IV pump and saw that he was not due for another dose for two hours.

"It only works for a short time now," I said, mostly to myself.

My mom glanced up from her issue of *Vogue*, a pained look on her face. "Here, you take this," she said, handing me the magazine.

We talked for a few minutes, then she was gone.

The next afternoon I was home, finishing my last load of laundry, when the phone rang. "Are you sitting down?" a familiar male voice said without taking time for introductions.

"I am now."

The doctor in the Complex Care Unit said, "I have great news! The marrow results came back today. Your daughter Hannah is a perfect ten-for-ten match. It's unusual to get such a close match. Do you know what that means?"

I sucked in my breath. "I think so," I answered cautiously.

"Hannah is not only a good donor match for her brother, but her marrow matched perfectly in ten categories out of the ten we measure. It's the best possibility for a successful engraftment."

I still didn't completely get it. "Explain engraftment."

"Well, you can think of it like a handshake. Andrew's body will need to recognize his sister's cells as being good cells and not try to destroy them. When his body allows her marrow cells to set up camp and multiply, then it's called engraftment. We always hope for one hundred percent engraftment, but it's not always the case."

Now that his words were sinking in, a million questions began zinging through my brain, but I couldn't catch a single one.

"Do you have any other questions?" he asked.

"What does this mean for Hannah?" I blurted out when my mind slowed enough to form the words. I wondered if I would be putting both of my children in harm's way. I couldn't bear the thought.

"It's usually pretty straightforward for the donor. She will have several more blood tests before we can move forward with transplant. On the day of transplant, she'll be put under anesthesia, and we'll draw the marrow from her hip bones."

I felt lightheaded and realized I was holding my breath. Leaning back against the dryer, I blew my bangs away from my face. Was this for real?

The doctor prattled on while doubts continued to plague me. "Young patients like your daughter bounce back quickly. She'll be tired, but she should be able to go back to school right away. We can go into more detail later." He paused for a moment, leaving the connection silent. "Congratulations! This is great news!"

I hung up the phone, put my mind on autopilot, and finished folding the laundry before calling Jon at work. It was clear we were on a speeding train and there was no getting off.

I took a deep breath and dialed. "You won't believe the phone call I just got!" The words came tumbling out as I told Jon every detail of my conversation with Andrew's doctor.

After a moment he whispered, "Amen."

When I saw Andrew that afternoon, he was listening to a new audio file Sue had made for him. I told him without too much detail that his sister was a perfect DNA match, that she would be able to give him some of her healthy cells. I don't know what I expected, but his response surprised me.

"Will she save me?" he asked.

My breath caught in my throat. *Will she save me?* How was I to answer that when I didn't even know the answer myself? I stroked my son's hot cheek, reaching over to tuck the blankets tightly around his long, slender body. I pressed my lips to his forehead and whispered, "I love you."

Jon and I decided to share the news with Hannah that evening. She responded with a shrug. "Good. Now we can get on with being a normal family again," she said, plunking down on the sofa with a tattered library copy of *The Great Gatsby*.

I glanced at Jon from across the room.

"It's not quite as simple as that." Jon delivered the words gently. "There are no guarantees. We don't know what your brother's body will do with the new cells, nobody does, but there is a really good chance it will work."

"What do I have to do?" she asked cautiously, eyeing both of us over the top of her book.

"I think it's a simple procedure, and the recovery is quick. You will be asleep for it."

She paled.

"You can think about it, Hannah. You don't have to do it. But if you decide to be his donor, no matter what happens, you will be giving him a chance at life."

"Okay. Fine. Whatever," she said, her face turning crimson, a hint of tears shining in her grey-green eyes.

The look on her face told me it was not fine.

She picked up her school bag and turned to go upstairs. "I've got homework."

I made a move to go after her. "Let her go," Jon said, patting the space on the sofa next to him.

I watched TV with Jon as a running dialogue of our unspoken conversation churned in my head. I tried to imagine what Hannah was thinking—the words she hadn't spoken. Finally, I got up and followed her up the stairs. "I wish you hadn't walked away," I said, sitting on the edge of her bed. She was facing the wall scanning YouTube videos on her phone.

"How am I supposed to react when you say something like that? I don't really understand what I have to do, anyway."

I didn't blame her for feeling so confused. I barely understood what we were getting ourselves into either.

"I'm afraid it will hurt, like all those operations Andrew has to go through. He screams sometimes in the bathroom at night and I can't shut out the noise. Why does he have to do that?"

I thought of the countless biopsies, needle sticks, infusions, and scopes he had endured over the last year searching for clues. Like Hannah, I remembered the nights he lay on the bathroom floor and cried. I sat there feeling sick, my mind devoid of any comforting words.

Hannah turned to search my face, looking for answers. "You think I can't hear it," she said. "The next day you act like nothing happened. You expect me to pretend to be normal. But nothing around here is normal. I'm scared. I wish you would get that!"

She tossed her phone to the foot of the bed, where it slid off and landed on the floor with a thud. I tried to snuggle next to her like I do most nights, but she refused, so I rolled to my back, hugging the edge of the bed.

"What do you want me to do?" I spoke into the dark room. I had a desperate desire to make her feel better, to take the pain away — although I knew perfectly well that I couldn't.

Hannah stared at the mobile hanging from her ceiling — a leftover science project from a long ago astronomy lesson. "Mom, why don't you look at me?" she said, turning my face towards her. "I feel like you don't even see me when I talk to you. Why do you do that?"

How could I answer that when my brain was working in slow motion and my heart was breaking?

"I'm so sorry," I answered, swallowing back tears.

I was too tired to come up with anything better, so I circled an arm around her shoulders — protecting her from the scary unsaid thoughts flying around the room.

Her voice was quieter now. "You say you're spending time with me, but I know you're far away. You're with Andrew. He's the one who takes up the most space in this house."

She was right. He *did* take up the most space in our house, and it was suffocating us all.

Hannah rolled toward me, reaching out her hand. "You always look at me with sad eyes. Why can't you just be happy?"

I thought about her question for a while. "I'm happy that I have you and Andrew and Dad. My heart is just heavy. Very heavy."

Her response was to pile blankets and stuffed animals on top of us both, creating what she called a 'nest.' Her chemistry book was pinching my leg, but I didn't dare move. I used my foot to nudge it over to the other books piled on the bed.

"Can I ask you something?" Hannah whispered into the darkness. She moved her body toward mine, tucking her legs behind me, spoon-like. "What's going to happen to my brother? Tell me the truth."

There it was. She had asked the question I was afraid to answer, and now it was out there floating around the room, bumping into walls, knocking things over. I let out a puff of air, my mind unable to focus on the seriousness of her question. In truth, at that moment, I was fantasizing about a really hot shower, perhaps some dinner, then sliding into bed and falling into oblivion.

I wrestled with my heavy eyelids and turned to face her. Brushing an errant curl back from her face, I said, "Truthfully, Teeny, I don't know what will happen. He has the best doctors in the country, and we live in the best city for a bone marrow transplant—especially one as complicated as your brother's. I believe God made you a perfect match for him. And I also believe God keeps his promises."

"Does God promise to heal Andrew?"

"I don't know. But I *do* know that God promised to never leave us. And I'm betting our lives on that."

It wasn't a perfect answer, and I was still trying to believe it myself, but it was all I had to offer.

Chapter 16

Finding out Hannah was a perfect marrow match for her brother was a mixed bag of blessings we had to sort out. She carefully sidestepped any conversation with me for the next week, until one afternoon after school we decided to go to the mall for a little retail therapy. Hannah was unusually quiet in the car, so I casually turned off the radio and waited. There's a universal understanding between teenagers and parents: It is only acceptable to talk about important things to a parent when they are driving or otherwise occupied. No eye contact is required; it's easier that way.

Hannah was thinking, loudly. "Mom, you know the other night?"

I knew what she was referring to. She'd been circling me all week, never quite ready to talk. "You mean when we found out you could be a donor?"

"Yeah. Well, you just surprised me. I didn't know what to say. It freaked me out a little," she said staring out the window.

I knew better than to respond, so I waited. Don't respond immediately: That's another universal teenager rule I found infuriating to follow.

"It's just that I don't really understand," she said, finally turning to look at me.

That was my signal to talk. And we did. We talked about everything that was happening in our home, how it felt like Andrew had been sick forever, and why they couldn't just do the bone marrow thing today and get it over with. She never mentioned the sticky notes I left for her on the mirror, yet during our conversation, it became clear she had read them all.

"How much do I love you, Hannah?" I said as we circled Bellevue Square mall for the sixth time.

"From the North to the South, and the East to the West, and everywhere in between," she replied with a hint of a smile in her voice.

I took her hand and squeezed. "That's right. Please don't forget that."

The next day, I told Julie about my conversation with Hannah while we chatted on the phone. Frightful was in my lap, pecking at an apple core. Again, I noticed she had lost a few feathers. *Should she be molting this late in the season?*

"I'm glad she talked to you. That's half of the solution," Julie said.

"But I still feel like a terrible mother, like I've abandoned her. When I'm home, I barely have the energy to attend to what she needs. Then we dropped a huge bomb on her the other night. I was too overwhelmed to think about how she would feel about being his donor."

"She'll get past it, I promise. Just start saving money now for her therapy."

I laughed despite myself, realizing there was probably much truth to her words.

Julie quickly changed the subject. "Why are they making you wait so long for the transplant meeting? Can't they move faster?"

I had asked the same question, but the harder we pushed the doctors, the more they pushed back. We were learning that 'discovery' was not a quick process. So we waited, and practiced patience with gritted teeth.

"To be truthful, I think they're still unsure what to do. There's no category to put us in, and I think that makes people a little nervous is my guess. We're scheduled to meet with Dr. Burroughs, a specialist in pediatric non-malignant transplants, next week. Even then, there's no guarantee she'll accept our case."

"What if she doesn't take Andrew on?"

Frightful starting pecking at my fingers. I shooed her off my lap and she let out an indignant *squawk!* in protest.

"It's crossed my mind, but I can't think about it," I said.

The line was quiet as both of us considered the possibility.

Julie was first to speak. "Andrew is strong enough for this. I'm choosing to believe that."

After we hung up, I thought about what Julie said: *Andrew is strong enough.* Yes. I believed that. But was I? Was my heart strong enough to watch my son go through hell and not know if he would make it back?

Both Andrew and Jon were asleep when I arrived at the hospital. For three days, Andrew had undergone tests on every body part they could biopsy, examine, scan or draw blood from. He had become withdrawn and even refused to engage with Sue when she visited.

I stood over my son, placing my hands on his frail body. "You are strong enough," I whispered.

Jon opened one eye, then sat up. I joined him on the cot, resting my head against his shoulder. "How'd it go today?"

"Okay, I guess. I tried to explain to him about the transplant, but either he didn't want to know about it, or he doesn't understand. He told me Frightful would give him some of her power."

Something inside me tightened, a cinching of my guts. "What did you say to that?"

He shook his head, "What could I say? He's determined. He believes she has some sort of power."

Jon left a few minutes later and I took his place on the bed, feeling the lingering warmth of his body while waves of anxiety floated around me, refusing to settle. Had the Frightful thing gone too far? Were we allowing our son to escape reality by talking to a bird, even believing that bird could somehow save him? Had I bought in to this fantasy, too? At some point I must have sunk into sleep, because I was pulled out of my dreams at 3:15 a.m.

Sue's steady voice filled the room, soft and lyrical. Even with my eyes wide open, I could only make out the shadow of the IV poles and the lump of Andrew in the hospital bed. What was she doing here? Was I still dreaming? I lay still, searching for the familiar landmarks: clock above the door, whiteboard next to the bathroom, blue rocking chair at the head of the bed. Once I was oriented, I noticed the faint glow of the iPad coming from under Andrew's sheet. He was listening to one of the recordings we made of Sue.

"Do you think Shadow will live?" Andrew asked over the top of the story.

Sue's voice continued its narration of *Super Fudge*.

"Shadow is scared. He is really sick."

Knowing that Shadow was Andrew's alter ego because his health issues were too scary to face alone, I held my breath and felt my heart shatter. Sue kept reading.

"They think I don't understand, but I do. I don't want to die."

I stifled a sob, recognizing how brave my son was to admit the truth…to own his fear.

"I miss Frightful. Why can't I just go home?"

Long after Sue's voice stopped and the sound of Andrew's breathing filled the room in its place, I lay awake, broken. **Andrew had always had the ability to purge his feelings in a story. So why had his nocturnal conversation destroyed me? Why couldn't I shake this feeling that m**y world was unraveling and there was nothing I could do to stop it? I carefully studied my sleeping son, his breath long and deep, his body limp, wondering where he had gone. Where was the quirky boy with the obsessive talk about chickens, dinosaurs, World War II, and dirt bike races? The kid who would ask me every morning when I woke him up what he was going to wear and what I was planning to make for dinner that night? Had he disappeared inside his pain and become lost?

I saw little sign of light from him until a huge, muscular man walked into our room two days later.

"Not another vampire!" Andrew moaned when he saw the plastic bin full of needles in the Phlebotomist's hand.

I stared at him, stunned by his connection between a simple blood draw and the blood sucking tendencies of a vampire.

"I'm not just any vampire," the man replied.

"What kind are you?" Andrew asked with general interest.

"I can do magic tricks," he said with a grin.

"What are your superpowers? Can you run at the speed of light? Can you fly?"

A deep rumbling came from the man's belly, followed by a huge toothy grin that spread across his face. He made a show of grabbing the wall for support as Andrew's nurse poked a head in the door.

"Everything okay?" she asked.

"Yes ma'am," he said with a wink in Andrew's direction.

"So you're a real live vampire?" Andrew asked again to clarify.

"At your service. Now, if I can just see this arm."

Andrew pulled a skinny arm from underneath the blanket.

"Oh yes, you have a perfect vein here," he said in a spooky voice.

He showed Andrew his empty hand, then closed his fist, tapped his hand twice and peeled each finger back to reveal a tiny butterfly needle.

"Watch closely," he said.

Before either of us noticed, the vampire had flicked the needle into the soft crook of Andrew's arm. Seconds later, he stuck a Scooby Doo Band-Aid on his arm and left.

"He was the coolest vampire I've ever met," Andrew said in awe.

Sue came by to read later that afternoon, her bright smile and easy manner instantly put us both at ease, forcing the events of that haunting night to the far reaches of my mind. Andrew shared his vampire story, which I noticed became more and more spectacular as the story went on. Soon the two of them were transported into Andrew's secret world, Sue leading the way with her soft and confident voice.

Sue was reading *Catching Fire*, which she had downloaded on her phone. It buzzed in her hand and she saw a single word: *Shadow*.

Puzzled, she continued to read. Her phone buzzed again.

A text read, "Shadow is scared."

"Is that you, Andrew?"

She put down the phone and peeled back a pile of blankets on the bed next to her.

Andrew cradled his iPad in his hands, offering up a limp smile that hung on his face a moment before fading.

Sue put down her phone. "Tell me more."

"Shadow is bad-ass," Andrew said, his face becoming closed and serious.

Sue picked up the little action figure from Andrew's bed and studied its oversized star-shaped head, black and red body, slanted eyes and fearsome scowl. But it was the figure's white fists that intrigued her. They were large and strong, held out in front of its body in defiance, as if ready to fight. She handed Shadow back to Andrew.

"Shadow misses his birdy-bird. He doesn't know if he'll get to go home," Andrew admitted to Sue. "Shadow lost his best friend."

Sue remembered reading about how Shadow had lost his friend in the Sonic Series. It was easy to see how Andrew had melded two lives — his, and the little hedgehog. Sometimes facing his life alone was too frightening, and he needed his hero's strength, bravery, and power.

"What would Shadow do if he were home?" Sue asked.

"That's easy. Go for a motorbike ride with Frightful. She loves bike rides. She doesn't have a helmet, though, so she rides in my coat so the wind doesn't get in her eyes."

That day was the first time I realized Shadow had become Andrew's alter-ego, the side of him that was wrestling with the terrifying reality of what was happening to his body. From then on, Shadow became the central character in Andrew's stories and was not limited to space and time, but often traveled from book to book, making friends wherever he found himself, friends who had the power to help, to heal, to rescue.

A week later, Jon and I sat in the sixth floor conference room at the SCCA (Seattle Cancer Care Alliance) overlooking Lake Union. Although it was only a transplant consult, we were secretly hoping for a tentative date to be set for the procedure to occur. We knew Hannah was a match, but we were waiting to hear if Andrew's body could sustain a transplant. As far as Andrew was concerned, Shadow was 'bad-ass strong,' which meant Andrew was 'bad-ass strong' as well, and we were counting on that.

At exactly one o'clock, Dr. Burroughs stepped in, trailed by two Physician's Assistants. They quickly laid out a stack of Andrew's medical files, pulled up his current blood test results from the computer in the room and vanished. Jon and I looked at one another expectantly, then across the table at Dr. Burroughs.

Dr. Burroughs was a petite woman in her mid-thir. Her demeanor was gentle and approachable, but we were n fooled. Her grey eyes spoke of intelligence far beyond that or her Anthropologie sweater set, sensible skirt, and heels. She was all business and spoke in a language that Jon and I would be required to learn. Quickly.

It was immediately clear to us that Dr. Burroughs was a brilliant doctor and that she had come well prepared to our meeting. She discussed the process of transplant and the very real life-threatening risks that go along with it. We learned about various degrees of graft versus host disease (GVHD), a condition where the donor cells refuse to cooperate and attack the host, causing a variety of horrific complications that can cause death. She also warned us about the very real possibility that Andrew wouldn't survive the chemotherapy and radiation conditioning required before the transplant.

She was direct, and she didn't mince words. "Andrew's case is difficult, making these risks even higher. I won't do it unless I can determine it is at least a 'reasonably safe' option."

The threat of losing him seemed more real now. Somehow, I had been able to keep that fear and potential reality at bay. But here it was, filling the room, and I couldn't avoid it.

"How will you make that determination?" queried Jon.

"The great news is that he has a perfect sibling donor. There is no better match and no better chance at a good engraftment. But my first concern is to take a closer look at his liver. I'll schedule a biopsy for this week," she said, opening a file from the top of her stack.

We knew his liver had been seriously compromised over the last several years; we also knew a bad report would be a game stopper. I wondered if God could wave his arms and miraculously fix his liver. I made a mental note to tell Julie to ask her prayer warriors to work on that one. It couldn't hurt.

Dr. Burroughs continued on, describing a two-week long ~ensive evaluation Andrew would have to go through prior to ~ransplant. Jon tapped my foot under the table. This was where we hoped she would set the transplant date — preferably now.

"We'll need to examine each of his organs and body systems, including biopsies of his skin," she said.

"What are you looking for?" Jon asked.

"The skin biopsy is to evaluate for Trisomy 8," she replied.

I don't know why, but I shivered at the thought. I remembered Dr. Torgerson telling us that Andrew most likely had concentrations of Trisomy 8 in all of his vital organs.

"After the results come back, *if* he remains a candidate for transplant, we'll come up with a treatment plan."

Dr. Burroughs looked us both in the eye, her side of the discussion finished.

I sat on the edge of my chair waiting for mention of a date. Nothing. "When…?"

I was interrupted.

"You *do* realize we're forging new medical territory here," she said, reaching across the table, clasping my cold hands in hers. "The team is still debating the best way to approach this, and not everyone has the same ideas."

I was surprised she touched me. Everyone around us was so formal and clinical. I felt the sting of tears at the back of my eyes, and blinked hard to keep them from falling. I glanced at Jon sitting beside me. His eyes were wide, but there was a determined look on his face. Earlier in the meeting, he told Dr. Burroughs it felt like we were stepping out of a boat into a raging river, not knowing if it would take us down river to placid waters, or over a waterfall. Dr. Burroughs had simply nodded.

Jon sat up taller, placing his hands on the desk, looking Dr. Burroughs directly in the eye. "We want to go forward with it, no matter what the risks are. Andrew's quality of life is hardly an acceptable existence."

"And we believe in miracles," I added, trying to convince myself of just that.

Dr. Burroughs nodded without breaking eye contact. "I understand. I really do," she said with a gentle smile. "I can see that you both have Andrew's best interest at heart. I will do everything I can to make it happen."

I went home that night feeling a strange mixture of hope and fear. A friend of mine had been telling me for months to just meet Jesus halfway on the bridge, that He would be waiting there with His hand outstretched to guide me all the way home. But I couldn't see that damn bridge, let alone stand up and walk across it. So I just sat right where I was and prayed the only prayer I could: *Help!*

Chapter 17

We spent our days waiting for said miracle to arrive. Each morning at rounds I eagerly asked for the results of the liver biopsy. Every day they shook their heads, "Not yet." Just when I was ready to choke someone, the results came back. The slides showed fibrosis, scarring, inflammation, and areas they referred to as inclusions — small cellular deposits in the liver tissue that weren't normally there.

"My colleague at The Hutch (Fred Hutchinson Cancer Research Center) is suggesting we consider a bowel resection to remove the diseased parts of his colon," Dr. Burroughs told Jon and me one afternoon in her office.

My body went cold. "But no one has *ever* found any indication of bowel disease," I retorted. "What would that gain us? And what does that have to do with his liver?"

She paused, arranging her thoughts before speaking. "Andrew has a highly compromised liver. It's clear from the biopsy. Chemotherapy alone could do irreparable damage." She looked at us both from across the table, sizing up our response. "As for surgery, there is concern he has fibrosis of his bowel from chronic damage. It could cause problems down the road if he were to develop graft versus host disease (GVHD). But not all of us are in agreement regarding surgery. We have to look into it further."

I didn't know what 'further' meant, and I had no idea how we would explain this news to Andrew. Plus, it sounded like more delay, and I knew we had a short window of opportunity before Andrew became too weak for a transplant. To do nothing and watch him die was unthinkable. To lose him without having tried a transplant was unbearable. I was a cornered mama bear, willing to kill, or be killed, in order to save my son.

I pressed my knee into Jon's under the table, searching for some tangible sense of support. For ten years, we'd been waging this war. I couldn't remember the last time I felt peace in my home or head. Especially my head. My migraines were an accumulation of the angst I felt every day around my son. As a child in Sunday school, I had been taught that God would provide peace, but so far, I couldn't find it.

"You know how we feel," we said in unison.

"I sympathize with your feelings," Dr. Burroughs replied kindly as she studied our faces. "I have never met another couple so unified in their decision. I understand the position you're in, and as I said before, I will try to do everything I can to make this happen."

After the meeting, Jon and I walked together to the parking garage, he on his way to work, me back to the hospital. *Bowel surgery?* Our conversation with Dr. Burroughs kept churning in my head as we picked our way through SUVs wedged into compact spaces under the SCCA building.

Jon pulled me into his arms, wrapping them around me, warm and strong. "Are we doing the right thing?" he whispered into my neck.

"I hope so."

Standing on the hard pavement, I wondered if there was a purpose to all of this. What lesson were we supposed to learn from this misery?

While we waited for answers, Andrew continued to decline and eventually stopped asking about Frightful. In hopes of conjuring a smile, we took pictures of each hen, printed them on sheets of paper and taped them to the walls. Sue recorded more stories, and Hannah made FaceTime calls to an iPad that now sat on the windowsill, sandwiched between stacks of books. Pain had become an unwanted guest that moved into our hearts, following us throughout the day, slipping into our dreams, keeping us hostage at night.

Andrew's ability to engage with us was gone, painkillers his only solace. I sat next to his bed for hours, my hand on his back, feeling the rise and fall of his breath as he pulled life into his lungs. I convinced myself that as long as I didn't let go, he wouldn't let go. When he wasn't in bed, he resided on the cold tile floor of the bathroom with a paper-thin hospital gown loosely wrapped around his skeletal frame. We set up an oscillating fan on the back of the toilet to keep his feverish body cool enough to tolerate. The ulcers in his mouth alone had become so big and deep that they eroded a hole through the front of his lower lip. We could only imagine what the rest of his gut looked like.

With each day that passed, the screaming inside my head became louder. I went through the motions that were expected of me, even though I was completely paralyzed inside my own body. Most of my day was spent watching Andrew and the nervous residents whispering outside our door, clutching their clipboards in hopes it would somehow shield them from the pain inside our room.

One afternoon, Andrew whispered to me, "Am I dying, Mom?"

I closed my eyes, feeling my heart threaten to stop its beating. How was I to answer that question? Would the truth kill me? I crawled onto the floor next to him, took his hand in mine, and explained to him what I believed to be true. I believed that he was not alone—that he was held tightly in God's arms, and that He would never let him go. An image came to mind, one similar to others I had seen while in the middle of the worst nights at home. With words, I painted him a picture of warriors surrounding his bed, raising their swords against an unseen adversary. I told him of the saints all over the world who were waking the heavens with the sound of their prayers on his behalf.

I admitted that I didn't know if he was dying, but God did, and he was safe.

We lay there for a while before he slipped his hand out of mine. "Okay, I just wanted to know."

That was my first flicker of time. One of those golden moments where time simply stops and you understand that you are part of something much bigger than yourself. In that moment, I understood heaven was not a place with golden streets and pearly white gates. It was here and now, and somewhere behind the veil I couldn't quite reach. Heaven was in the room with my dying son, and it was a part of us both. I saw those mighty warriors I spoke of — surrounding his bed, hovering over his body, protecting him from harm. I had witnessed something supernatural, and I accepted it without a shred of doubt. And in that split second, I realized that it did not matter how long he lived on this earth. He would forever be okay. He was loved. And then I felt peace. Something I had been groping and clawing for since the moment he was born.

That feeling lasted one fiery moment, a breath that caressed me like a lover, leaving these words etched onto my heart: All is well. It always has been. It always will be.

Later that afternoon, a social worker stopped by.

"You should have a plan in place," she said. "It alleviates any extra stress if the time comes where you have to make some difficult choices."

What she didn't say was: *You should prepare for your son to die.* The feeling of peace I experienced earlier vanished when she shoved reality in my face. I had come to peace with 'Death' as a concept, but not with Andrew dying. My son was lying in bed, emaciated and on the brink of death, yet I wasn't ready to let him go yet. I wasn't ready to make any other plan besides 'survive.'

She eyed me carefully. "You and Jon need a break. Can someone stay here with Andrew for the night?"

And just leave him? I shook my head, then nodded as tears pricked at and started to fall from the corners of my eyes. *He had to make it.* Julie reminded me every time we talked on the phone that Andrew was strong, that he had a purpose in this life and had not yet begun to fulfill it. It always left me feeling somehow inadequate, and maybe a little angry that she was so confident, but today, I clung to those words, forcing myself to believe them.

At four o'clock, my dad arrived with his C-Pap snore machine in one hand and his briefcase in the other. "Hi Kris, your mother said I am here to spend the night with Andrew."

I grinned inwardly at the thought of my mom informing him where he was sleeping. "Sounds like you're on your way home to have dinner with Jon and Hannah. Take your time in the morning. I'll be here."

His presence was a comfort to my soul. Like my mom, my dad is full of energy, has a fantastic sense of humor, and is always up for a good prank. But where my mom shows her love in the doing, my dad shows it in the being. He is a gentle and kind man who ponders things deeply and sometimes struggles with an oversensitive soul. I think I am most like him.

I gathered my things to leave, imagining his six-foot-three, lanky frame hanging over the end of the short little fold-out bed, and loved him all the more for being willing to stay. I noted that he had not brought a change of clothes with him. Perhaps there was a toothbrush stashed in his briefcase? Hugging him tightly, I thanked him before closing the door behind me.

On the way home, I wrestled with my conversation with Andrew. *Am I dying, Mom?* Had he understood my answer? His response had been calm and mature, possessing an assurance that was surprising for an eighteen-year-old, let alone a child with autism.

When I got home, Jon and Hannah were crashed on the sofa watching a rerun of *Cheers* on Netflix. I tried to keep my composure for Hannah's sake, but when Jon asked me about the afternoon, the tears that had been threatening all day came out in a torrent of emotion.

Hannah's face fell. "I'm outta here," she said, scooping Charlie into her arms and slipping from the room.

"That bad?" Jon asked.

"My dad has no idea what it's like."

"He'll be fine. He's stronger than you think."

I wasn't so sure. The nights were the worst—the 'witching hours', we called them—when the pain was the most exaggerated and we were sure the darkness would overcome us before the light of day came to save us.

When we went to bed, I noticed for the first time the bare trees outside our windows. December had arrived and I couldn't recall the leaves changing in the fall. Frost was splintering its way across the skylights and moonlight bathed the room, leaving elongated shadows of the evergreen trees across the carpet. At another time in my life it might have been romantic, but tonight it made me feel uneasy.

As Jon and I crawled into bed together for the first time in weeks, I tried to think of something to say. Where would I begin? How would I tell him about my day, what Andrew had asked? I stared at the ceiling, not daring to meet his eyes. The sound of our breathing matched one another, deep and strangled—the sound of unshed tears.

Jon broke the silence, "If transplant isn't an option, I don't think I can bear to see him in such pain anymore. It seems inhumane," he said, staring through the skylights at the few stars that could be seen. "I told Dr. Burroughs today that I wished it was okay to put people out of their misery like we do with our beloved animals. She was shocked I would admit that to her."

He turned to face me. I caught my breath, shocked as much as the doctor. I couldn't believe he was bold enough to say the words, or to even think them, for that matter. That thought was locked too deep in my heart. I knew I would never be able to look at it.

I rolled into his arms, pushing my nose and forehead against his, his eyes filling my vision. Watery and blue. I stayed that way for a long time, wondering what had happened to us — senior class sweethearts, best friends, lovers. Had we gotten lost? By necessity, we had become an extreme-parenting machine, living from one life-altering decision to the next. There had been little room for lighthearted play, or dates, or sex, for that matter. I wondered if we would ever get that part of ourselves back.

I remembered that a teacher friend once told me that when she observed parents of special needs kids, there was usually one parent who just accepted it and moved on. The other would go digging, trying out every therapy available, looking under every stone for anything to make the child's life just a little bit easier to bear. I thought about that for a long time. It gave me permission to accept the ways that Jon and I were different.

"I pray for mercy every moment of every day," I whispered into the crook of his neck.

I felt hot tears in my hair and realized they were coming from Jon. Curling tightly behind me, he held me while we sunk into our grief. Lying perfectly still with my eyes closed, I listened for each breath, a reassurance that Jon would still be there in the morning. Somewhere during the night, I sunk into another one of my Technicolor dreams — a dream so vivid I could taste and smell and feel the ground beneath my feet.

I watched as a mother dropped her child at the foot of a great man. She turned away, walked a few paces, then turned to scoop up his limp body, carrying her burden further away. Again she came into view, this time, carefully placing the child at the feet of a wise man. She kissed the child's hand, then left, only to come back a short while later to carry him away again. Variations of this scene played over and over in my dream until at last I saw the woman turn her head to face me. I recognized her. She beckoned for me to come to her, and I helped carry her burden. This time she put the child into the arms of a wounded man — a man in whose face she could see all the burdens of the world. The woman walked away. The woman was me.

I woke up with Jon's arms still around me. Through the trees, I could see the first slices of dawn, a blush of pink, the stars having faded away. The witching hour had passed, we had survived another day. Somehow, I had given myself permission to let go.

Chapter 18

Jon and I stared at one another across the breakfast table, searching for answers to questions neither of us knew how to ask. Finn lumbered in, pressing against my leg for a handout, and I fed him a few crispy cheerios that had stuck to the side of my bowl.

"Where's Hannah?" Jon asked.

"She left with your dad about an hour ago."

Jon's dad had taken over my carpool duties two weeks before, and had resorted to bribing Hannah and three middle school boys to behave by buying them ice cream on the way home from school each day. So far, it was working well.

"Did you sleep?" I asked Jon as he was nursing his second cup of coffee. I sensed he was hoping for relief in the form of caffeine.

He shrugged. Something like pain and confusion shadowed his blue eyes. Confusion I understood. There were so many things I questioned, wondering if we should have found another way, waited, or made different choices. The question of *what did we do wrong?* suspended in the air nearly every time we spoke.

He answered my benign question. "Yep. And you?"

I nodded, concentrating on my cup of tea. I wanted to tell him about my dream, but kept it to myself.

As we sat at the breakfast table, I wanted words. I wanted to spill them from my broken heart and have someone be able to contain them. I wanted someone to tell me everything would be okay, that I would not die from the grief and terror that was eating me alive piece by piece, that I would not drown in the dark waters of my dreams. I wanted our words to tangle together, fix our pain, and solve the problems of our loneliness.

But he couldn't do that. His own pain had buried the words too deep and he remained silent. I glanced up at Jon and paled. He was looking at me with the grief of the world etched across his face, yet neither of us dared to speak it. My need for words would only burden him more.

I remembered what a friend said to me as we were just beginning this transplant journey with Andrew. "Always look up," she'd said, pointing her finger to the sky. "Look up to the One who continually offers refuge and hope."

That morning, I prayed over my bowl of soggy cereal:

Where are you God?

I can't see you.

Am I all alone?

I finished my cereal, somehow hearing:

I am here.

I will never leave you.

As I walked into the hospital lobby later that morning, I was seriously freaked out by my cereal conversation with God. Had I wanted to hear those words so badly that I had made them up in my mind? Was I going crazy? It was possible. I wondered how many parents ended up in the psych ward after trials like this. I was sure it had happened. So many blows to the psyche over time can leave a person doubting whether or not they have a grip on reality.

Andrew was sleeping again when I slipped into the room. My dad was sitting upright in the chair, asleep too, with his briefcase on his lap, his C-Pap machine on the floor next to his feet.

I bent down to wake him. "How was the night?"

His head bobbed and he rubbed at his eyes. "Just fine. We did just fine."

My dad slept though all sorts of chaos when I was young, so I wasn't surprised he didn't notice any disruptions throughout the night.

After he left, I made myself comfortable and began writing a few emails to friends and family to keep them up to date. Although I generally left out the gory details of our existence and shared only the surface facts, my closest friends knew how to read between the lines: Things were getting bad.

My phone buzzed in my pocket as I was trying to compose a positive thought to complete an email to one of Andrew's old teachers. I pulled out my phone along with a bunch of wadded up used Kleenex, and a slip of folded paper. I recognized it immediately. It was a few lines of scripture I had written on a grocery receipt: *Have I not commanded you? Be strong and courageous. Do not be afraid; do not be discouraged, for the LORD your God will be with you wherever you go. – Joshua 1:9*

I remembered writing the note weeks before. It was intended for Hannah — words of encouragement for the times we were absent. But here it was, in my hand now, reminding me that God was somehow with us. I tucked it back in my pocket as a familiar voice came on the line.

"Hi, Kristin, how is Andrew? Is this a good time to talk?"

It was Carol, a long-time friend whom I hadn't talked to since we moved into the hospital months before.

"Sure. Andrew is sleeping and I'm just writing some notes. How are you?"

"Well actually, I'm downstairs. Do you think you could get away for a short while to meet me for lunch?"

A lunch date? I was overjoyed at the prospect of seeing my friend as much as escaping the room. I checked in with the nurse, grabbed my purse, and quietly slipped from the room.

"I woke up this morning thinking of you," she told me as we ate. "Suddenly I felt I should drive down here."

I was speechless.

"Now tell me, how are you *really*?"

I felt my carefully put together facade crumble immediately. The walls I had built around me, to protect me from the reality of my life, were broken and I couldn't contain the raw truth. "Not so good," I admitted through a stream of tears.

We sat in the far corner of the coffee shop, hidden from others on their daily quest for a caffeine fix. "Just when I think it can't get any worse, it does. Every night when I go to sleep, I wish I didn't have to wake up."

I began to tell my story through snotty sobs, tugging it from the deep, dark places inside of me, places I rarely went, places I avoided for fear I would never be able to return. I told her how one minute I felt so strong, my convictions feeling like peace, then the next moment I felt hope slipping from my grasp.

Carol paused, biting her lip and tucking her auburn hair behind her ears, measuring her words carefully. "Do you know the difference between the words resign, and relinquish?" she asked.

I shook my head. What did that have to do with anything?

"To resign, is to give up, or give into. It leaves you with a feeling of hopelessness. But to relinquish, that is the act of handing over." She waited, forcing me to look up at her. "Like handing over Andrew, perhaps? It will give you room for acceptance and hope."

I shivered. It was like she was inside my head. Like somehow she knew about my dream from the night before. I thought about how I had struggled for months to define that difference for myself, running from the feeling of hopelessness, afraid that if I let go of my hold on Andrew, it would be an indication of giving up. And I was not willing to give up. Handing over authority to not only Andrew's medical team, but most importantly, wholly entrusting him to God, was my only avenue for survival. I couldn't contain the fear anymore.

While we ate our lunch, Carol listened. And during that time, she was carefully picking up the pieces of my broken heart, handing them back to me with a renewed sense of hope. She offered me room to grieve, to share my fears, and to unravel in a way that I couldn't do in my upside-down daily life.

When we finished, she handed me a little blue box. "I made this for you," she said with a smile.

I opened the gift, hardly believing what was inside—a sterling bracelet with lettered beads that read, *Light of the World.*

After lunch, I called Julie, hoping for a generic conversation about the latest novel she was reading. Julie devours books like a chocolate lover eating a sheet cake in a single sitting. Her life changed the moment Amazon put books online and she cradled a Kindle in her hands for the very first time. Her husband is a jealous lover in a three-way relationship, always competing for her attention.

"Hi," I said when she answered the phone. Tears were too close to the surface, so I didn't dare say another word.

"I can tell something's up. What's going on?"

I hated it when she could read me so clearly. "I had a conversation with God this morning over my bowl of Cheerios." It wasn't the first time God had intercepted my path, but it was the first time I had ever heard the voice of the Divine.

"Well, what did He say?"

I told her about my morning, how I thought I might be losing my mind. Then I told her about my about my lunch with Carol.

I heard a smile in her voice. "Check your email, I'm forwarding something to you right now."

I opened my laptop, waiting for the ping of an incoming email. When I opened it, there was a giant photo, a selfie, taken from the top of a mountain. A woman's hand holding a cardboard sign read: 'Psalm 34: 4-6, in honor of Andrew.'

"Who's that?" I asked Julie.

"A new friend of ours. When I told her Andrew's story, she felt helpless. She said she wished she could do something.

So this morning, she hiked Camelback Mountain in Scottsdale, in honor of our Andrew. You're not alone. Please don't forget that."

I hung up the phone and searched the Internet for the scripture. I found it and sat back in the rocking chair to read.

"I prayed to the Lord, and he answered me. He freed me from all my fears. Those who look to Him for help will be radiant with joy; no shadow of shame will darken their faces. In my desperation I prayed, and the Lord listened..." - Psalm 34: 4-6

Seek. Look. Cry out. It was clear that this God of the bible, the one I tried so hard to trust, had heard these pleas before. Had He heard my cries? Were they important enough? Was my faith strong enough? I didn't know. I spent so much time wanting a God with skin on, one I could touch and see and feel and hear. I wanted to be scooped up in His arms and told that everything would be okay, and I was angry that that hadn't happened. But then I remembered what Becki told me days before, "God will show up in the mess. Watch for it."

While looking at the picture again and reviewing my day, I saw for the first time that the people in my life were the presence of God I longed for, carrying me when I was too weary to go on, holding my hand as I walked through hell. They showed up when I needed them most, even when I didn't know I needed them. They were my living, breathing, skin wearing version of the flat-felted God I had given my heart to as a little girl. That night as I went to sleep, I thanked Him for showing up in my life in a very real way. And then I begged for mercy for us all.

Chapter 19

As I walked through the hospital lobby doors into the frigid December air, I calculated that six weeks had passed since Hannah's blood work confirmed a match. I wasn't sure what we were waiting for. Another surgery? A single doctor willing to put his or her career on the line for an experimental transplant? The stars to align?

Making my way to the parking garage, I noticed the planters outside the main entrance were devoid of flowers. In their place, construction paper Christmas trees and snowmen were glued to the front of wooden tongue depressors and spiked into the frosty soil. A sign taped to the wall read: 'Happy Holidays from Mrs. Grant's second grade class'.

When I arrived home, our neighbor's Boy Scout troop was scaling the front of our house with a colorful menagerie of Christmas lights. A lone Christmas tree stood in front of the garage door with tiny notes of encouragement tied to the end of each branch. Putting up a tree, or decorating for the holidays, was far from my mind, so when I saw the boy's playful banter on my front lawn and realized my book club had decorated the tree, I nearly cried. I stood wondering if these were the ways God was showing up for me—a Boy Scout, a neighbor, my book club friends, the barista at Starbucks who knew I liked honey in my peppermint tea, even the stranger in the grocery store who bought our family dinner.

A rain-soaked boy approached, asking me where to hang the next string.

"Right around those windows," I said, pointing to the kids' rooms on the second floor.

Hannah would be thrilled. Our house had become an empty shell, a place for Jon and me to dump-and-run, leaving unopened mail, discarded clothes, and empty fast food containers in growing piles around the house. Neighbors were taking care of the animals, de-pooping the front yard, petting our lonely and surly cat, and collecting eggs from under two of our chickens that had gone broody on us and were violently pecking anyone who dared to come near. Even Frightful seemed out of sorts. Her usual barnyard chatter was all but silenced and her silky feathers were now splotchy and thin in places.

My mom dropped Hannah off one evening and hollered from her car, "The house looks beautiful! When did you have the time?"

I told her about the night I found the Boy Scouts climbing the front of our house. "They just showed up and lit up our world. It makes me happy when I come home at night," I said.

"What a great idea!"

She flashed me a smile and gave me two thumbs up before backing down the driveway. It came as no surprise to me that my mom and six-year-old niece showed up at the hospital the next morning with wrapping paper, ribbon and stockings.

"We're bringing Christmas to you!" she said.

My niece had made a fist full of cut-out paper snowflakes and a cross-eyed felt reindeer she named, "Moose." Moose was roughly taped to the window below a cascade of snowflakes. He was missing a leg.

"He's in the North Pole, Auntie. There's lots of snow," she offered as an explanation.

By that evening, each cabinet door was carefully wrapped in paper and shiny bows, creating a mass of giant presents across the room. Stockings hung from cabinet handles and a little tree was tucked in the corner by the window. Our room was a crazy rainbow of mismatched love, and I reveled in it.

The next afternoon, Grandma Connie brought Hannah to visit. Rounding the corner excitedly, Hannah held up her art project. "Hey, Andrew, I made an angel for the Christmas tree. Check it out!"

Andrew was awake, but made no reply from under the blanket. He had withdrawn so far into himself that we had a hard time eliciting any kind of response. When my mom and niece played Christmas music the day before, he had not uttered a word.

"Andrew?"

I watched as a mixture of frustration and fear passed across my daughter's face. She stood frozen in place, her angel slipping to the floor, forgotten.

Connie handed Hannah a shopping bag. "Why don't you give this to your brother?" she said.

Hannah dropped the bag on his bed and sat next to her grandmother. A pair of yellow-felted chicken feet poked out from a wad of tissue paper.

I opened the bag for Andrew, pulling out a life-sized stuffed chicken. "It's Frightful!"

Andrew pulled the blanket from his face and studied the tawny brown mottled chicken. His slender hand reached out, squeezing thumb and first finger together. His remaining three fingers poked up in the air like a fan.

"You miss Frightful, don't you?" I asked, acknowledging his symbol for bird. I carefully sat on the edge of his bed, moving the tubes and IV lines out of the way. "Should I tell you a story about her?"

He nodded, a look of anticipation spreading across his face.

"Well, I know she misses you, too, because every day when I leave home, she's squawking at me. Just yesterday she was perched on your bicycle seat when I went into the garage. I could tell she'd been waiting all morning because there was a fresh smear of chicken poop down the side of your bike. She let out a low croon, like she does when she sings to you. I told her to be patient and that you would be home soon."

Andrew placed his hand in mine, the bird symbol still pinched between his first finger and thumb.

"I'll bet she wants to be held like this. Don't you think?" I pulled his hand to my face, kissing the pad of his thumb—beak to lips. "We hold Frightful all the time, but it's not the same. She flutters and complains. What's your secret, Andrew? How do you make her so happy?"

Andrew's face dropped. He pulled the sheet over his head, sinking back into the bed. I worried I had pushed him too far.

Hannah's face turned pink and she stood up to leave.

"How about we put these lights on the tree?" Grandma Connie said, pulling out a colorful string of lights and handing them to Hannah. My mother-in-law glanced at me and mouthed the words, "She'll be all right."

Together, Hannah and I carefully placed the miniature lights on the tree. I picked up the abandoned angel, handing it back to her. She twirled it between her fingers while unspoken words flew back and forth between the two of us:

I'm scared.

I know you are, sweetheart. I am, too.

I don't like being here.

I understand. I hate being here myself.

Everything sucks.

Yes. Yes, it does.

I grabbed my little girl in a tight hug, ending our silent dialog. I understood why she didn't want to be in the room with a brother she hardly recognized. It tore at our hearts, causing us to grieve as if we had already lost him.

Searching out Connie on the other side of the room, I caught her eye. "Thank you," I mouthed back to this kind mother who not only loved my children, but had raised her son to love me in the same way.

* * *

On Christmas Eve, my parents stayed with Andrew while we shared an impromptu dinner with Hannah at my in-laws house. Although I appreciated their gesture and attempt to normalize the holidays for us, it didn't feel right.

"It feels strange to be here without Andrew," I said to Jon as we were finishing up the dishes.

"I know. It's too quiet," he whispered back. "I keep expecting to hear Andrew making silly bird noises in the back room."

"Or digging under the tree, while your mom hollers at him to stop shaking all the presents," I added.

Connie's Christmas tree sat in its usual place by the windows. Brightly colored gifts spilled out on all sides — a mockery of the holiday we were supposed to celebrate. Hannah had plopped down on the sofa, feigning interest in a book. My father-in-law tried to engage her in conversation all evening, but the one-word answers had become too tedious.

At one point, he coaxed her into the den. "Let's see what crafts Grandma has stored away in here…"

Hannah leaned against the bookshelf, her arms folded tightly across her chest while Jon's dad dove head first into the closet, pulling out a *Thomas the Tank Engine* book, an old baby doll, and a Ziploc baggie full of Legos. Hannah turned to leave.

"Wait a minute! There's nothing too difficult for Grandpa Man. I'm part superhero you know."

Jon's dad had earned the name Grandpa Man, the day he tied a beach towel around his neck and flew through the house Superman-style in order to get Andrew to stop screaming in his bouncy seat. It worked, and the name stuck.

"It's a fact," he said.

Hannah scowled, but reached for the Legos. Her grandpa clasped her hand, searching her eyes, "It's going to be okay. We have to believe that."

The two of them played together for a while, communicating with each click of a Lego:

I love you. Click.

I love you back. Click.

When it was time for us to leave for the hospital, I kissed Hannah goodnight and slipped out of her temporary bedroom. "Sweet dreams, love. I'll see you in the morning," I said, reaching for the door.

"Mom, will we all be home for Christmas next year?" came a voice from the dark.

It was the million-dollar question. I didn't want to think about it. There was no room inside of me.

I walked back to the bed and smoothed a few wayward curls from her face. "It's what I pray for every day, Hannah." I left quickly so she wouldn't see my tears.

Jon and I were quiet on the way to the hospital. He flipped on the radio. A jazz rendition of "Jingle Bells" assaulted my ears and I reached over to turn it off.

He caught my fingers, intertwining them with his own. "Let's just pretend," he said and started belting out a jazzy "Jingle Bells."

"My ears! You're hurting my ears!" I cried in mock pain, but when he didn't stop, I decided to join him in a little holiday cheer.

Forty-five minutes later, we emerged from the elevators on the third floor, leaving behind a mural of a smiling pink hippo and a sign reminding us it was flu season. A note card clipped to the sign said they had not had a case in seventeen days. Someone had written across the top of the sign, "Wash your hands please!" We each added another squirt of Purrell to our hands.

Jon opened the door just enough to see **my mom pressing the little Shadow action figure into Andrew's palm. She had wrapped his fingers around the tiny body and held them there** as if it would somehow ease the pain and bring him back from wherever he had gone. We paused to allow them a moment of peace. When we opened the door again a few minutes later, my mom's phone cast a pale glow on her round face, illuminating her freshly pinked lips.

My dad stood, unfolded his long legs from the low-slung bench and grabbed me in a bear hug. "We love you, Kris. We worry about you and Jon like you worry about Andrew and Hannah," he said.

"I'm fine," I lied.

"Well, just the same. I'm here to tell you it never goes away. Your kids will always be your kids."

He ruffled my hair into a miniature rat's nest like he had done since I was a little girl. I smoothed it out and turned to my mom to say goodbye.

"Merry Christmas, love," she said, leaning in to kiss my cheek. Then, in a moment of heartfelt affection, she reached around my shoulders and drew me into a tight embrace. A moment later, the door clicked shut.

The room became eerily quiet except for the noisy breathing of our drugged child and the incessant whir of the IV pump. Even the constant movement outside our door had all but disappeared. It felt like we were the only people in the world.

Jon and I squeezed together on the twin-sized bed under the window. It was going to be a brutally long night. Moose eyed me with his one good eye. "I'm trapped, too." The HEPA filter turned on causing one of the snowflakes to break free from its tape and begin jumping around the windowsill.

"We didn't send out any Christmas cards this year, did we?" Jon asked.

"Are you kidding? What would we possibly say?"

"Well... how about, 'Life really sucks for us, but we hope you are having a Happy Holiday!'"

I snorted, catching myself before waking Andrew.

"Or better yet," Jon added, cackling at his absurd cards, "The Adams' have gone to the dark side. Not sure if we'll be coming back. Merry Freaking Christmas."

This time, a snort escaped my lips. Jon, laughing, clamped a hand over my mouth. Our imaginary holiday cards were the perfect way to express the insane predicament we were in. The more obnoxious they became, the more we laughed, allowing us both a much-needed sense of relief.

By the time sunlight broke through the edges of the shade on Christmas morning, Jon and I were twisted up on the narrow bed like two pretzels.

"I wish we had a chiropractor in the family," Jon groaned.

I watched while he stretched his back on the only open area of floor big enough to accommodate his six-foot frame. He was headed to his parents' house to get Hannah, then home to pick up our dog Sawyer, for a surprise visit to the hospital.

He leaned forward to kiss me on the forehead. "We should be back in a couple of hours. I'll call when we're close so you can bring Andrew down to the side doors in the lobby."

I forced a tired smile. Andrew was restless, but still asleep, so I took the opportunity to go to the cafeteria for coffee and anything else I might find palatable. IV poles and abandoned wheelchairs cast long shadows in the empty hallways, and I suspected that every doctor, specialist, and patient that could possibly vacate the premises was long gone. Although it was the middle of the usual breakfast hour, the cafeteria was nearly empty.

Plunking down my coffee, a banana and some yogurt at the cashier station, I searched for the credit card I had stashed in my shirt pocket.

"It's all free today, honey. Merry Christmas!" chimed the cashier.

Unbelieving, I looked around and saw a few other parents milling around with surprised looks on their faces. They had been told the same thing.

"Thank you," I said, completely overwhelmed by that simple gesture of kindness. I found a quiet place to sit and ate my Christmas breakfast alone.

Two hours later Jon called from the road. "We're about ten minutes away. How is Andrew?"

"About the same."

"Hopefully, the surprise will be a good thing. I'm not sure what to expect," he said.

I watched Andrew stare at the wall, unblinking. Unless one of the doctors probed him for answers, he had rarely spoken during the last week. I feared we had lost our quirky boy with the obsessive talk of dinosaurs and chickens to a dark place we couldn't reach. Where was the kid who watched the 2008 Daytona dirt bike race on YouTube over and over? The carnivore who would eat meat every day if I let him? He had crawled inside of himself and, somehow, I knew he wouldn't be coming back for a very long time.

"I don't know what to expect, either. But regardless, I'll be downstairs in five minutes."

I bent down to pick up Stuffed Frightful who had been kicked to the floor. I smoothed the fur back from its face and looked into its glassy eyes. They were nothing like the yellow eyes of our living raptor-girl, Frightful. Her eyes seemed to possess some understanding of things unseen, and in that moment, I missed her dearly.

Andrew and I made our way to the lobby and waited in the alcove between the two sets of doors. Each time they opened and closed again, the familiar scent of evergreen blew in, reminding me of the holiday we were missing. To protect Andrew from the crisp air outside, I had wrapped him from head to toe in his SpongeBob comforter. Inside, I tucked Stuffed Frightful into the space between his legs. I wondered what he thought about our excursion, but Andrew never asked me why we were there.

Minutes later, our Christmas celebration pulled in the drive. All four grandparents were in one car, and Jon, Hannah, and Sawyer in the other. When his grandparents came through the doors and gave him consecutive hugs, I saw Andrew flinch with the emotion he had filed away. But the sight of Hannah emerging through the side door of the van with our dog Sawyer made Andrew cry.

Hannah reached past Sawyer, handing me a brown paper lunch sack. On one side was a felt marker drawing of a Christmas tree, hasty blue circles tipped the branches. The words, "From Frightful," were scrawled across the back.

"For Andrew," Hannah said when I made a move towards her.

Andrew became increasingly restless in the chair and I glanced at Jon, afraid we would have to abort our mission. From past experience, I knew we had a few short minutes before he became overwhelmed, and a good thing turned bad. Jon quickly enlisted the front security guard to take a photo of our family gathering. There was no posing, no time to prepare a staged smile. At the last moment before the camera clicked, Sawyer jumped into Andrew's lap and a huge smile spread across his face. The picture was taken, then the moment was gone. It was our Christmas gift.

Andrew fell back into a drugged sleep the moment we wheeled back into the room. Jon would not be back until evening, so I stretched out on the cot and opened the bag from Hannah. Inside was an unappealing wad of toilet paper as big as a grapefruit. I couldn't imagine what she had put in there. I unwound the ball of white cottony paper with a shiver of anticipation—like a Christmas surprise. The moment my fingers gripped around a hard ball, I knew what she had done. The last piece of paper broke away, revealing Frightful's gift. An egg. Powdery blue, like the Parisian sky in my pastel drawing. Its velvety shell warmed to my body as I cradled it in my hands.

The promise of life yet to come, I thought. A feeling of hope and a deep sense of gratitude overwhelmed me as I thought of Hannah and Jon, our family, our friends, doctors and nurses — and most of all, the bird that loved my son.

I peeled the covers off Andrew and searched for his hand. In it I placed the warm egg, folding his fingers around it like my mom had done with the Shadow action figure. He opened his eyes and smiled.

"I knew she wouldn't forget me."

Chapter 20

I chucked the Christmas tree into the garbage two days after Christmas. Done. It was a holiday I wanted to forget. Hannah and I spent the morning packing up ornaments and cleaning the house, and we were both ready for a break. The morning was crisp and sunny, so we bundled in our winter jackets and walked the dogs through the neighborhood.

"What do you think of coming to the hospital with me this afternoon?" I asked.

I was met by a withering look. "Mom, I don't think so. I really don't like to see my brother like that. It scares me," she replied without looking at me.

I took her hand and we walked in silence for a few minutes. I felt the same way. My heart wrenched each time I saw my son's skeletal body curled under the sheets.

"It scares me, too," I said, squeezing her hand.

Ignorant of our conversation, both dogs happily led us on our familiar walk through the adjoining neighborhood and park. The swings were empty but for a silver coating of frost. There was no more mention of a visit. Instead, I cherished the time with my daughter watching the dogs play in the crackling leaves that had been tossed by the wind into a lacy pattern at the edge of the grass. I closed my eyes, inhaled deeply, and took a snapshot of the moment in my mind. I wanted to remember this feeling of bliss. I knew I would need it in the weeks to come.

Arriving at the hospital that afternoon, I found a handwritten note on the tray next to Andrew's bed informing us that the action items from our last meeting in mid-December had not yet been addressed. We would have to wait until after the New Year's holiday before any of them would be worked on.

"Happy Holidays!" it read in a curlicue scrawl at the bottom of the page.

I snapped. *Good Lord! Is this a joke!?* I stalked into the hall looking for someone to kill.

We'd been waiting weeks for the team to determine whether or not Andrew could survive a transplant, not to mention that our insurance company had yet to approve the million-dollar endeavor. Once those two items were taken care of, the doctors had to determine a protocol—a select grouping of medications they *hoped* would eradicate the diseased cells in his bone marrow before the transplant could be done.

"We don't understand the etiology of his disease, and we have never encountered cells that look quite like these," they told us more than once.

Sometimes, as I sat there listening to their rationalizations, I felt again like we had been exiled from the land of ordinary people to a land of misfits. So far, no one had been willing to put their neck on the line. Nobody wanted us, we were a hot potato, uncomfortable to hold, and frankly, unappetizing.

I stomped down the hallway only to find the nurses station quiet and empty. At the elevators, I ran into one of the interns currently working with Andrew. "Do you know who left this letter for us?" I growled.

"Can I see it please?" she said gently, afraid I might bite.

I handed her the note. What could she do about it? She was just an intern, rotating through, gone in a couple of weeks.

She quickly scanned the letter and handed it back to me. "I will try and find out for you, Mrs. Adams," she said sweetly, "Why don't you wait in your room…"

"Nope. I'll wait right here!" I cut her off.

Anger bubbled up from my gut as I went into super-bitch mode. *I can play this game, too!* I smiled at her with just a glint of rabid-mother in my eyes.

Pointing to a door that read STAFF ONLY, I grabbed the nearest chair, positioned it in front of the door and sat down. She quickly disappeared into the mysterious place beyond the sign. I slumped in my chair, suddenly exhausted. I was tired of being nice. And compliant. And a pleasant parent. This was my son's life we were wagering, and I was done waiting for our file to rise to the top of someone's in-box.

By the time a more senior doctor came back through the door, I had made a few decisions. I played my next words like a coveted poker hand. "I was thinking. Does the hospital have an Ombudsman? Or what about a patient advocate? Are they kind of like a lawyer?"

The slightest widening of his eyes let me know I had hit my mark. "Let's chat in here, shall we?" he said gently as we walked in to an empty conference room.

He asked me to repeat my decade-long story again, and I lost my bravado. "I am too tired for this," I said through my tears, "I need someone to help me. RIGHT. NOW. Someone who can make things happen. I'm not sitting through another conference. We need to make a decision."

He looked at me, hard, perhaps to determine how desperate I was. "Wait here," he said, skipping back into the hall.

Where would I go? I was just as stuck as Moose. He returned with a pencil and notepad, scratching the name and number of the hospital administrator onto the small slip of paper. "Maybe he can help?" he said, handing it to me.

Five minutes later, I exited the elevator on the fifth floor. I felt a glimmer of hope as I slowly read the numerals on each passing door. At the far corner of the hallway, I found the office. It was hardly more than a refurbished coat closet with a slim vertical window cut into the door. The room was just big enough for a desk, computer, and a few file cabinets. His door was ajar and I was able to poke my head in and introduce myself. He was not at all surprised to see me. It was clear he had been notified by the doctor downstairs.

David Archer was somewhere in his mid-sixties with a full head of silvery hair, a wide smile, and a kind face that immediately put me at ease. The cup of coffee on his desk left a comforting and familiar aroma that further melted my anger.

Reaching into his bottom drawer, he pulled out a box of Red Vines and handed them to me. "Would you like a couple? I find they help me think."

Incredulous, I helped myself to two licorice pieces and handed the box back to him.

"I'm just going to pull up your son's chart here, and I want you to give me the highlights. Then I want you to tell me about today, and I will see where I can help."

We talked for over an hour, me telling him about our reluctant team of doctors and the fact that our insurance company was still not on board. When I had finished my story, the coffee cup was empty, and the Red Vine box had a measly three ropes left.

For the next week, it was quiet. Then one morning, I heard the words we had been praying for since Dr. Torgerson discovered the problem with Andrew's cytokines: "The transplant has been approved."

I was shocked. Our assorted group of doctors, specialists, and nurses formed a semi-circle surrounding Andrew's bed during rounds—some familiar, some new. I searched each face looking for some clue to their private thoughts and noticed David Archer in the doorway, smiling in my direction. I knew he had been our champion—the one who set fire under each of the players who were reluctant to sign their names to such a complex medical endeavor. *Thank you, God.* I felt a heavy burden lift from my shoulders. It was quickly replaced by, *what in the hell have we done?*

With a compelling letter from Dr. Torgerson explaining Andrew's irreversible mutated marrow cells, our insurance company had agreed to the transplant. And with that, we were immediately transferred over to the SCCA (Seattle Cancer Care Alliance) unit within Children's Hospital. It went unnoticed to the casual observer, but to us it was a monumental shift. That morning, we were introduced to an entirely new team of doctors who immediately started Andrew on an aggressive pain regimen. They flooded his system with a cocktail of narcotics, anti-emetics, and frequent doses of Benadryl. He swallowed carefully compounded doses of Magic Mouthwash—an oral rinse heavily laced with liquid lidocaine. For the first time, he had some temporary relief from his mouth and esophageal ulcers.

On the heels of our new medical team, a brisk rap on the door was followed by two purposeful women. They walked straight into the room and introduced themselves as our palliative care team. Just as the medical team had done not thirty minutes before, they took charge of the situation.

"I am Karen, and this is my co-worker, Elizabeth."

They reminded me of the women in my kids' playgroups — approachable, understanding, and with an air of humility that comes from being a mother.

"We have read Andrew's chart and have spoken at length with his doctors. You're exhausted. We can see that. We're here for you. *They* will take care of Andrew," Karen said, waving at the team of doctors congregating in the hallway.

I stared at her with my mouth draped open. I had been on the losing side of a medical battle for so long that I couldn't think of a single thing to say. This was the first time someone had taken care of *me*. My hands started to shake as I clutched them in my lap.

"What am I supposed to do? I'm hardly qualified to make all of these decisions." I pointed at the stack of papers in my lap. "What if we make the wrong decision and lose our son? How can a person live with that?"

My body started to shake from inside and my breath came out in a fearful gasp—the very same feeling I had in the emergency room the night I told the nurse my son was dying.

I looked at both of them, hoping they would tell me what to do. Instead, Elizabeth told me her story. Ten years earlier, she had been a mother watching her child go through a transplant. The pounding in my chest slowed as her words filtered through my ears and wove their way slowly to my overtired heart. Just the knowledge that someone knew what I felt like was a balm to my soul.

Elizabeth moved to the seat next to me and wrapped my hands in hers. "There are no guarantees, but I can promise you that we will be here on the other side...whatever that might look like."

I shivered at the thought. We had just stepped out of Jon's metaphorical boat into the rushing river. I had no idea where we would end up.

Taking charge of the conversation, Karen pulled a small notebook from her purse. "Who can you trust with Andrew? Who is he most comfortable with?"

Julie. I told them about my best friend, how I hated that she lived so far away in Arizona.

"Let's call her," Karen said, handing me her phone. "You need her right now."

Without hesitation, Julie booked an open-ended flight from Phoenix. She would arrive in two days, right before Andrew's scheduled surgery to place a Hickman Line (central line) into his chest. The plan, I learned that morning, was to be ready for transplant by the first week in February. I made quick calculations in my head. In conjunction with the preparatory medications for transplant, and TPN (intravenous nutrition), it would give us only three weeks to build up his reserves.

"Now, you need someone who can manage your daily life from here. Who would that be?" Karen sat with pen poised above paper.

I couldn't think of a single friend who would be willing or able to take on such a task. Or was it that I was too afraid to ask? I felt I had used up my lifetime allotment of favors, creating a friendship deficit that left me owing others more than I could possibly repay.

But with Karen's encouragement, a couple of days later, I called my friend Anne and invited her over. I sat on the sofa, nervy at the thought of what I was going to ask her. She walked into my home, sat down, and eyeballed me. I could see her taking in every aspect of the room. There were pairs of dirty socks and shoes clustered at the foot of the couch where we stripped them off at night, a stack of magazines, and unopened mail used as makeshift coasters for used coffee cups. A half-eaten box of Frosted Mini Wheats sat on its side, and the cat had made a nest in the laundry basket next to me. Anne noticed all this without taking her eyes off me. I felt exposed. My house was always immaculate and picked up every morning before I started my day. Now, here I was sitting in a pile of debris and I hadn't the energy to move. I stared back at her, a nervous smile creeping onto my face at the absurdity of it all.

"What can I do?" she asked with a genuine tone of concern.

I swallowed hard, trying to find the right words. I hadn't seen her in months and couldn't think of where to begin explaining my life. I started with the list of jobs I was sent away with after meeting with the palliative care team at the hospital.

"So... you are the first person I thought of," I said with my heart galloping around in my chest. *Please say yes.* The truth was that she was the *only* person I could think of who could do the job. Anne is the most organized, get-it-done person I know. I had known her since our boys were in the first grade together, and even then I knew she was a force that made my Type-A tendencies look like mere laziness. I lost my bravado quickly when she didn't reply immediately. "I need help. My world is falling apart."

She leaned over, a kind look of concern on her face, and took the yellow paper from my hand. She quickly glanced through my notes as she fumbled for a pen in her purse.

"This is no problem. Let's start right now. Do you have a list of contacts you can print out for me from your address book?"

I let out an audible sigh. For the first time in months, I felt like I could breathe, like we just might make it, and maybe, just maybe, we would come out the other side in one piece. Anne spent the afternoon going over a list of people who could help us. She divided them into people locally, out of town, neighbors, family, friends, and church members. We wrote a select list of people who might be willing to spend the night at the hospital with Andrew, and people who could take care of Hannah.

"Do you know how to start a blog?" she asked.

I shook my head.

"Let's set one up now. Then I want you to invite everyone on your contact list. You can keep people updated medically, and I will be in touch with people who can help. That way, you won't be so overwhelmed with phone calls and emails. Keep things simple, focus on your family, and let me take care of the everyday things."

Again, I let out an audible sigh.

"But what do you think anyone can do?" I asked, as she was packing to leave. "If I see another casserole, I might barf."

She raised an arm in the air, "Leave it to me. This woman has mad plans!"

I returned to the hospital to hear my mom talking with Andrew.

"I'm not gonna do any more surgeries," Andrew told her.

The doctor had recently explained the purpose of a Hickman line, and the procedure that would entail. Andrew had paled when he heard he would have two long lines hanging outside his chest near his heart, one for medications, the other for blood draws and infusions.

Feigning interest in an outdated *People* magazine, my mom casually said, "You know, that sounds exactly like what Iron Man did. He was out of energy and he needed superhuman strength to get his job done." She flipped the page, scanning the best- and worst-dressed Hollywood starlets while Andrew chewed on this new information. "Seems to me that this new wiring will help you get your superpowers back, Andrew."

"Does this mean I can fly?" he asked.

"Maybe. I really don't see any limits to the possibilities."

He pulled Stuffed Frightful from somewhere under the bed sheets and whispered in her ear. The two of them came to the conclusion that this was a very good idea.

Chapter 21

The air had turned bitter cold, but I didn't care. Perched on the stone steps in front of the hospital one morning, my cold fingers fumbled for the buttons on my down jacket. Frustrated, I looked down and realized there weren't any. I awkwardly grabbed at the zipper, yanking it up to my chin. *Was I losing my mind?* Every thought felt fuzzy and held in suspense as I fearfully realized I couldn't even recall the thirty-five minute drive home the night before. I wanted out. Out of here. Out of hospitals and disinfectant smelling hallways and doctor's meetings about my terminally ill child. I told God all the faith I had mustered for this transplant was not enough to make it through. I wanted out.

I rubbed at my face and wound my scarf tighter around my neck, stuffing it inside my shirt. Somehow this one small cozy moment made me feel like I could keep my head attached to my body, a simple way to tame the thoughts racing through my mind day and night. I carefully shifted my weight on the icy step and pulled my phone from my pocket to check the time. Forty-two minutes until the transplant meeting. There was no way I was going back to the room — not yet. I was suffocated by the insanity of needles and drugs and white coats.

Cradling a hot cup of peppermint tea to my frozen cheek, I mindlessly rooted through my Starbucks bag for the last pieces of a stale blueberry scone. My phone rang as I finished my tea. It was Anne.

"I have a schedule set up for the next three nights at the hospital. Check your email for the list and let me know if it sounds okay to you, then I will confirm with each person."

My mouth hung open, the scone suspended midway to my lips. It seemed impossible she could do all that so quickly.

"I also have Hannah taken care of through the weekend. A gal from church is picking her up at your in-laws on Sunday and bringing her to confirmation class. The youth leader will be bringing her home. Your neighbor is taking care of the chickens, buying them feed, and cleaning the pen today."

"Really? Are you sure? Were they okay with that?"

I knew the youth leader was someone Hannah trusted, but the coop was a mess and the chickens seemed to have gone mad with the lack of care they were used to. I didn't know if my neighbor knew what he was getting into.

"Oh, and ladies from your book club are dropping off a huge bag of fruit, vegetable soup, and homemade bread. No casseroles. I thought you'd like that."

I didn't know what to say. Anne chattered on, sharing that within hours of my first blog post, she had been flooded with a barrage of phone calls and emails. When people from out of town called, she suggested they send gift cards to local grocery stores and delis, where we could escape from the less than palatable hospital cafeteria. A hot meal schedule was posted on-line, and she directed others who wanted to help with meals where to sign up. She even scheduled hospital visits.

"Can you think of anything else you need?" Anne asked, her voice interrupting the thoughts in my overtired brain.

"No, I don't think so," I said between chattering teeth. The wind had picked up, bringing an icy moisture that hinted at snow. I began to shiver and pulled my scarf up over my head. Blowing my breath out slowly, I watched the warm air curl up from my mouth like steam out of a teapot. I didn't know what to say. "Thank you, Anne," I breathed into the phone before hanging up.

Back in the room, I untangled myself from my winter ensemble and tossed my phone onto the bed next to the window.

It hit the far wall, making a loud *thunk* before sliding down the back side of the cushion.

"What was that?" Andrew asked through closed eyes. He raised his hand and made his symbol for bird, reminding me to ask Hannah to FaceTime Frightful in the coop. Before I could answer, he was asleep again with Shadow's tiny body standing on the pillow next to his sweaty head.

Leaning back in the rocking chair, I closed my eyes and tried to slow my racing thoughts. I wondered if God had overlooked the fact that I was being tested beyond my capacity. Did He know my very human heart felt like a heavy weight that just might rip a hole in my chest?

For years, I was told by others to trust God and have faith. I had tried. Not only had I tried to trust the doctors and trust in a cure for Andrew, but I also tried to have faith in a God who had allowed this to happen. Trust is hard, but faith is a bitch. Faith requires diligence. It required me to get up each morning, and say, "I believe," even when my life was messy or downright tragic. In the end, the surest sign of faith was how I chose to live. Because I believed that when faith was put in to action, it had the capacity to bring light into the world.

I was just falling into sleep when a nurse came in to see if I was ready for the meeting.

"It's time already?" I grumbled. Looking at her kind face, I mustered a weak smile and added, "Thank you."

Jon was frantically wrapping up a meeting at work, so I would have to brave this consult on my own. *I've done these countless times. I can handle it*, I coached myself. Steeling myself for battle, I fumbled for a pen, gathered my notes, and walked in to the medical conference.

"Hello, Mrs. Adams. Please sit right here."

Dr. Lewis motioned to a seat near the door. He was a friendly but formal man who I suspected had been a transplant doctor for several decades. He was the one who would harvest the marrow from Hannah, and I was glad for his experience.

Nine other people, most of them clad in white coats, were staring at me from the other side of the table. The too-small conference room was stuffy and vibrating with energy, making my skin feel prickly and my blood thud heavily in my ears. Desperately scanning the room for a friendly face, I spotted David Archer, the hospital administrator, sitting in the far corner. He gave me a comforting smile, and I could breathe.

"Okay, let's make introductions and then we'll proceed," Dr. Lewis said.

Everyone introduced themselves and slid their business cards to the center of the table, a gesture eerily reminiscent of a high stakes poker game. I shivered at the thought.

Dr. Lewis addressed the room. "Andrew's transplant remains one of the more perplexing ones we have performed. We're not clear what the etiology of his underlying disease is, so it's been difficult to figure out how to treat it. Considering his current state of health, it's critical we find a good regimen his body can tolerate. We carefully selected the group of medications used for the chemotherapy in order to protect his liver as much as possible. We also have to carefully calculate the amount of radiation he can receive. If we do too much, he won't survive."

I felt the bile rise in my throat and the room got a little smaller. The woman next to me handed me a bottle of water just as the fuzzy feeling in my head threatened a takeover.

"Thanks," I said weakly.

"The most tenuous time coming up will be from the day of transplant to thirty days out. He will be required to remain in the hospital as long as he is unable to eat. Once his ANC (blood neutrophil counts) begins to rise and he is able to maintain an adequate calorie count by mouth, we will consider discharging him." He looked over his glasses at me, making sure I understood him clearly. "Even if he goes home, he will be required to remain within a twenty-mile radius of the hospital for at least one hundred days post-transplant so he can be transported to the hospital quickly if any complications arise."

I didn't volunteer that we lived twenty-seven miles from the hospital.

Addressing the rest of the room, he continued, "As you all know, Andrew is currently in-patient here at Children's. Since he has been so ill, he has undergone his pre-transplant testing here instead of the SCCA downtown. The GI team determined that he will not need a bowel resection as briefly discussed, so that allows us to continue on schedule for transplant in early February." He took his seat.

A blond woman in the far corner took the floor next. "Andrew's sister, Hannah, is an excellent donor match, which is a good indicator for a successful engraftment. Her test results came back well within the parameters of what we hope for, and she seems eager to help her brother. Since we will only be able to do a partially ablative regimen on her brother, we are proposing we give Hannah some medication to help mobilize her marrow to produce a higher percentage of stem cells."

"What do you mean by partially ablative?" I interrupted, realizing this was new information.

"It means only a certain percentage of Andrew's marrow cells can be eliminated, instead of the desired one hundred percent. Because of this, we need to make sure the donor cells are as effective as they can be so he has a good chance at a strong engraftment," she said.

I nodded, pretending to understand exactly what she just said. For the next hour, members of each department added their own reports and opinions while I practiced my yoga breathing to keep the room from spinning.

At the end, Dr. Lewis turned to address me. "If you are in agreement with the plan as presented, I will need you to sign these papers so we can move forward."

I looked at the stack. It seemed to loom above the desk at a dizzying height. I couldn't imagine what could require so much paper. The first documents were consent for Hannah's treatment and surgery. I scribbled my signature on the pages, wishing Jon was there with me.

"These are consent forms for each of the medications required for Andrew beginning today, until about thirty days post-transplant," Dr. Lewis said, handing me the first stapled pile. Yellow sticky notes with the words, "Sign Here" protruded out at all angles up and down the right edge.

"Why is this all in red?" I asked.

"That's the drug warning information required by law. You can skip a few pages back if you like, and sign there."

My eyes froze on the first page. The word "WARNING" was written in huge red block letters, followed by a two-page list of all the cancers, diseases, maladies, and complications the drug was known for. One drug mentioned that it would permanently damage the reproductive organs, most likely leaving the patient sterile. The notation under the warning label read, "This medication is best not taken unless absolutely necessary."

Oh God, what in the world am I consenting to? The white-coated strangers in the room flooded my vision, crowding around me like a twisted carnival nightmare. Prickly sweat started at the top of my head and began running down my back and shoulders. Looking up, I caught David Archer's eyes on me. I must have looked horrified or half-crazed, because he held my eyes, not allowing me to look away. Then he gave me a steady and encouraging nod. My hands reached for a pen; I scrawled my name on the paper.

For the next thirty minutes, additional drugs were discussed at length and introduced to me by names I would never remember. Each had warning pages in red, some more frightening than others. My water bottle was empty and my chin cradled in my fists as I willed myself not to cry. I knew my shirt was speckled with nervous sweat—the kind that smells like fear. I hoped the lady next to me didn't notice.

"This is another medication we use called MMF," Dr. Lewis droned on.

"Oh, that must be known as the Mega Mother Fucker drug!" I said without hesitation.

A heavy stillness settled over the room. I was mortified and embarrassed, yet strangely liberated. I felt powerful in a way that my son could not. Those realizations overcame me just seconds before I snapped, collapsing into crazy, snot-spitting hysterics. Grabbing my belly, I gasped for air as I continued to laugh maniacally, tears streaming from my eyes. Each time I tried to regain my composure, Dr. Lewis would say, "Okay. Now let's continue..." Then I would look up at him with his serious face and faint scar that sliced its way from the corner of his mouth to just below his chin and wonder how it got there. When he opened his mouth to speak, I started in with the insane laughter again.

I had no control over my response. I was a woman shedding ten years of fear, pain, grief, and a death grip I held over my need for control. The moment I rolled off my chair into the fetal position on the floor, I heard someone say, "I think we are done with our meeting today."

Twenty minutes later, I was still huddled under the table in the middle of my breakdown, alone. There was a tentative knock on the open door.

The woman who handed me the water bottle an hour earlier came in and crawled under the table. "You did well today. I will never think of the MMF drug the same again," she said with a huge grin. "I like your name for it. It's very fitting."

I looked at her through my puffy eyelids and mustered a smile. She was right. It was fitting. We sat awhile, under our wood and metal canopy.

"Today was also good for *you*," she said.

I nodded. She was right again. That afternoon, I had surrendered my son in a flood of tears and laughter, and it was good. Very good.

Chapter 22

Once my blood stopped pounding and the roaring in my head ceased, I crawled out from under the conference table and stripped off my sweaty shirt. Anyone walking by would have to deal with my bare back and grungy bra. Both smelled like all my other clothes, reeking of anxiety no matter how many times I ran them through the wash. Making sure the hallway was empty, I weaved my way back to the room, collapsed on the bench below the window, and slept for the rest of the afternoon. I awoke to Seattle's version of a snow-ice-ball-freezing-rain that caused the entire city to shut down. Everything was wrapped in a heavy coating of ice, topped by several inches of innocent looking fluffy white snow. The muddy streets and colorless trees had cloaked themselves in soft white robes, but nobody was fooled; the treachery that lay beneath the beautiful landscape was enough to keep the bravest of souls off the roads. It was clear I wasn't going anywhere.

The next day, little came in or out of the hospital, the streets silent with the congestion of abandoned cars. For hours, I listened to the whirring blades of a helicopter, presumably bringing patients to the hospital's helipad just outside my view. Andrew slept, only waking when the nurse checked his ID before changing medications. Eventually, boredom and hunger forced me downstairs to the coffee shop, where I came upon two women negotiating the purchase of one-half of the last raisin bagel in the Starbucks goodie case. When handed their goods by a traumatized barista, they stalked off to their own perspective corners, hurling dagger-eyes at one another. It struck me: I was trapped in a giant stone fortress with an angry pack of ravenous parents, doctors, and nurses, desperate with stress and hunger, willing to fight for the last bit of dried up food. I backed out of the cafe and hightailed it back to my own room.

With the exception of these hunger-induced battles, the hospital was quiet. I quickly passed the darkened gift shop with a hastily scrawled note taped to the door saying it would reopen after the storm. Even the smiling hippo in the elevator seemed morose at the lack of visitors. The corridor outside our room was occupied only by the cleaning staff disinfecting an empty room. I lingered outside our door for a moment, secretly watching Andrew enjoy the snow falling outside our picture window. Stuffed Frightful was tucked under his arm, the Shadow action figure contorted in a sitting position above his head. He would be loath to admit he was enjoying himself, so I pretended not to notice as I entered the room.

"How's it going?" I asked.

"Bored."

He cut me off from any further conversation by becoming suddenly absorbed in a movie on the iPad, so I made myself comfortable on the bench and opened my book. Moments later, I heard a rustling, then the familiar sound of plugs being pulled from the wall and the squeak of wheels on the IV pole.

I kept my eyes glued to my book as Andrew crouched down on the bench next to me. "I think I would like one of those excavators for my birthday," he stated plainly, as if we had been in the middle of a conversation.

I turned to stare at him. *Are you kidding?* I thought. With all of the lines and poles and beeping machines attached to him, he rarely got out of bed on his own. Now he was sitting next to me, telling me he wanted construction equipment for his birthday?

I watched Andrew stare at the massive earthmovers on the ground below. His face was gaunt, the palest white; his mouth a flaming red from the ulcers that cut through his flesh. But there was a new life in his eyes I hadn't seen in months, an inner strength that astonished me.

"You want an excavator?" I asked. I recalled a time when he wanted to *be* one.

"I could help Dad clean the yard with it. You know, Mom, they look exactly like the T-Rex at the Field Museum in Chicago. Same big jaw. Huge teeth." There was a long pause. "Yep. I would like one of those."

I stared at him incredulously. He gazed back, looking into my eyes, like a regular kid having an everyday chat. Stunned, I wondered how long had it been since I sat next to my son having a conversation? Six months? A year? I couldn't remember.

A few days before the snow, the SCCA put him on a new regimen of drugs, preparing him for transplant. They had also installed a timed narcotic pump. Andrew had been dosing himself as needed and seemed much more able to cope with the pain. It was clearly working. Looking at him, I decided I liked narcotics. Very much.

I redirected my attention to the scene outside our window. A massive blue crane had been erected the day before the storm while the construction crew prepared stacks of materials to be assembled in the new building.

"What about this new crane?" I asked, hopeful for more conversation. "Wouldn't it be cool to be up high in one of those and lift giant steel beams?"

Andrew looked at me like I was an idiot. "No. They don't have teeth."

Three days later, I was still abandoned at the hospital. I watched as cars and busses performed a complicated ballet on the hill of ice in front of the hospital and decided I wasn't interested in joining that treacherous dance. On day four, however, after hours of gazing out the window at muddy streets slathered in ice, I sent out a desperate alarm on my blog: Stuck in hospital with hungry ravenous beasts. Wearing same underwear since Tuesday. No relief in sight.

Twenty minutes later, a woman I had never met walked into the room swinging a Walmart bag. "I heard you placed an order," she said with a huge catlike grin. I sat there confused, not having a clue who she was.

"Who *are* you?" I asked.

"My mom is a friend of your dad's from Rotary. She read your blog and called me here at work. So...I went digging around our donation bin and found you the perfect outfit! The underwear is especially nice."

She dumped the contents of her bag on my lap, revealing a sweatshirt, sweatpants, new socks, and two pairs of size extra-large granny panties covered in tiny pink flowers. I laughed out loud when she took them from the package and modeled them for me. They would cover me from butt to armpits, but I had to admit there was a great sense of appeal in having something clean to wear. I couldn't wait to put them on.

I slept in my new sweat suit—a mass of grey fleecy cotton rolled up at the sleeves and ankles, wrapping me in a temporary state of bliss. The next morning, the icy temperatures broke, allowing forty-five degree rain to wash the last of the ice and snow away. When I opened the shades, I saw a message spray-painted onto one of the vertical steel beams directly outside our window. It read, "Hi Andrew!" in huge green letters.

"Look out the window!" I called to Andrew as soon as I registered the message was for us. He lazily opened one eye, then sat up in bed when he realized what it said.

"Is that for me?"

"Oh yeah it is! There are all sorts of people cheering for you. You're famous!"

I marveled at the thought of someone rappelling off the side of the building to create spray paint graffiti for Andrew.

"I told you I wanted an excavator," he said flatly.

I gave him the what-the-hell-are-you-talking-about look I reserve just for him. "What does that have to do with the message?" I asked.

"You know. Construction people. They're cool," he said with an obvious air of disgust at my lack of understanding.

Grandma Connie called later that morning, having heard through the grapevine that one of our blog followers had connections at the hospital and, presumably, had made arrangements for the message to be written. I wondered if there was any connection with the woman who brought me the granny panties.

At noon, when Jon arrived to relieve me, my heart gave a leap at the sight of him. "I heard you're famous, Andrew!" he said, walking in to the room.

"I'd like an excavator," Andrew replied.

Jon grinned and grabbed me in a bear hug. "Thank God you're here," I said, burying my head in his chest. He smelled like fresh laundry, lavender soap, deodorant, and hair gel. I could have stood there and smelled him forever.

Dr. Lewis poked his head into the room right as I was telling Jon how I wished I could relieve him of his clean clothes. "Andrew can leave the hospital today for a short ride in the car if you like."

I glanced at Jon, thinking he had arranged it. He shook his head, looking as surprised as I felt. Turning back to Dr. Lewis, I noticed his eyes were smiling, lighting up his face in a way that made me ache for my grandfather Joe, someone I had loved dearly. It didn't seem possible this was the same formal and humorless man who had lectured a room full of white coats and me earlier in the week. When he handed Jon a stack of papers, I noticed his fingers were long, smooth and graceful, those of a surgeon.

"Your son's pain seems to be controlled right now. I thought it would be good for him to get some fresh air. Once you move upstairs this weekend, it will be a long time before he's able to go outside again."

"When can we go?" Jon asked.

"Any time. I signed a ninety-minute pass, so let your nurse know when you're ready."

"Can I visit Frightful?" Andrew asked Jon, his voice small and hopeful.

Neither of us knew how to answer. There was no way to get home and back in time, let alone the agony of forcing him to stay in the car while he peered through the window at the home and friend he missed. It would have crushed him.

Andrew must have come to the same conclusion, because he said, "Maybe Stuffed Frightful could go for a ride?"

While I helped Jon place Andrew in our van, I wondered how long would it be before he could leave again. What would our lives look like? Would we just pack up, go home, and carry on with life? Or would we be too bruised from the trauma of the past few years to be able to move on? I couldn't think too much about those questions; they would only lead to other questions I wasn't willing to ask. So I forced myself to concentrate on today. Today Andrew had a sparkle in his eye, and our conversation had filled me with hope. Today Jon would take his son for a drive, and I would go home to our daughter, make dinner and pretend our life was normal.

Hannah was flopped on the couch with her cat sprawled across her legs when I walked in the door. The TV remote sat next to a box of Wheat Thins, a chemistry book, and a balled up pair of socks. Sitting next to her, I ran my fingers through her curly blond hair, remembering how I used to put it in pig tails when I sent her off to grade school.

"How was your day?" I asked.

She shrugged, keeping her eyes focused on the TV. I reached over to pet Charlie and quickly avoided being scratched. "Doesn't look like Charlie had a good day," I mumbled, wandering into the kitchen to thumb through a stack of mail. Peeking through my lashes, I noticed she had draped his obese body across her shoulders; a frown, or maybe a look of frustration, crossed her pretty face.

"Mom, my friends at school have been asking about my brother, and I don't know what to say. Nobody even knows what a bone marrow transplant is."

"People ask me that, too. Sometimes I don't know how to explain it. They assume he has leukemia, and I have to explain: No, not cancer, but something that acts a little bit like it. Then I really confuse them," I said.

Hannah joined me in the kitchen, pawing through an assortment of leftovers I put on the counter. After deciding against all of them, she went in search of instant oatmeal.

"Well, what am I supposed to say?" I heard from the back of the pantry.

I thought for a moment. "Maybe you could tell them that the cells in his body keep getting the wrong messages. His body thinks there is a threat, so it makes lots and lots of killer cells to go fight off the bad ones, but there are no bad ones to kill. The only way to fix it is to give him new healthy cells to replace the ones that are sick."

She looked hard at me. "You know, you really talk like a mom — no high school kid will ever believe that. I get it though. I'll think of something to say," she said through a mouthful of sticky oatmeal. "I don't think I'm hungry after all. Do you want it?"

Without waiting for an answer, she handed me the bowl and disappeared upstairs.

I knew she was scared. In three days, she would begin a series of injections that would force her body to produce an abundance of stem cells. She had been warned that it could be very painful, and she was a little tweaked. So was I, for that matter. I was putting both my kids in harm's way, and I felt like I had no other choice. Hannah was in her room with her headphones on, so I went to my studio and called Julie. I couldn't wait for her upcoming visit. I needed her.

"It's me," I said when I heard her pick up.

"How are you? You home?"

"Yes. There's still a bunch of snow outside, but the roads are clear."

I heard the faraway sound of a lawnmower puttering to life, the opening and closing of a door, and the faint bark of her dog in the yard.

"Hannah goes in for injections in *three* days!" I blurted into the phone.

"I know."

I was becoming frantic at her lack of conversation. I wanted her to throw out some comforting words, convince me this was the answer to all our prayers, and assure me it would all be okay.

"Andrew moves to the Transplant Unit the same day, then the next day he begins chemo. She's freaked out, Andrew's resigned, and I think we are insane to try this!" I said.

I swallowed back tears and wiped my nose on my Walmart sweatshirt sleeve. A whiff of stale sweat reminded me that I really needed to take a shower. I turned to stare at the rain slapping against the studio window.

"Can I be honest with you?" Julie asked.

"Please," I begged.

"Stop thinking. Stop questioning, and just be. He is having the transplant. You knew this was the right thing the moment Dr. Torgerson told you about it. Remember that."

I gave her the silent treatment, the distance between Seattle and Phoenix yawning even further between us. Did she think it was that easy? She wasn't putting *her* kids at risk. I imagined her biting her lower lip, a habit of hers when planning what to say next.

This time, she spoke more gently. "You and Jon are great parents. Be confident in the fact that you're making the best decision you can at this moment. I don't know why life has been so hard on your family, but you've made it this far. Trust that Andrew will make it safely to the other side...no matter what that looks like."

I let out a deep breath, blowing crumpled bangs out of my eyes. She was right, and I knew it. My constant wrestling match over my feelings surrounding Andrew continually made me lose my way. I was living in a Ping-Pong game of emotions. *Hold on. Let go. Hold on. Let go.* One moment, I was willing to let go and accept any outcome; the next, I was scrabbling to retain my chokehold on control. If I had control, then the fear couldn't overcome me. Or so I thought.

I fingered the yellow, pink, and orange sticky notes framing my computer screen, reminders of things I would never get to.

"Did I tell you about the dream I had about leaving Andrew with the wounded man?"

"You did. I remember you using the word surrender," she said.

"Yes. I really felt like I had let go of my worry. I also felt an incredible peace about everything. I somehow knew the dream was a gift." I started to peel the sticky notes off my computer, flicking them into the garbage. "But I feel like I lost it somewhere. The peace. You know what I mean?"

"I do. We're human, and we keep forgetting that we don't need to carry our fears around with us. We're pretty dense sometimes," she said.

I dumped a stack of junk mail in to the garbage and crushed it with my foot. "I'm afraid I won't find it again," I told her, feeling the sting of tears.

"Just keep letting go. If you pick up that beastly bag of worry again, set it down, and know it's not yours to carry." Julie made kissing noises on the other end of the line. "Only eight more days until I get there. Then I'm all yours, sista!"

"I can't wait," I said, feeling layers of tension leave my shoulders at her abrupt change in mood.

The line clicked off and my faraway friend was back in sunny Arizona. I turned to study the landscape outside my windows. Even in the heart of winter, Jon kept the yard immaculate. I knew he spent his precious few hours away from the hospital or work raking and cleaning up the dead leaves and branches in the yard. It was his walking meditation, his way of finding some sort of peace.

I heard one of the hens attempt to crow in the coop, followed by a jumble of friendly clucks and cackles as the others were roused. Maybe it was Frightful calling to me?

"Cher-cher. Cher-ROO!"

Trust me. All will be well.

I closed my eyes, picturing Frightful's silky coat, her puff of black beard around her beak, and her eyes that seemed to know things about my son I couldn't fathom.

I thanked the Divine for sending my son a feathery friend and for sending me courage through a friend who told me the truth.

Chapter 23

A feeling of relief followed me into the Transplant Unit three days later. The moment we walked through the doors, I knew there was no room for indecision. Remarkably, I had made peace with not only the transplant itself, but with the possible outcomes. What no one could prepare me for, however, was the journey between the first step and the last. That part, I was still clutching on to my desire for control. So every morning when I woke up, I had to let go all over again.

While we checked in at the front desk, a young patient came sliding around the corner. Amelia was wearing sparkly slippers, mismatched knee-high polka-dot socks, and a shiny bald head. She shimmered with energy. She could have been eight years old, or sixteen. I had no idea.

She immediately walked up to Andrew in his wheelchair and introduced her socks. "This one with the red dots is Carly and the one with the blue dots is Gertrude," she informed him.

Andrew cranked his head around, eyes begging me for escape.

I grinned and whispered in his ear, "Be polite."

He held up Stuffed Frightful for her to examine.

"Name?" she asked.

"Frightful. Except it's not an actual real chicken."

Amelia reached out a hand, glittery orange fingernails tapped at Frightful's fuzzy bird head. "Nice to meet you, Frightful."

The nurse showed us to our new corner room just as Amelia disappeared inside the room next door. I spotted a tired looking woman sitting outside her door, knitting.

"You must be Amelia's mom," I said, smiling my friendliest smile.

I needed allies and friends. We would be living in this place, Jon and I, which was both unreal, yet extraordinary. It was a place where children were bald and plastic lines emerged from pale creamy chests. A place where anything could happen, and usually did. We'd been in the hospital long enough to know that we were best to not try to align our survival stories or measure our pain against another's. For some, God felt victorious over the situation, and for others God seemed to have abandoned them entirely. That is a dance that continues our whole lives long, I suppose.

Amelia's mom dropped her knitting and pointed to a ripped vinyl chair shoved against the far wall, "You see that blue chair down the hall, honey?"

I craned my neck around, catching sight of the hulky chair.

"You gotta grab that thing while you can! I know that skinny little foldout excuse of a bed you have in that room, and it's no good!"

I raised my brows, my mouth falling open a little. What was I supposed to do? Drag the beast into our tiny room and lay claim to it?

Amelia's mother motioned to the nurse with a flick of her knitting needle. "Would you show this nice lady that fine piece of furniture?"

The nurse sprang into action, wheeling it over to us. Two pieces of duct tape held together a tear at the base of the chair, the wooden armrests gouged by years of abuse. There's not a chance I would have ever picked it out of the hallway. Andrew sat in the wheelchair, just as bewildered as I, while my new neighbor showed us the fine details of this 'wider-but-better' fold-out chair that would be our bed for many weeks to come. When the demo was over, the nurse whisked it away to be sanitized.

"You'll be thanking me," Amelia's mother winked, before picking up her discarded knitting.

I smiled politely and followed another nurse as she wheeled Andrew into our new room. I had been in many rooms like this before. There was always a token window, allowing a patient a glimpse of pale sky, the top of a tree, or maybe, if one was lucky, the fluffy white contrail of a plane escaping to somewhere impossibly wonderful. The HEPA air filtration would whir through the room at timed intervals, gently fluttering at the edges of a magazine, or kissing the exposed skin of a patient, lifting a stray hair or two.

The walls were meant to be cheerful with their blocks of wood, scenes of teddy bears on a train with giraffes, hippos, puppies, and such. Crammed in between the happy entourage of smiling companions were the wires and cables and computers— the brains of the room. Then there was the message board, where a conglomeration of important facts and figures was written. It fed us the information we desperately waited for: Our new doctor, the name of our nurse, the number to dial Nutritional Services for the food we weren't allowed to eat, procedures scheduled for that day and the next. There was a chart we would mark each time we were able to coax our child out for a walk or into the shower. When it was full, we would receive a star or a happy face for the day and somehow feel complete.

"Everyone here is bald!" Andrew squawked as the door shut behind us.

"It's the new popular hairstyle," I replied absently, wondering where Jon was. He was twenty minutes late.

"Well it's a dumb one because they don't have any hair!" Andrew replied.

He was as much on edge as Hannah had been the night before. Her first injection was approaching, and one student at lunch had accused her of lying when she said she was donating bone marrow to her brother. That caused a cascade of emotion to pour out of her, mostly directed at our kitchen cabinets. "What's wrong, Hannah?" I had asked, being sure to stay out of the line of fire.

"We never have any good food in this house! And the dogs stink, and I'm not feeding them anymore. They will just have to starve! Like me!" She threw a box of macaroni on the counter and burst into tears.

"Should we toss the cat, too? His litter box could peel the paint off the walls," I said, hoping to make her laugh.

She scowled. "Not funny."

I walked up behind her, circling both arms around her middle. "I'm just so tired of it all," she said.

"I know you are. We all are. These next few days are going to be tough, but I'll hold you tight and never let you go." I had hoped to quell both our fears.

Oh Jon, where are you? I thought then, and now. We were rarely in the same place at the same time, alternating between home and hospital, and he trying to stuff a paying job into his already overworked days.

Andrew broke into my thoughts with one of his bits of trivia. "Did you know that chickens are omnivores? They eat seeds and insects, but they will eat mice and lizards, too. T-Rex is a carnivore. He eats meat. I like meat. Beef. But only with A1 sauce." He became more agitated by the moment, rocking in bed, looking for his narcotic button.

The black and white grade school clock on the hospital wall began taunting me, ticking away, hands remaining in place, as if we would both be suspended in this state of anxiety forever. I fumbled around the top of the bed for the TV remote, hoping for a way to distract him.

"Let's check out the Travel Channel. They should have something good on."

Sure enough, his new favorite, *Man v. Food*, came blaring onto the screen. His demeanor changed instantly. A huge exhale, a slumping of his shoulders, and the relaxing of his jaw told me I had hit the mark. An impish smile curved at the corners of his mouth as he settled into the new bed, chattering away at Stuffed

Frightful about the twelve-patty cheeseburger the TV host
was attempting to eat.

Jon arrived, shucking his coat onto the foot of Andrew's
bed before scrubbing at his face with cold hands. "Sorry I'm
late. The bridge was backed up for miles. Did I miss
anything?"

"Only Amelia and her polka dot socks," I replied.

He cocked his head to the side.

"Don't worry. You'll meet her later."

"She's bald, B-A-L-D," Andrew said without taking his
eyes off the man on TV trying not to throw up the twelve beef
patties he just ate.

I noticed him rocking again and shook my head at Jon,
mouthing the words, "Don't ask."

Our new nurse poked her head in the room. "Mr. and
Mrs. Adams, are you available for a tour of our ward?"

We nodded, following her out of the room and down the
first of four short hallways. It was distinctly different from
other areas of the hospital we had inhabited. Hand sanitizing
soaps and sinks were outside each of the rooms, along with
carefully folded bins of one-time use robes, facemasks, gloves
and booties set at intervals along the way. Doors were
decorated with posters and pictures of things the cloistered
patient on the other side treasured or enjoyed. It was clear to
me this was the place where long-timers dwelled.

The sporadic windows I could see in each hallway
showcased the new adjoining building under construction.
Our nurse noticed me ogling the construction site outside.
"The entire floor they are working on now will be a new state-
of-the-art cancer treatment and transplant facility," she said.
"We will be the first ones to move into the new building
sometime in the next six months."

I hope we're not here, I prayed silently, looking back at her
with my practiced smile.

We continued our tour of four separate pods with nursing stations in the center of each, then on to the hidden beauty of the place—a small forgotten playroom. A nearly dead sofa sat at an awkward angle in the middle of the room facing into the center of the ward.

While Jon spoke with the nurse for what felt like eternity, I curled up on the sofa. From my vantage point, I took in beautiful shiny bald heads ranging from creamy white to rosy pink to a deep chocolate brown, all with scars and bandages—the war paint of heroes. Sparkly wild mischievous eyes peered out from a pale round face and a child zoomed down the hall on a bicycle with four wheels, a nurse cradled a baby in her lap, a central line was decorated with Elmo stickers, and a basket was filled with hand-knit hats.

Music played, crayons clinked in a glass jar, and a visiting writer recorded the stories of brave souls in a room bustling with candy stripers and paper snowflakes. A boy walked by in nothing but a Darth Vader cape and a pair of pajama bottoms. But perhaps the most vivid picture of all was a barefoot little girl in a Seahawks T-shirt skimming her ankles, waving to the back of her hero, Russell Wilson. It was all so spectacular, these beautiful faces rising up from the ashes of heartbreak and uncertainty.

Jon motioned for me to join him, and I reluctantly left my magical couch. Our lady in blue scrubs continued the tour by introducing us to our nursing staff. "You will have a day crew and a night crew. They'll stay with you while you're here, so they can get to know Andrew and your family well."

Jon and I shared a look of relief. What a comfort it would be to see familiar faces each day, rather than a continual rotation of staff, requiring us to educate them with Andrew's particular needs.

"One last thing. Visitors check in at the front of the ward and won't be allowed in the room unless we have your permission," our nurse said.

I thought of 'Books on Tape' Sue. She would be staying with Andrew in his new home. "We have a friend coming to stay with Andrew tonight. I'll be sure to let her know."

Back in the room, Jon sat next to Andrew, watching *Iron Chef*. A prep station exploded in flames when a bottle of wine spilled into an ignited gas burner.

"Whoa! That's so cool!" they said in unison.

"I'll bet they show it again after the commercial," Jon said, plucking Stuffed Frightful off the bed. He thumbed her glassy eyes and pinched the felt beak in the same way Andrew did.

"I wonder if they'll do it in slow motion. That would be even cooler," Jon said, trying to keep Andrew engaged.

Andrew flipped off the TV and reached for Stuffed Frightful, disappearing under the blanket with his stand-in friend.

Jon turned to me and asked, "Will you be okay if I leave for work now?" He brought his hands to my face, smoothing my brow with his thumbs, cupping my cheeks. I relaxed my face into a smile. "That's better. I've missed your smile," he said.

I nodded. "Me, too."

After Jon left, I settled in to wait for Sue. I knew she would be able to get Andrew out of his current state of agitation.

"Nice new digs buddy!" Sue said when she arrived.

Andrew pulled Stuffed Frightful from somewhere in his bed and dropped her into Sue's lap. "Frightful doesn't like it. The people here are weird and bald."

"Maybe bald is a new hairstyle?"

Andrew scowled and glared at me. I shrugged my shoulders and gave him the 'I-told-you-so' look.

The following morning, I asked Sue how the night went, cringing at the thought of what I might hear. Andrew had been surly and agitated when I left and I hoped Sue hadn't received the brunt of it.

"Pretty well, I have to say. Andrew and I read until midnight..."

"Until midnight?"

I had left the hospital just after six-thirty the night before, meaning she had read for over five hours.

"Well, yes. We started with *Harry Potter*, then decided that *Fudge* was a more interesting story. We added Shadow and Frightful to create a new and exciting adventure. Apparently Frightful can fly at the speed of light," she said, reaching for her coat and purse.

Andrew was still sleeping when Sue left, so I made myself comfortable and set out to read a *People* magazine I had pilfered from the lobby.

When Andrew woke up, he was clearly upset that I had replaced her at his side. "Hey, Mom," a tired voice said from under the covers, "I was thinking you might want to go to University Village. You could shop and stuff. You would like that, wouldn't you?"

This sounded fishy to me. When had he ever thought to suggest something that I might like to do? "Thanks, but I'm happy here. I've got a juicy magazine," I said.

I flashed him a picture of Johnny Depp, heartbroken after his latest break-up. He wasn't impressed. "I really need some private time. And by the way, would you please leave me your phone?"

Now I was really curious. I couldn't imagine what he had planned. Sunshine bathed the room and I looked longingly at the scrap of Lake Washington we could see from our window. Maybe a walk would do me good?

"Okay, I'll go for a quick lunch and a little shopping," I told him, then reluctantly handed him my phone.

Two hours later, I came back refreshed. The door to our room was ajar, and my son, who can multi-task better than anyone I know, was propped up in bed with his *Calvin & Hobbes:*

Attack of the Killer Snow Goons book draped across his lap. Stuffed Frightful was squashed under one arm and my iPhone was perched on a pillow next to him. The soothing sound of Sue's voice spilled out of the phone, filling the room.

He glanced up and saw me. "Oops! Gotta go," he said, abruptly clicking off the phone.

I gave him the squinty eye. "How did that private time work out for you?"

I was met with a sheepish grin and a request for a nap. I wanted to be mad at him, but truthfully, I admired his tenacity and his scheming. It had been a long time since I had seen that side of his personality.

Andrew fell asleep immediately, leaving me to my thoughts. I made a pillow out of my coat and planned to check my messages. I don't think I even made it past the first message before the phone dropped on my chest and I quickly entered one of my Technicolor dreams…

In a lake again, this time Lake Washington, the lake I drove across every day on my way to and from the hospital. The surface was choppy, whitecaps beat the cement bulkhead of the bridge and sheets of spray slammed onto the deck. I stood at the bottom of that massive lake, somehow understanding that this time the water was feeding me, nourishing my mangled heart, bringing me life. I allowed the water to wash around me and through me and, eventually, I became the water, and was carried into the ocean. I flowed through creeks and streams and back into the lake of my dreams. I buoyed the woman on the raft, sending her into the world armored with the things she would need to keep her safe. I lapped at her feet as she sat with her two friends, wondering for the first time who they really were.

I woke from that mid-day slumber with a need to pray, to talk to someone or something that would listen to the sound of my weary heart. And when I did, I felt a feeling of lightness I hadn't felt in years. For years, the fear of losing what I treasured most had attached itself to me like a piggy-back rider, making me carry its indeterminable weight with me wherever I went. Those were dark days, as deep as an indigo night. Even when I ventured into the light, I could hardly see, squinting until my eyes were mere slits in my scrunched face. But little by little, I had chipped away at the fear, shedding some of its awful weight. I left it in ditches, in dark corners, and at the edge of the lake. I watched it tumble down through the water, tangle in the weeds, catching in one of the magical trees to finally be swept away in a current that came from nowhere.

With my eyes still closed, I sensed Andrew moving in his bed. I heard the *cruk-cruk-cruk* of a chicken, and the scratchy sound of Hannah's hand near the microphone as she adjusted Jon's iPad. Then I heard Andrew's voice:

"We're coming home soon, Frightful."

Chapter 24

The next five days were a cascade of activity as we began the countdown to Day Zero. The process of killing off Andrew's immune system with chemotherapy had been brutal, leaving Jon and me to float through our days and sleepless nights, numb, yet deeply aware of the magnitude of our decision. After ten years, we had finally reached this moment. With no other options, we desperately held on to a flicker of hope, knowing something momentous was happening, understanding our lives would never be the same.

Day Zero: 4:10 a.m.

Something woke me up in the middle of the night. A charged energy and feeling of anticipation hovered over the room. It was Transplant Day.

I sat up gingerly in my narrow bed, carefully avoiding the wooden bars that had been digging into my hips all night. Andrew groaned, rolled over, and threw up. Five solid days of chemo and barf made my own stomach clench and heave each time his did. In order to keep my growing anxiety at bay, I grasped at every bit of scripture I could remember, reciting pieces of hope and courage as a mantra in my mind: *I will never leave you…I will be with you wherever you go…I am strong when you are weak…I have plans to give you hope and a future…I am close to you when you are brokenhearted…you are not alone.*

My cell phone buzzed and I groped for it under the blanket. It was a text from Jon: *On our way. All good.* Attached to the message was a photo of a sleepy-eyed Hannah, wrapped in her favorite quilt. She was due to arrive in an hour for surgery to harvest the marrow she would be donating to her brother. Although fifteen, Hannah still felt like my affectionate little girl sitting on my lap, leaving butterfly kisses on my cheek, whispering, "I love my Mommy" into my hair. I ached to be with her, but I couldn't be in two places at once.

Andrew rolled over again, knocking over a stack of comics and the already full barf bucket.

"How are you feeling?" I asked, knowing it was a ridiculous question.

"Like a dirty rotten potato," he mumbled from beneath the blanket.

It had been a miserable night. The pain, nausea, and vomiting had been a constant companion, and the new cocktail of poisons compounded the problem, making the level of misery unbearable for everyone involved. After a few moments, he fell back asleep, and I mustered the courage to slip out to the bathroom.

Avoiding the crash cart on the way in, I bumped into our nurse. "The EMT's will be here to take him to the University for radiation within the hour," she said.

I will never leave you...I will be with you wherever you go...you are not alone.

When I finished untangling my hair, I saw the door crack open and Julie crept into the room. She had flown in from Arizona the night before to stay at the house with Jon and Hannah. "How did it go last night?" she asked.

One look at my face told her what she needed to know. She handed me her cup of coffee and grabbed me in a tight hug. I was so glad to see her, and I burst into tears.

My phone buzzed again with another text from Jon: *Arrived. Being prepped for surgery. We are fine.*

Getting ready to go, I texted back.

I could hear the EMT's talking in the hall, waiting to take Andrew to his first of two TBI (Total Body Radiation) treatments at the University of Washington Hospital.

"Radiation from eyeballs to toes," Jon and I had crudely joked the week before after a three-day stint of no sleep. The radiation would kill any remaining Trisomy 8 cells lingering in his bone marrow after the chemotherapy had done its work. It would also kill just about everything else.

Julie stood next to me as we stared at my eighteen-year-old son. I couldn't help but be angry. He was supposed to be in high school, planning for college, poring over acceptance letters, scheming and dreaming big dreams about what he wanted to do when he grew up. But what I really wanted was to see him on our porch talking to Frightful. She was his confidant, the seer into his soul, the keeper of his dreams.

Day Zero: 6:00 a.m.
"There's only room for one person in the ambulance, miss," the EMT said to Julie. "Can you meet us at the University Hospital?"

She grasped my hand and squeezed, then left to get her car. Despite the sedative Andrew was given an hour before, he was wide awake when they loaded him onto a narrow gurney. They bundled him like a sausage and cinched the straps firmly across the bed. He panicked, shouting to the taller of the two, "You're choking me, you conformist!" A fleeting look from the tall guy told me this was a line he hadn't heard before. Neither had I, for that matter. I followed them down an unfamiliar hallway with a long line of fluorescent lights before Andrew and his gurney were hoisted into the back of a waiting ambulance.

Once in the ambulance, I convinced them to loosen the straps. Andrew calmed down enough for me to answer Jon's phone call.

"Hannah's doing just fine. How are you guys doing?" he said before I had a chance to speak.

Andrew began twisting his body out of the straps and I placed a hand on his chest.

"We're okay. Tell me, how is Hannah *really*? Is Dr. Lewis there yet? Have you seen him?" I asked, pelting him with questions.

"Relax. She's fine."

Like his mother, Jon remains calm and almost stoic in tense situations. He has an uncanny ability to remain level headed when most everyone else around him is responding to the crackle of panic in the air. It's one of the reasons I love him so much.

"What does 'fine' mean?" I asked.

"When she walked out of the changing room in the hospital gown, she had her quilt wrapped around her like Cleopatra. The nurse suggested she leave it with me, but Hannah said, 'Not a chance!' I watched her wad up the hospital blanket and chuck it on the floor as she settled into bed."

I could picture her dramatic entrance and laughed despite my growing anxiety.

"They're taking her in now. Dr. Lewis said it would be about two hours start to finish. They're planning to take the marrow from her hip bones," he said. My stomach flipped.

"I'll call you as soon as she's in recovery."

Day Zero: 6:40 a.m.

"I'm scared, Mom," Andrew said over and over again as the ambulance pulled into the side entrance of the University where Julie was waiting for us. I held his hand and refused to admit I was terrified, too.

"It should take about forty-five minutes or so," said the EMT who had ridden in the back of the ambulance with us. "We'll wait here in the hallway and take you back when he's finished."

Andrew's reaction to being loaded on the gurney told me they had underestimated the amount of drugs required to sedate him. Although he seemed okay in the waiting room, I saw a fresh wave of panic spread across his face when a pack of radiologists in white lab coats arrived all at once and began barking orders.

"I'm not going in there," he told Julie.

She stayed by his side while I signed papers and met with the lab coats.

"What is he supposed to do?" I asked the radiologist.

"He will need to lie completely still for twenty-five minutes while we map the perimeter of the body and then apply the radiation," Mr. Lab Coat said.

My mouth hung open.

"Oh, and he will need to be alone in the room. We will wait in the control room and give him directions through the speakers."

"Yeah, right. How do you suppose you're going to have a terrified autistic boy stay still while strapped down to a cold plastic table and respond to a voice from outer space?" I growled.

"We do this all the time. He'll be fine," he said.

Not a chance in hell, I thought.

The radiation room felt eerily reminiscent of the gas chambers Andrew had seen on his black and white World War II documentaries. The lead walls were covered in cement from floor to ceiling, the entire back wall painted with a giant nuclear symbol with the word DANGER printed in huge block letters. An eighteen-inch thick lead door on railroad tracks sealed off the room from the outside. When Andrew was wheeled around the corner and caught sight of the image, it sent him into a full-scale panic attack. In one swift movement, he extricated himself from the radiation table, Houdini style, and rolled off the side. Julie and I heard Andrew's screaming through the monitors.

"I'll be outside waiting in the ambulance," the EMT said, clearly disturbed.

My knees began to tremble and I couldn't breathe, and for some reason I started to itch all over. We were on a strict time schedule. I knew he had to have this radiation *now* in order for enough hours to pass before having the second treatment. Hannah was at the hospital having her bone marrow aspiration, and Andrew had to be ready for the marrow when it arrived that evening. I swallowed hard when the cup of coffee I drank earlier that morning threatened to make a return appearance.

I stormed into the control room, demanding to talk to Andrew. Begrudgingly, the technician agreed, and the doors were opened again.

"I want Frightful!" he shrieked when I reached him. He curled in a ball on the floor, but no matter how hard I tried to console him, he continued to scream for Frightful.

A minute later, I heard a kind voice from behind and looked back to see one of the nurses entering the room. "Let us help you get back on the table and I will bring you some comfy pillows to hold," she said to Andrew in a soothing voice.

Andrew covered his head with his arms and rocked back and forth. "I want Frightful," he sobbed.

"Who's Frightful?" she asked.

"My best friend."

A confused look passed across her features, telling me she was wondering what cruel parents would name their poor kid Frightful. I allowed her to ponder that one while I scooped Andrew off the floor by his armpits. Several long minutes later, with a little distraction, we were able to coax him onto the table with a promise to stay still. When I walked back to the control room, I was met by a posse of scowling radiologists. It was against the rules for anyone other than staff to be near the equipment. *Tough shit!* I thought.

"I'm staying in here and talking to my son over the speaker," I announced.

I glared at each of them, daring someone to challenge me. No one argued, so I stayed and told him stories. We talked about Shadow and Iron Man, Harry Potter and Fudge. I told him Sue was planning to visit and had a new Frightful adventure to share. I talked about our dogs, Finn and Sawyer, and his chickens at home, all probably wondering why we weren't collecting the eggs they so carefully laid for us. After nearly an hour, I heard these sweet words announced over the speaker: "We're done now, Andrew. You did a good job."

Day Zero: 10:45 a.m.

Jon and I were scrunched in the far corner bench of the Starbucks downstairs. Two cups of untouched coffee waited on the little table in front of us, a half-eaten sandwich stuffed back into its plastic container. Remarkably, the coffee shop was quiet, and it was a welcome relief to have some privacy.

I picked up my coffee, made a show of blowing on it, and asked, "How's Hannah?"

Jon's shoulders drooped a little. "She was still in recovery when I arrived, so I spoke to Dr. Lewis and the anesthesiologist for a few minutes. They made four separate holes in the back of Hannah's hip bones and from there, accessed her marrow by angling the needle in different directions within each opening."

I stifled something between a grimace and a sob. Jon put an arm around me and picked up his coffee with the other. "When I left, they had just sent the raw marrow to Fred Hutch downtown to be strained for bone fragments and impurities. This afternoon it will go through additional testing and processing to prepare it for infusion tonight."

I could tell he didn't feel like talking, but I wanted to know more, so I blew on my coffee again, peeled off the lid, then stuck a finger in and sucked the foam off. He didn't take the hint. "So? Was there anything else? Did you see her?"

"I did. When they wheeled her in the room, she gave me a weak smile, but I think she was still struggling with the anesthesia. I held her hand for a long time, but I doubt she will remember my visit." He put his coffee back down, untouched.

Struggling to take it all in, I concentrated on the monstrous front loader behind the barista, pushing a pile of steel beams away from the coffee shop windows and into the path of the waiting crane.

"How did she look?" I finally asked.

"Not real great. She's pretty wiped out. They tried to get her to stand up a few minutes after she was wheeled in, but she was immediately sick, so they laid her back down."

I wondered if they would still try to send her home that afternoon.

"They were planning to give her a bag of fluids to help perk her up. She's still scheduled to go home this afternoon, although that's hard for me to believe," he said, answering my unasked question. "I stayed with her and talked to her for a long time. I told her how proud I am and that she's my hero." He took a deep breath. "I didn't know what else to say."

We sat together a few minutes longer as the early lunch crowd began to trickle in. He already knew about my terrible morning with Andrew — there was everything and nothing more to say. Time was in motion and we were rapidly approaching the waterfall on which the transplant team had put us months ago.

Day Zero: 11:15 a.m.

I heard Hannah's voice down the hall talking to a nurse. It sounded hesitant, small, like that of a girl far younger than fifteen. A second nurse pointed to the door of her room where I hesitantly peeked around the corner.

"Hi, Hannah," I said. "Are you feeling any better?"

She gave me a weak thumbs-up, and my heart flipped in my chest as I admired my daughter's bravery. She looked just like Jon had described her; ghostly white, not a trace of pink in her face. I noticed she was still reclining and had what looked like a second IV bag hooked up to a pole behind her chair.

I suddenly had a desire to unplug my child from the blinking machine and run out of that place as fast as I could. I wanted to run until my chest burned and my mind was numb enough to forget what had become of our lives.

Instead, I took her hand. "You are so brave, sweet girl. I love you from the East to the West."

Day Zero: 12:05 p.m.

I was enjoying a moment of quiet on the nearly dead sofa in the playroom when a young volunteer found me. "There are two women waiting at the front desk asking to come in and visit."

I suspected one would be 'Books on Tape' Sue. Anne told me she was planning to stop by around lunchtime. I couldn't think of who else might be visiting.

"We're here to see the hero of the day!" Pastor Becki said, when I spotted her at the front desk.

Sue smiled at me. "I brought a friend."

"And lunch!" Becki threw her arms around me before handing me a bag from my new favorite deli. Becki's energy was such a departure from the events of the day that I couldn't think how to respond.

"Can we see Andrew?" Sue asked.

The three of us slipped into the room unnoticed. Sue found a chair next me on the cot and Becki reclined in the rocker next to Andrew, who was in a drugged sleep. Becki kicked off her shiny orange flats and curled up in the chair. "Lunch time!" she said.

She reached in her voluminous purse and pulled out bags of gummy bears, gummy worms, and Sour Patch Kids candies, spreading them across the bed. I couldn't imagine what she was up to.

"Gummies are Andrew's favorite, aren't they?" she said, popping a lime green gummy worm into her mouth. The nurse who had just walked in ogled. Becki handed her the bag of gummy bears. "Bring this to the nurses' station. We're celebrating Andrew and Hannah today!"

My mouth hung open. The last eight hours had been surreal, the morning at the University of Washington a living nightmare. Hannah just came out of surgery and Julie was playing referee between the doctors, and Jon and me. I had no idea where Jon was. I wanted to crawl into a hole, but Becki was offering me gummy worms in celebration.

"Maybe Frightful wants one?" she asked, winding a green and yellow worm around the felt beak.

I snorted. Becki's eyes crinkled at the corners, glinting like someone who never stopped expecting to be amused.

"I'll have some, too," Sue said.

A handful of colorful worms flew at us both, landing in our laps and on the bed. I bit into one, studying Becki as she laid a hand on Andrew's shoulder, whispering something about Frightful in his ear. I smiled. What was it about her that always brought light into a room? And how could the silliness of flying gummies break the tension of months of worry? By the time we reached the bottom of the bag, I found myself belly laughing at some crazy story of hers about stealing her mother's car when she was thirteen, so glad that some of her light had rubbed off on me.

When the room quieted, Sue handed me a polished slice of stone—flat across the bottom, an irregular hump at the top—a handheld mountain.

"For Hannah," she said.

I turned the warm, smooth stone over in my hand. A gathering of white crystals meandered across the bottom and skimmed the top edge. The center was a non-descript translucent grey. My face must have revealed that I deemed it nothing particularly spectacular.

Sue waited patiently. "Hold it to the light."

I held it to the window. For the second time that day, my mouth hung open. Tiny fractures, filled with minerals of gold, ruby, and rich caramel brown, wove their way across the top of the mountain. The center lit up like an early morning sunrise, rays of white streaking the sky in anticipation of a warm summer day. The transformation was completely unexpected.

"It's an agate. I collect them near my childhood home in Goldendale, deep in the Columbia hills."

"When did you find this?"

"With my grandfather when I was a child. Every spring, we visited his ranch and checked the dry creek beds for water. For a few short weeks a year, the run-off from the winter snow would create little creeks. We found all sorts of things: arrowheads, bits of bone, and buckets of agates."

"You've had it all this time?" I asked.

"It was waiting for the right home. Hannah is your light today. She is here to transform the darkness."

The room was quiet now except for the grind and swish of the IV pump. I looked over to Becki, a gentle smile lit her face. She understood the seriousness of the situation we were in and equally understood the need for laughter in order to heal.

As they prepared to leave, Becki hugged me, whispering in my ear. "I will hold your pain for a little while so you can rest."

When both women walked out the door, my heart felt the tiniest bit lighter. Although Andrew slept the entire time, I would be willing to bet that somewhere in his subconscious, he enjoyed Becki's laughter and Sue's voice and was comforted.

Day Zero: 2:40 p.m.

I carefully opened the silver locket and took it out of the box. It had a tiny inscription on the back: "Giving the Gift of Hope." Inside were pictures of Andrew and Hannah, taken from a photo of them holding their new baby chicks from that long-ago Sunday drive. I hoped Hannah would like it. Jon and I had wrestled with what to do for her. Nothing seemed adequate.

When I arrived to check on Hannah, Julie was sleeping next to her, slumped in a folding chair, her Kindle open on her lap. She didn't look much better than Hannah.

I kissed the top of Hannah's head, breathing in the scent of her. Her face was still so pale. A grey-green tinge had crept into the edges around her mouth and nose.

"Any better?" I asked.

She shook her head.

"Your Dad and I wanted to give this to you. Do you want to see it?"

She shook her head again, but put out her hand. I placed the jeweler's box into it, folding her fingers around it much the same as with Frightful's Christmas gift to Andrew. She started to cry. A nurse came in to check on her and assured me that everything was okay. Her vitals were strong; she just needed rest.

"For later then," I said, kissing her closed eyelids before slipping from the room.

Day Zero: 7:00 p.m.

Peace descended on the room like a slow, easy exhale — something completely unexpected after the crackling energy of the day. Flood lamps lit the top of the crane and the first three floors outside our window. Sparks from various torches cascaded down the side of the building like our own personal fireworks show. *Very fitting*, I mused.

From my vantage point on the cot, I watched Jon struggle to untangle a set of earbuds. Julie had curled herself into a ball near the window with a cup of tea. Somehow, the three of us had managed to navigate this day of insanity and were back in the same place we started.

"How did the radiation treatment go?" I asked Jon. After a disastrous morning, he had been elected to take Andrew to his second radiation treatment.

"Better, I guess. An anesthesiologist was waiting at the University when we arrived, but the anticipation was a killer. He flipped out much like he did this morning with you and Julie."

I flopped onto my back to study the tiny holes in the ceiling tiles. Neither Julie nor I spoke as we recalled our hellish morning.

"Did anyone tell you guys when the infusion is supposed to start?" Julie asked.

"I heard one of the nurses say they expected it between seven and eight," Jon said, giving up on the earbuds.

More than the surgeries, chemo, radiation, and preparatory medications that Andrew had been subjected to, the infusion of the marrow tonight would require us to take a giant leap of faith. There were no promises—and no turning back.

"It's going to be okay," Jon said, answering my unspoken thoughts.

"I know it is. I have a sense that things are already better, even though it doesn't look like it," I said. The fact that there was movement—something tangible somebody was willing to try in order to save our child—brought a huge sense of relief.

Thirty minutes later, a small red and white cooler was delivered to the nurses' station outside our room. Jon and I watched as three nurses checked and verified the information printed on each bag of marrow.

"You can show these to Andrew if you like," his favorite nurse said. "I think he would like to see it. He told me yesterday he was going to get his powers back. I didn't know what he meant, but I think this is it."

Jon and I knew exactly what he meant. On some level, he understood that Hannah's gift was powerful. He never mentioned it to either of us, but I heard him tell Frightful that Hannah was getting super-charged so that her cells would be ready for battle. And today, the war would begin.

"Andrew, Mom and I want to show you something," Jon said, placing Hannah's gift on the bed, knowing it could forever change my son's life.

Andrew reached out to touch the silky bags, tracing each letter of his name with a trembling finger. I thought he might say something, but the door clicked open. My parents and Father Heric, the beloved priest from Hannah's school, entered the room. Hannah had asked him to be there, and at that moment I thought we could use all the help we could get.

Father Heric sat next to Andrew. "I would like to say a blessing on your sister's marrow. Is that okay with you?"

Andrew nodded, his eyes roving across the room, from me to Jon to Julie and my parents. Jon set up the iPad at the foot of the bed, which allowed his parents to join us via FaceTime connection. Our little party gathered around the bed, and Hannah's gift to her brother was blessed.

Andrew scrawled a word in the air with his finger.

"I don't know what you want," I said.

He pinched his thumb and finger together in his symbol for bird.

"I know she's not here. But she's here in spirit," I said.

His face fell. I knew he wasn't buying it.

Father Heric knew all about Frightful from Hannah and asked, "Do you want me to bless your chicken, too?"

Andrew moved his hand forward and back, *yes*. Father Heric blessed Frightful, thanking her for keeping watch over her friend, and for bringing him comfort when he needed her most. That simple gesture of grace cracked me open. More than anything else that day, that short informal prayer thanking a backyard chicken for loving my son unconditionally was exactly what we needed.

Moments later, a bundle of nurses came in to present Andrew with a hand-illustrated poster of his three favorite heroes. "This is your new birthday, Andrew," one of the nurses explained. "You will now have two birthdays, the one you were born on, and today, Transplant Day. We call it, 'a new birth.'"

A new birth. It seemed appropriate. In so many ways we were learning to trust and believe in what we could not see. In this place, superheroes took the form of chickens, bone marrow recreated itself, gummy bears kept us sane, and the people who loved us most had become the three-dimensional version of the God I gave my heart to when I was a little girl.

Shortly before Julie and I left to go home to be with Hannah, Andrew's nurse came in to hook up the infusion. For such a monumental thing, it didn't look monumental at all—just a mere bag of blood passing from a bag into my son's body. Andrew stared at the marrow as it moved through the clear tubing that was connected to his chest. When it reached the end of the tubing and the infusion began, I heard him say, "Bring it on!"

Chapter 25

Julie glanced at my crumpled form in the passenger seat of her rental car. My face was pressed against the cold window with the air conditioning blowing on my face.

"Are you okay?" she asked.

"I don't know. I have a screaming headache," I replied, scrubbing at my cheeks.

Julie took my hand and we drove the rest of the way home in silence. I was secretly hoping Hannah would be fast asleep so I could stumble into my bed and sink into oblivion. But as we pulled in the drive just after midnight, the house was blazing with lights. My sister met us in the driveway in her stocking feet.

"Hi Kris! Hi Julie! How'd it go?" she asked, rubbing at her arms to keep warm.

Jennifer and her husband had taken Hannah home from the hospital an hour before the infusion began. Watching my brother-in-law lift her into the car, I felt more assured when I saw a tinge of pink creeping back in to her face.

"Hannah has been pretty uncomfortable all evening, but I think she's feeling a little better now. She's in bed, hopefully sleeping," she said.

"Thank you, Jen," I said, meaning every word, but having no energy to elaborate.

I dropped my coat and bag on the kitchen counter, kicked off my shoes, and shuffled in to the living room.

"When did they begin the transplant?" Jennifer asked, trailing behind.

I slumped down on the couch to lean against the back cushions. My head was throbbing. I was in no mood for conversation, but I knew my sister had been waiting to hear how things had gone at the hospital.

"They started the infusion about two hours ago," Julie told her, "and they expect it will continue all night, providing his body tolerates it."

Neither of us mentioned the crash cart or that a team of nurses was hovering around the room like bees. There were still people on his medical team who questioned whether or not he would be strong enough to make it through the night. Jon and I were confident, though. We both felt we were doing the right thing, moving forward with a certainty that was either divine or desperation.

Julie finished filling in my sister on the details of the day until she was satisfied, then made a beeline for my bed and was asleep when her head hit the pillow. Dumping my grimy clothes on the laundry room floor, I fumbled through a bin of clean clothes and came up with one of Jon's old t-shirts. The fabric was soft and worn, smelling faintly of the man I loved so much. I crawled into it.

I navigated the stairs in the dark and found my way to Hannah's room. Scooting into the far side of her double bed, I allowed my bones to settle into the mattress while my mind whirled through the events of the last twenty-four hours. I stared out Hannah's window, knowing that on the far side of the yard, the chickens were roosting in the coop, squeezed next to one another, tail to beak in a group hug of warmth. I gazed into the blackness, searching for the darkened outline of the house across the street, wondering if my neighbors suffered with burdens I would never know about. Rolling towards Hannah, I closed my eyes and uttered a desperate prayer: *Lord, let me do right by these children. Don't let me screw up.* Then I recited for the millionth time what had become my mantra: *For I know the plans I have for you declares the Lord, plans to prosper you and not to harm you, plans to give you hope and a future.*

Yes. Hope. A future. I would hold on to that with everything I had.

Hannah shifted under the covers and circled an arm over me. "How is brother?" she asked, her voice raspy and weak.

"He's doing well, sweetheart. He told the nurse he was getting his powers back."

After a minute, she whispered, "I love my brother."

"I know you do." I kissed her warm cheeks and left her to sleep.

It was still early when the Waste Management truck screeched to a stop in front of my neighbor's house and began its clunky ballet. Next to me, Julie rolled over, taking the remaining scrap of comforter with her. Carefully rearranging the blanket, I turned to my friend occupying the space where Jon usually slept. She cracked an eye, smiled, and immediately fell back into sleep. Flopping onto my back, I allowed my mind to race through the past thirty hours. It was impossible to grasp everything that had happened, my brain blended it all together in a menagerie of color and sound and emotion. Julie had remained a steady force through it all, and I wondered if I would ever be able to repay her in kind.

Leaving Julie to sleep, I quietly slipped into Hannah's room across the hall. She was in her signature sleeping position: face down, neck and head wrapped in her quilt, bare legs hanging over the edge of the bed. Charlie, who had arranged his ample feline self at the foot of her bed, was purring loudly. Hannah whimpered and rolled over.

"I hurt, Mom. I feel like I was kicked by a horse."

I went rummaging through the bathroom clutter to find the pain medication the hospital had sent home. "This should take the edge off," I said, handing her the pills and a glass of water.

We lay together, silent, gazing at the ceiling of her room. She still had rainbow stickers and glow-in-the dark stars stuck all over the sloped ceiling where she could reach. A construction paper mobile hung from an old hook that once housed a lace canopy from a time when she considered becoming a princess.

"You know, I think I'm done with a pink room," she said, breaking the silence.

I turned to look at her, her pale face still puffy from yesterday's surgery. I watched her eyes take in the little girl's room—the silky bows at the top of a mirror, a quilted picture of a fairy, and a corner cabinet filled with stuffed bunnies.

"What are you envisioning?" I asked.

Her words came out slowly, deliberately, as a picture formed in her mind. "I really like purple. And maybe some black. I'd like to do something creative around my windows. Do you think we could make some curtains?"

We imagined all the possibilities for something new. I stayed until the drugs drew her back into sleep, realizing for the first time in two years that I was thinking about something beyond the immediate crisis. We had made plans, and in a tiny flash of understanding, I realized we were on the other side— of something. In a breath of gratitude, an imperceptible shift occurred, a seismic rumble that left open a great chasm of possibility. In my imagination, I threw my arms in the air, shouting the words Andrew had said the night before: "Bring It On!"

Jon was more than ready to leave when I walked into the hospital room later that morning. The night had been uneventful, the crash cart forgotten and unattended in the hall, used yellow isolation gowns stuffed in the hamper at its side. A good sign.

Tossing my overnight bag in the corner, I chucked my clogs, stripped the ponytail elastic from my hair, and collapsed onto the fold-out bed as Jon filled me in on the night's events. The marrow infusion took ten hours, with no adverse reactions.

Andrew had been comfortable. He would remain sedated for the next few days to gather strength for the weeks to come.

"We're going to be okay. We're in a new place now," I told Jon through closed eyes. The bed seemed to have heavy arms, drawing me into its depths, lulling me in to a coma-like state.

Jon leaned down to kiss my closed eyelids. "Yes, we are. Good thing we can swim."

I smiled at his reference. We were free-falling in Jon's imaginary waterfall and I had finally stopped trying to turn tail and swim upstream.

After Jon left for work, I sat vigil with Andrew while his blood counts rapidly dropped. I couldn't concentrate to read, music felt like a cheese grater in my brain, and visitors were discouraged. I didn't feel like talking anyway. Mostly I just sat. And was still. I stared at the colorful posters I had made for Andrew: "Be Strong! Be Courageous!" and I realized they were really for me.

The transplant poster, made by his nurses the night before, hung proudly on our door, symbolizing to our small world that we had joined the ranks of a new tribe. The looming images of his heroes spoke *his* words, *his* truth, and I was struck by how poignant his sign was. Andrew had chosen three heroes to represent his external power; power that gave him the strength to withstand all that was happening to him: Katniss Everdeen, Shadow, and Iron Man. Each played an important role in his made-up stories with Sue, and represented the powers Andrew needed as he faced each new horrifying challenge. Katniss, like Andrew, had to be brave — to look death in the face and defy it. Shadow had lost his best friend, much like Andrew was missing Frightful, and channeled his grief into superpowers that he used to conquer evil. Iron Man had been transformed through an electronic port in his chest that kept him alive and gave him superhuman strength.

Even though Frightful wasn't there, she was his best friend, his internal power, his comfort, the one who spoke to his soul. It was an amazing team. At the top of Andrew's poster, a comic-style word bubble read, "Bring It On!"

Until I had time to study that poster, it seemed like a random grouping of characters from his favorite tales. I had overlooked the meanings of their stories.

"Is Shadow still scared?" I heard Sue ask Andrew one day. I was grateful Sue understood that it was too terrifying for Andrew to face the pain as himself. He needed Shadow to carry the burden of his fear in order to cope.

"Yeah. He thinks he could die. But Katniss is there, and she is helping him," Andrew told his only friend who was not a doctor or worried family member.

"What does she do to help?"

"She is brave. She won't let anyone hurt him. She'll nuke them first," Andrew replied.

Sue sat with Andrew that afternoon, weaving their dialogue into stories that gave him the power, strength, and courage he needed to survive.

During that first week, Andrew was examined every hour. Blood was taken each morning and evening to determine how well his body was tolerating the bombardment of poisons to which it had been subjected. We were banking his life on the belief that his sister's cells were doing their silent work in there. While Andrew and Sue created new stories of heroism, I imagined those new cells with Iron Man's armor, blasting through the debris left by the radiation and chemotherapy, waging war on the mutant cells that had warred against my son since birth.

In the language of transplant, each day was carefully numbered from Day 1 to Day 100. After Day 100, they would reduce some of the immunosuppressant medications in anticipation of his rising cell count. The Hickman line could be removed around that time, and maybe we would be allowed to venture past his twenty-mile limit from the hospital. But regardless of what things looked like on Day 100, Andrew would still be required to remain sequestered at home for an entire year.

On Day 4, Andrew's mucosal lining began sloughing off in his mouth and gut as cells began dying too quickly—a wickedly nasty effect of the intense radiation. The only thing we could do was adjust his pain medication and suction his mouth to keep his airway clear and wait for it to slow. He was in misery.

On Day 8, I woke up to the realization that I had had my last fight with the fold-out chair.

"That's it! No more!" I shouted to the Naugahyde beast. My back was constantly in a spasm and my hip mashed into the wooden seat support no matter which way I turned. I lumped the scratchy bedding onto the seat, folded it in half, and drug the makeshift bed to the nurses' station in the hall. Stomping back to our room like an angry child, I fired out a message on my blog: "Need something to sleep on. Nasty foldout chair bites back!"

Within the hour, Anne called. "I have someone dropping off an REI camp cot this afternoon." Knowing what I was thinking, she quickly added, "They swear it's comfortable."

I was willing to try anything. When I crawled into bed that night with a new cot, foam topper, and a silky soft blanket, I had a smile on my face. I sent a text to Anne: *If you want to be my permanent Life Coordinator, you're hired! Thank you!*

The next morning, the loudspeaker interrupted my boredom with its daily announcements. I silently cursed it for bringing me back to reality. I'd been staring out the window at the construction site for nearly an hour, enjoying my temporary escape.

The nurse popped her head into the room. "There's a group of moms in the playroom area with the knitting gals. You might enjoy visiting with them."

"Thanks, but I don't knit," I replied.

I wondered why she thought I did. The last time I wrestled with a pair of knitting needles was with my favorite neighbor lady when I was eight. She taught me how to knit a poncho, which was all the rage at the time. I have since professed it a very boring hobby.

"It might be nice to get to know some of the ladies," she persisted.

I had no energy to contemplate being social, so I nodded politely and waited for her to leave. After a while, curiosity forced me into the common room, where I met the most bedraggled and haggard group of women I had ever seen. It was clear most had slept in their clothes and that a tangled ponytail was the popular hairstyle. Showers were optional and makeup unheard of. Their eyes were tired and worried and full of hidden fear, but their faces lit up with the delight of being together. They were my people.

Knit For Life came to the ward every other week to spend time with the moms in one of the open playrooms. They arrived with bins of yarn, needles, and an abundance of patience for teaching this assorted group of bone-weary women to knit.

"Do you know how to knit?" the instructor asked when she spied me lingering in the doorway.

"I'm not sure. When I was in grade school, my neighbor was a knitter and she spent a summer teaching me the basics. It's been so long, I'm sure I don't remember."

"Pick out some yarn you like and I'll give you a lesson," she said with a genuine smile.

Bins and bins of beautiful colorful sparkly yarn were offered to me. I caressed each skein while ideas and designs zoomed through my head as I planned what I wanted to make.

Fifteen minutes later, she came back. "Have you made up your mind?"

Embarrassed, I looked at the pile of colorful balls I had hoarded in front of me. "I can't quite decide which ones I want."

"You can have as many as you like. Why don't you sit here and I'll get you started making a scarf like the other gals?"

"Actually, I was thinking of a hat," I told her.

I described what I had envisioned. Although she looked skeptical, she didn't discourage me. Handing me a set of circular needles, she carefully taught me how to cast-on stitches to begin, and showed me the difference between a knit and a purl stitch. My grade school lessons came flooding back as I remembered the gentle hands of my neighbor holding my awkward eight-year-old hands tightly in hers, directing the needles to tie their intricate knots. I concentrated on my new needles with the same expression of delight as my new companions. I listened to the women's voices, woven together in a disorganized song of relief. We shared our stories while twisting yarn into a tangled shape we could hold onto while our lifeboats teetered on the waves. It was like God had taken the deepest part of our sorrow and knit it into a pattern of hope. The beauty of it all left me with a feeling of joy.

Hours later, while Andrew slept, Stuffed Frightful and I practiced the art of being still. I focused on my belief that God was the great art director — knitting the new cells into Andrew's weary body. I also finished my first hat.

On Day 10, Andrew's immune system was wiped out.

"He is vulnerable," Dr. Burroughs said, "An infection would be bad."

His organs — especially his liver — were closely monitored. He received his first blood transfusion. I closed my eyes, becoming as small as the cells, entering the battle on his behalf. And I prayed. Constantly. To the ears of the wounded man I had given my son's life to:

Lord, take my hand. Guide me on this narrow path. Don't let me fall. Be my light when the way is dark, full of questions and fear. Help me understand your ways so I can know peace. Don't let me give into despair. Give me rest in the chaos. Bring joy to my spirit. Allow me to comfort Andrew as I walk with him through this hell. And Lord, if this illness takes him, then please promise me you are real and we will meet again.

To diffuse my growing anxiety, I was knitting hats as fast as I could get my hands on new yarn. While my fingers worked, I obsessed over my bold prayer: *If this illness takes him...*It was the first time I had actually said those words and I thought maybe I could survive that. As I finished each hat, I thanked it for keeping me occupied. Some hats I kept, while others found their way to the box at the front nurses' station where people could donate small gifts for the patients.

During this time, I learned that waiting was about being still. Waiting is not in anticipation of, but rather a deep inner stillness and acceptance, of what is occurring *right now*. Knitting became my waiting, my way to be entirely present. It was a time when the only thing that mattered was the next purl stitch, and then the next and the next.

"When will you make *me* a hat?" insisted Julie during one of our daily phone conversations.

"As if you would wear it in the Arizona desert!" I said.

"That's not the point and you know it," she shot back.

The truth was, they were really quite ugly. A mishmash of colors, textures, and yarn, the stitches reflecting my moods, sometimes tight and precise, more often uneven, with dropped stitches here and there.

Julie's phone calls were my escape to the outside world. After reassuring her that Andrew was okay, she described to me in detail the latest novel she was reading. We laughed and talked about all the inconsequential things in daily life. In my mind, I was with her in the sunshine.

"I'd like to invite Hannah to stay with us for a while," she said one afternoon. "What do you think? Do you think she'd be willing to come?"

"She would love it!" I said, knowing I would have to nudge her out of the house for her own good.

Two days later, Hannah was on a flight to Arizona. I hoped she would emerge from her shell enough to enjoy the change of scenery, and knew Julie's family would be there to support her and dote on her in a way that Jon and I could not.

Chapter 26

Anne began sending me a schedule each day, outlining the details of my life. I reveled in having a life coordinator. It gave my mind a rest from having to make any more decisions than necessary. According to my notes, Diana was due to arrive at any moment to relieve me for the night. Andrew still talked about digging for pirate gold at Lake Michigan, and Diana had become synonymous with that memory. I hoped he would be happy to see her.

I glanced up to see our nurse motioning to me from the hallway. "Diana is here!" I told Andrew.

I began sorting through my overnight bag stuffed with skeins of yarn and copious amounts of dirty clothes that had mysteriously multiplied in our room. "She's going to spend the night and hang out with you. How does that sound?"

No response came from the pile of blankets.

"She's looking forward to reading to you. What sounds good? Maybe a Harry Potter book?"

A bona fide grunt came from under the SpongeBob comforter, followed by Stuffed Frightful, who was suspended by her scrawny neck. I took that as a positive sign.

Diana walked into the room a moment later, shedding her coat and purse on the cot before going over to the bed. "Hey, buddy! Cory says hi!"

Andrew poked his head out from under the covers at the mention of his childhood friend. Diana thumbed through our windowsill library, selecting a Harry Potter book with one of Hannah's handmade bookmarks sticking out the top. I was so eager for my escape that I raced around the room, forgetting what I had planned to bring home and what to leave at the hospital. I must have been babbling out loud, because Diana caught me by the shoulders, forced me to look her in the eye, and told me to take a deep breath. Was I that fritzy? Had I forgotten to breathe again? I felt the prickle of crazy-tears at the back of my eyes, threatening to spill. Not today. I didn't have the energy.

Diana let go of my shoulders and took my hand in hers, opening my palm. Into it she dropped a flat, round stone—a Petoskey stone. "A promise to keep," she said, folding my hand over the little stone.

How different this stone was from Sue's translucent agate. It was a solid brown stone—fossilized coral—with creamy clustered starbursts that reminded me of honeycomb.

"Do you remember?" she asked.

I did remember. Clearly. The trip that ended my innocence. Not only had I been wrestling with the reality of autism, but I was also reeling with the new diagnosis of Trisomy 8. They had both left a heavy burden on my shoulders, but for some reason, when I found that stone, a shred of hope entered my world.

Andrew forced our attention back to the room with a rustling of sheets and a forced groan. "That's one of Hannah's rocks," he said, waving a hand in my direction.

"What is?"

"Duh! The rock in your hand. The Petoskey stone," he said, rolling his eyes.

"Andrew! Please stop." He had been grumpy all afternoon, and I was getting tired of it.

Diana started to laugh. "I didn't think you would remember."

"Aren't you here to read?" He was sitting up now with Stuffed Frightful under one arm and Shadow clutched tightly in the other.

Diana let go of my shoulders, but held my eyes with a look that commanded: *Go. Relax. Breathe.* Turning from me, she curled up in the rocking chair, opening the Harry Potter book to the last place marked. It was there she discovered Harry and his friends Ron and Hermione in the middle of one of their many escapades. She began reading.

Andrew piped up after only a few short sentences. "Shadow was with them and he broke his arm. Hermione had to use a repairing charm to fix it, and Professor Snape almost caught them. Snape is bad."

"Who is Shadow? I don't see him here," Diana said, frantically looking through the pages.

Andrew look annoyed. "You're supposed to put him in the book. He's a hedgehog anyway. Don't you know that?"

She stole a glance in my direction. "Okay. So, let's see.... Shadow broke his arm." She turned the page. "Oh, no! Hermione, I need help! My leg is hurt!"

Andrew dropped Shadow and reached for the book. "You're doing it all wrong! Shadow doesn't talk like that. He's a baby."

Diana had barely begun reading again when he interrupted her. "Diana, I don't think you can read like Sue. But you are good at other things," he stated frankly. "I remember when we ate popsicles together. It was fun."

"Popsicles?"

"Yeah. When you came over and put peanut butter in my mouth."

Diana's eyes grew wide as the memory flooded back—a frustrated little boy strapped in a high chair, learning how to form words with his uncooperative tongue.

"You remember that? You were only three!"

Diana worked with Asperger kids frequently in her speech pathology practice, so she was familiar with their blunt, direct manner when addressing others. They generally had no filter, no manipulation, and no hidden agenda. It was annoying, uncomfortable, and refreshing to be with someone who was an open book—someone who told you the truth as they saw it. Andrew's encounter with her was no exception.

Unfazed by Andrew's comments, Diana suggested he might like to hear a story from when he and Cory were little. "Remember when we were in Michigan and you kids were playing Hide and Seek?"

Andrew nodded and settled into the bed, a hint of a smile lighting his eyes.

Leaning back in the rocking chair, Harry Potter forgotten, Diana brought back that summer day. "Cory was the 'finder.' Do you remember that?"

Andrew nodded as Diana watched the story unfold behind her closed eyes. "...seven ...eight ...nine ...ten! Ready or not, here I come!" quipped Cory.

Unfortunately, Andrew didn't understand the concept of hiding, no matter how much we all explained it to him. Hannah, delighted to be included in the boy's game, ran to the next room and hid in the closet behind a stack of board games. Cory took his hands off his eyes and turned around to see Andrew standing right behind him with a silly grin on his face.

"Come find me!" he declared to the room at large. The four adults looked at one another, bewildered.

Jon offered some coaching. "You're supposed to hide someplace that Cory can't see you. Then he'll try and find your hiding spot."

Andrew looked mystified, the unspoken words scrolling across his face. *Where would I go? Why would I want to be where no one can see me? Is this supposed to be fun?*

During the next round, Andrew found what he thought was the best hiding spot ever. Gleeful, he sandwiched himself between the cushions and the frame of the sofa like a peanut butter and jelly sandwich. A shock of red hair popped out between the cushion seams. He was far too big for the narrow seat, one skinny arm and one long leg hung out the side, dangling to the floor. Snorts of laughter made the furniture quake and could be heard in the next room where Cory was again calling out the number ten. Cory stomped into the room.

"I can hear you, Andrew. Stop laughing!"

He pretended to look everywhere, avoiding the lumpy sofa that contained a giggling boy. Finally, Andrew could stand it no longer. He jumped out of the couch and pointed at himself with both hands. "I'm right here, goofball!"

The gallery erupted in laughter. Andrew looked around, a smile spreading across his face.

On the last night of the trip, Hannah crawled into my lap, her blanket wrapped tightly around her. "I like the way my brother plays Hide and Seek. He does it his own way, and I always know what to expect."

During the drive home, I could feel the Petoskey stone in my front pocket right where the seatbelt crossed over it. *A sunbeam of promise.* A piece of hope. Something solid to hold onto. Diana's gift was a treasure that I would carry with me for the next hundred days.

Jon's car was in the usual spot in the driveway when I arrived. He had picked Hannah up at the airport earlier in the evening. I hoped that the past few days in Arizona proved a refreshing break for her. Julie's texts had all been positive, but Hannah's messages to me had been a bit subdued. I was worried about her.

"How's brother?" Hannah asked as I walked in through the garage.

She looked sun-kissed and relaxed. I hugged her tightly. She smelled…golden. Like sunshine and lemons and Coppertone. The thought melted away my irritation with Andrew.

"He's okay. Resting. I missed you huge." I tugged at her ponytail, hoping to elicit a smile. "How was Arizona?"

"Good."

"Good?" I hoped for more information.

"Yep. Good." She walked into the house.

Both she and Jon began foraging through a refrigerator full of questionable leftover casseroles. Nothing must have passed Hannah's sniff test, because she quickly migrated to the pantry. I watched her pull out pantry staples — Arborio rice, an onion, garlic and chicken broth. Jon tossed parmesan cheese on the table and scared up a bottle of white wine from somewhere.

"Will you make risotto?" Hannah asked hopefully. "I just want some normal food."

Normal. There was that word that seemed to plague my thoughts. We were anything but the normal I had always expected my life would be. My Pollyanna dreams had evaporated when we were dealt the autism card. Now, in the middle of a transplant, when I wasn't sure my son would survive, I felt anything but normal.

"That sounds perfect," I said, forcing a smile.

Jon slipped out of bed early the next morning to go to work. As soon as he pulled out of the drive, I heard the hens stir in the coop. One announced she was on the nest with a *tw-tw-tw-tw-tw*, while the others chirped and chattered as they filed into the outdoor pen. A soft lonely warbling sound came through my open window, and I rolled over in bed to peer through the bare branches of a dogwood tree. Frightful stood alone at the gate, her beak poking through the hexagonal chicken wire.

Coo-coo-rrr. Coo-coo-coo-rrr.

I had no idea what she was trying to tell me. I wished I spoke chicken.

Chapter 27

Frightful was still singing her mournful song when I got out of the shower.

"Will you pleeeeease let the chickens out?!" I called to Hannah as I combed through my wet hair. Finn was licking water off the shower basin with a slobbery tongue and I shooed him away with my foot. "Go drink your own water," I grumbled.

For whatever reason, I woke up irritated and pretty much everything was ticking me off, starting with the lamentations of a backyard chicken. I had promised to relieve Diana by 8:00 a.m. so she could get to work, and I was already late. I was poised to shout at the next person who dared get in my way.

Dr. Burroughs and I met in the hall when I arrived at the hospital.

"He's still pretty wiped out," I told her on my way into the room. Andrew was half asleep, picking at something on his lips.

"There's something in my mouth," Andrew spat.

"What is it?" Then I saw the tufts of hair stuck to his pillow and face.

"I'm losing my feathers." Andrew patted at his head.

It was Day 13, and like Dr. Burroughs predicted, Andrew began losing his hair. Although I was expecting it, my heart sank as I thought about shaving off his remaining silky red hair.

"Tell us how you're feeling," Dr. Burroughs said.

Andrew poked a finger at his belly button, laid a flat palm across his abdomen and squeezed.

"Can you describe it to me?" Dr. Burroughs asked.

"I want Frightful," he replied, screwing his eyes shut and rolling over.

"I think that's all we are going to get today," I told Dr. Burroughs.

During the next week, we began to see glimmers of improvement. Andrew's ANC (Absolute Neutrophil Count—the measurement used to gauge immune system functioning) slowly began to rise, and the team felt confident this was an early sign of engraftment.

Then something unusual happened. "Would you come in here, please?" I asked his nurse.

I pointed to a rash that behaved like a constellation of the Northern Lights. While Andrew slept, a pattern of bright red blotches rose up the side of his torso and neck, then disappeared. Reappearing on the other arm and side of his torso, it cascaded down his legs and landed at the top of his foot.

She looked perplexed. "I know the doctor is in the hall," she said, and hurriedly left the room.

Dr. Burroughs came in and watched as this random constellation continued for another five minutes while Andrew slept. Then, as quickly as it came, it disappeared.

"I'm not sure what to think," she said. "But I'm not worried about it. This is about the time we see funny things like this. I suspect it's an early response of his sister's cells. It's an indication that Hannah's cells are assimilating and active. That's a good thing!"

The next morning, Andrew's lab results were dropped off in our room. Dr. Burroughs had scribbled in the top corner, "Yes! A good thing!" and drew an arrow to the numbers that indicated Hannah's cells were doing their job.

By Day 21, Andrew's ANC had doubled, and the team felt confident this was the beginnings of engraftment.

On Day 26, Andrew asked for a Big Mac.

"What did you say?" I said, certain I hadn't heard him correctly.

"I have a spot right here. See?" He brought both hands to his belly making an "O" with his fingertips.

"Really?" He'd been on a feeding tube or IV nutrition for the better part of a year, and this was the first mention of food.

"Yes. And the Chick-a-dee would like a vanilla milkshake," he said, pointing to a picture of Frightful on the iPad.

And that was that. Gone was his infatuation with binge-eating superstars on the Cooking Channel. In came a renewed interest in all things foodie. Soon he was talking about recipes for soup and steak and Mexican chili peppers. The hotter the better.

"Do you know how many Scoville heat units a ghost pepper has? Over 2,199,999! That will melt your brain out!"

When I looked unimpressed, he found articles on the Internet about people who had mistakenly eaten one. "Look! Dead. Deader than a doornail. Your throat seizes up. Where do you think we could buy some? They're cool."

I couldn't keep up with his newest passion, so I just listened and nodded and made all sorts of affirming sounds.

"I've decided to become a chef and own my own restaurant someday," he told me one afternoon. "I'll even give you a coupon for half price off any entrée you want."

"Well, that sounds very generous of you," I said, stifling a laugh. I shook my head wondering what had happened to my kid, wondering if we had transplanted his brain instead.

Chapter 28

Despite all the talk of food, we weren't out of the woods yet, but we were past the harrowing decision-making phase and initial worries immediately following transplant. Now we were in the phase of watch and wait. Once a patient began to engraft, to 'adopt' the donor cells, there is risk for GVHD (graft versus host disease). This could take many forms and come on any time after transplant. Andrew was already showing signs of Hannah's cells having small 'skirmishes' with the roving rash, but it all seemed quite benign as of yet. So I hung on to my lifeboat 'hope', just as I had been doing for ten years.

But then my lifeboat started taking on water. In the beginning it was subtle, unrecognizable. I was tired, irritable, and my body hurt all over. My hair hurt when I wrestled with my daily ponytail, and I watched, unattached, as strands of hair fell out with the twisted rubber band. I wondered if I would go bald, too.

People came to visit and to relieve me for a few hours at a time. I smiled and thanked them, but there was nowhere for me to go. Even when I could escape, the smiling hippo in the elevator taunted me. "You'll be back soon enough," it seemed to tease.

My mom visited one afternoon, bringing her usual stack of fashion magazines and a treat from Starbucks. We sat for a few minutes as she sized me up carefully. I couldn't hide my sense of desperation.

Always the optimist, she put a smile on her face and began rummaging through her purse. "Here," she said, handing me her credit card. "Why don't you walk down to University Village?

Buy yourself something new and have some lunch. There's a new Italian restaurant next to the Eddie Bauer I think you'll like."

I knew it was a ploy to get me out of the room, to distract me, to force me to put a smile on my face. She was painfully uncomfortable when anyone was less than perfectly happy— especially one of her daughters.

Looking down at my clothing ensemble, I agreed that my adopted hospital uniform of REI cotton drawstring pants and fleece pullover was becoming offensive. I honestly didn't remember the last time I had washed my clothes. And it was true; I could use a hot meal. The plastic boxed snacks at Starbucks had become unpalatable, so I usually resorted to an apple slathered with the peanut butter I had stashed under my bed.

Bundled in my down puffy coat and scarf, I gulped in the crisp breeze coming up from Lake Washington as I walked to the outdoor shopping mall. It was pain relief in the form of air. First stop: Food. The food was hot, but I couldn't taste it. It didn't matter, though: I could feel the heat in my belly, and that was enough. Armed with my mom's credit card, I wandered the mall, peering into every shop window and ducking into my favorite stores when I thought there might be something interesting. Everything I saw looked like the tasteless food that was rumbling around in my stomach.

Two hours later, I walked back to the room. "I couldn't find anything," I said, handing my mom her credit card.

She looked speechless. "Are you sure? I saw tons of stuff down there this morning."

I plastered a smile on my face. "I did have a nice lunch, though."

She looked mollified, but I could tell she was worried. "I'm fine. I'm just really tired," I smiled, trying to convince both of us it was true.

Andrew began channel surfing the moment my mom left.

"Why is there always so much noise?" he asked, settling on a show called *Restaurant Impossible.*

"What do you mean?"

"Someone is making noise next door. I hear it when you're sleeping," he said.

Amelia had gone home two weeks before and was replaced by a girl I still hadn't met. Before leaving, Amelia's mother found me in the hall. Handing me one of her knit scarves, she said, "To keep your head on straight until you get home, honey." Then she took my face in her hands and planted a kiss on my cheek before scooting out the door after Amelia. I never knew her name.

Our new neighbor shared the wall that the head of my bed was tucked into. Sometimes I heard nurses coming and going while they adjusted the noisy machines, but other than that, they remained silent behind closed doors.

"What is it you hear?" I asked Andrew a little later, not sure I really wanted to know.

"Crying," he replied.

The rooms were soundproof for the most part, but I guess I'd been sensing something, too. Shaking off an odd feeling, I left Andrew and went in search of food downstairs. Coming back up only a short time later, I came upon the scene every parent desperately avoids: "Come on, Dad, let's go," pleaded a tear-stained son.

His sobbing father was being dragged out of the room by his armpits, supported by his eldest son and one of the male nurses. Moments later, the room exploded. I ducked into my room, wishing I could unhear the grief that was ringing in my ears. Andrew was still watching TV, completely unaware. With no place to go, I pulled the shades, collapsed facedown on my cot, and begged God for mercy: *Oh God, please don't let this happen to us! I thought I could handle it. I thought I had enough faith, but maybe I don't because I want to curl up and die. Please, please, please save my son. I'm not strong enough to bear this. Where are you? Do not leave me. Are you here?*

The words tumbled from me as I cried for the family next door, but mostly, I cried for myself, because truthfully, I knew it could have been me or Jon pulled out of the room by our armpits. When that reality gripped me, I wasn't sure I could let go of the fear that it may happen to us. Not really. I was as terrified as every other person I saw in that building each day. I knew that in order to survive, the mothers needed to knit, to bind and knot, twist and tangle. I knew the fathers kept their thoughts miles away while they sat in the hallway, feigning work on their laptops. I knew the visitors with the Mylar balloons, stuffed animals, and raucous laughter were all scared. I knew the code: Stay behind the smiling mask. I went through the rest of my day numb, refusing to accept that I had felt a child die. Over the course of the day, boxes and rolling bins were brought to the room next door and loaded with blankets, stuffed animals, and gifts — all artifacts one collects while living in a hospital.

Inside our little cocoon, business went on as usual. Our nurses gave no indication of what was going on only feet away from me. I said nothing.

That evening when I came back from dinner, the shades were open while a cleaning crew aired and sanitized the room. "How is the family from next door?" I dared to ask our nurse the next morning. Her look told me clearly she wasn't going to tell me anything.

"I was just wondering. I've been praying for them," I said.

She glanced up from the IV tubing she was changing, and smiled. "That's really nice of you."

Venturing into the hall, I saw that a young family with a two-year-old toddler had moved in. The toddler was on the bed playing with building blocks, the shades pulled up and the door open into the hallway, where a nurse was bringing in a breakfast tray. This family, of course, had no clue what happened in that room less than twenty-four hours ago.

The following, day Jon and I met with Dr. Burroughs. We had arrived at Day 28, and there were clear signs of engraftment.

"He's scheduled for blood work and a bone marrow aspirate this afternoon. We'll be checking for any remaining Trisomy 8 cells, as well as his chimerisms—that number will tell us what percentage of cells are his sister's," she said.

Uncharacteristically, Jon was scribbling notes. Usually, he sat in the chair, attentive, but left the note taking to me. I took the opportunity to share with her Andrew's continued requests for a Big Mac. "I didn't think a hamburger was such a good idea. But he does seem to be getting hungry."

Dr. Burroughs thought for a moment. "A Big Mac? That's a first! Let's begin to lower the calories in his TPN and start with something a little more basic like applesauce, some broth and maybe crackers if he'll tolerate it. I'll have the nutritionist visit you this afternoon."

Jon and I exchanged a hopeful look. This was tangible progress.

"I suspect he has some graft versus host disease (GVHD), so I am scheduling a biopsy of his gut," she said. "It's important to catch it right away if there's something brewing in there."

Jon appeared nonplussed. I slumped in my chair as the warm fuzzy feeling I experienced just moments before was stripped away. *Holy crap! When would it be okay, really okay, without the threat of decline?* I kicked Jon under the table, stomping on the top of his foot, wanting him to feel as bad as I felt. He took notes.

At home that night, Jon found me weeping into my keyboard, a half written blog on the screen. He was instantly irritated. "Why do you do this to yourself?" he asked.

"Do what?"

"Make yourself miserable."

When I wouldn't meet his eyes, he walked over to my chair, spinning it around on its swivel. "This has to stop. We are fine.

Andrew is fine, at least as fine as he ever will be. Can't you just relax? Today is a *good* day. This is who we are, what our family is." Anger burned its way under his shirt collar, leaving his cheeks streaked with red.

"But I am so done. I just want it to be over," I heard myself whine.

Jon brought his face inches from mine. "You know what? He could drop dead tomorrow. If he does, I will know we did everything we could to give him a good life. We have the best medical team in the country and they have checked him up and down, and God knows, inside and out. There's nothing more they can do."

He stared me down while I met his eyes, defiant. I *wanted* there to be something else to do, something that would make him never suffer again. I glared back at him, the worst bitch-glare I could muster.

This time he shouted: "So if someday he doesn't wake up, I will be okay. I will go on with my life. What about *you*?!"

My vision narrowed to see only the flaming end of his pointer finger, an accusatory gesture calling me to action. *Would I be okay?* I didn't know. Sometimes I really believed I would. But then, the day before, when the reality of death struck me in the face, I felt myself crumble inside. Having said his piece, Jon left the room. I knew he would be fine. But I wasn't. Not yet.

I spent the next day at the hospital, still furious with Jon. He showed up early, after lunch, to relieve me. "Go home and rest. I'll stay here for the night," he said.

He didn't have to ask me twice. I arrived home forty-five minutes later to two slobbery dogs and an absent cat. Hannah was still at school, the house blissfully silent. I collapsed onto the couch and felt my tense body argue with the soft cushions at my back. Panic began pushing its way through my limbs, winding its way through my gut and landing in my heart with its tight fist. I had experienced a panic attack when I was in college and I hadn't forgotten that horrible feeling. Lacking the energy to get off the sofa, I looked out at the grey sky with an anger I'd never experienced before, wondering how God could have allowed this to happen, to us, to the little girl in the room next door.

Finn circled my feet, finally laying his body against the length of the sofa. Sawyer, the smaller of our two dogs, came over to me, whimpered, and jumped up. His hot tongue licked my hands while he squirmed around, finally settling his front end on my chest. But the animals couldn't stop what I knew was coming. The feeling of panic increased until my heart began pounding in my ears, my muscles tightened and my hands and feet began to tingle. That's when I fetched my phone and dialed a familiar number.

An hour later, I was in Leah's office, face down, swimming in a pool of sticky snot. I felt her gazing at me, her signature cup of tea cradled in her hands.

"Do you want to tell me what happened?" She reached over to touch my slumped shoulder and I felt my body crumble again.

"I have no idea. I thought I was fine." I lifted my head to find a box of Kleenex in front of me. "Sometimes I'm swimming in grief, sometimes I can ignore it, although most days it hunts me, crawls into my head, and takes me out."

I told her about my fight with Jon, the girl next door, how my hair was falling out, and that food tasted like dirt. I told her I couldn't feel things, and that I forgot what people were asking me moments after they spoke. I loved Hannah with all my heart, but I was afraid I was a terrible mother. I just wanted to be alone. I was afraid.

"Do you think I could be sick, too?" I asked.

"Your heart is broken, dear, but that rarely kills anyone," she said, knowing where my irrational thoughts were taking me.

My foundation had been rocked. I wasn't sure what I believed anymore. All the things taught in Sunday school were meant to placate us, make us stop asking the hard questions. Where was this kind, caring, merciful God with the white flowing robe? Certainly not here! He didn't exist.

"I feel so alone!" I wailed.

Leah leaned back in her chair and blew on her tea. That pissed me off even more.

"Well, aren't you going to say something?!"

"It seems like you have more to say," she said.

I wiped at the table with a wet Kleenex, kicked off my shoes and folded my arms across my chest. I would give her the silent treatment, too.

After an excruciating minute where I squirmed in my chair and let my gaze scan anywhere in the room but where she was sitting, she said, "I'd like you to close your eyes."

When I questioned her, she said we were going to practice being still.

"With your eyes closed, you can see and hear the Divine at work," Leah said. "After all, Andrew's doctors are doing just that, aren't they?"

"What do you mean?"

"Well, they are trusting in a process that's still a mystery. They put their faith in the ability of new foreign cells to find their way beyond the bloodstream, enter through bones, and into the marrow. It's quite a miracle."

I thought about it for a while. "Hmmph," I grunted.

"You are stronger than you know. Don't forget that."

Leah asked me to go to my lake. "Pick up your pastels, paint a new picture of it behind your eyes."

I relaxed into the chair, letting out a deep strangled breath.

"Good. Now walk into it."

After resisting, I closed my eyes and let the feeling take me away. I found I could bear the pain when I allowed the water to pour over me like warm liquid, filling me to overflowing. I saw myself as a great artist, blending color to create a lake that possessed all color, but appeared as clear as a diamond. My lake shimmered with crystalline light. I discovered that the wretched feelings that threatened to drown me over and over again were strangely gone.

"Who is the water?" Leah asked as I described my journey in the lake.

The answer popped out of my mouth without thinking: "Christ."

"What does the water do?"

"Feeds the plants and trees and..." My mind was grasping at something, but I couldn't quite form it into words. *I am the living water,* Christ said. His disciples had looked at him like he was off his rocker. A little cracked.

"Jesus isn't flat," I said softly.

Leah remained still. The faint sound of her breathing told me she was there, waiting.

"But this is *not* how it was taught in Sunday school. In Sunday school, the Jesus character had glamorous hair, a flowing robe, and stylish sandals, and He most certainly stayed on the felt board where the teacher put him," I said, still searching for the truth.

"The Divine is too big to be put in a box and tied with a pretty bow," Leah said.

I almost choked. *Had I told her about my God-box?*

In that moment, everything I thought to be true or real or normal or right was stripped away, leaving my soul cracked wide open. For eighteen years, I had been living on a knife's edge, obsessed, because I couldn't fix my son. In the end, it was not about the fix, the healing, or even the cure; it was about me letting go of control and my belief that if my external world was orderly and neat, then my internal world would somehow match.

"But this is not how I thought life would be," I said, my voice barely above a whisper.

"That's why we need grace," Leah said. "Everyone suffers hardship or tragedy. But if you can look outside yourself, see that the world is good — even the raw and ugly parts — then you will truly live."

I fingered the silver bracelet on my wrist. Without looking, I knew what it said: *Light of the World.* Carol's message to me during our lunch came to mind: "When you hand over control, when you trust in this life, in God, then you will find peace."

"What are you thinking?" Leah asked me.

"I'm thinking it's time to redefine myself, and God, and be okay with it." I knew I couldn't save my son or control this world and keep him safe.

When I arrived home, there was a note on the counter from Hannah: *"Gone to Grandma Connie's house. See you in the morning."* Grateful for the respite, I walked through the house, flicking off lights one by one, creating a cocoon of blackness. I stripped off my grimy clothes, leaving them in a puddle on the kitchen floor. Wrapping myself in a blanket, I stepped through the front door and folded myself into Frightful's wicker chair. I imagined the hen in my lap, nestled between my knees.

"Who are you?" I asked the imaginary bird.

An impossible thought flickered at the back of my mind.

"You know Andrew's heart," I said.

And he trusts you with his soul, I thought, remembering the tiny mottled chick that opened up his world with a single peep. It seemed uncanny that she had come into our lives right when Andrew needed a voice. It was no coincidence. Of that, I was sure.

When I finally dragged myself upstairs to take a bath, I dumped an entire box of Epsom salt into the tub, then turned to study my naked body in the mirror. My skin was dull and dry, but my eyes frightened me. They were hollow, filled with savage grief. There was no room for any other emotion, the crinkle of a smile, or even the grimace of pain. They just were there, staring back at me. Turning sideways, I noted my belly was no longer flat and toned, and my butt seemed to have taken on the shape of a metal foldout chair. It depressed me even more.

Once I eased myself into the warm water, my body came alive. For the first time in months, I could *feel* something. For one precious hour, I pretended I wasn't me. I was an artist living in Provence, going to market in search of food and supplies to create beautiful things. I was a writer, living in exotic locations, having adventures that would certainly weave their way into my books. I was fearless, confident, wild. I embodied all the names I had ever been known by, and at the same time, was defined by none of them.

When the water cooled, I curled my knees to my chest, allowing myself to submerge completely. From the bottom of the tub, I opened my eyes to a world that was shimmering, moving, and alive, like the lake I painted in Leah's office. My silent and unseen tears mixed with the salts in the water, erasing the pain in my body, and I knew that somehow, in the small, dim comfort of Leah's office, I had been set free.

Chapter 29

Spring busted through the sidewalks, creating rivers of green along the cracks. Long tendrils of morning glory fingered their way through rock walls to invade the flower bed near the parking garage where I sat. It was my second spring at the hospital.

From under a weeping cherry tree, I watched the smokers who laid claim to the handicap parking zone and adjoining steps winding down from the parking garage. They smoked hungrily, at all hours of the day and night, congregating in their secret tribe. I'm not a smoker, but if I were, I would have sucked the cigarette dry in the first breath.

I recognized a handful of parents out there, although we didn't acknowledge each other. We were people from nowhere beyond the room number we occupied. We were homeless parents—some living in the parking lot in a rented RV, others wandering in and out of the parking garage, eating in our car—the closest thing we called home.

There was an unsaid rule in that sacred place: Don't mix the outside world with the one inside those doors. We all understood that there was too much heartache contained inside those walls. So we said nothing.

I sat in solitude under my flowery umbrella, gazing at my peek-a-boo view of Sand Point Way and Husky Stadium. Cigarette smoke curled its way around me—an absurdly comforting twang of cheap tobacco, coating me in an invisible layer of nicotine. I could taste it, and wished for that instant that I was a smoker, a chaser of the nicotine rush.

When I walked back into the room, Andrew was watching an episode of *Myth Busters*.

"Where were you, Mom?" he asked, his eyes still glued to the television.

"Sitting on the steps out front."

"That's where the smoking people are. You know, smoking will kill you. Black lung. Emphysema. Stroke. COPD. Bad news. You should tell them," he said with certainty.

I rolled my eyes and tossed a wadded napkin at him. "Where do you come up with this stuff?" I laughed.

"It's true. I saw it on TV," he said.

He was becoming so chatty and opinionated, I hardly recognized him.

"I like the new Andrew," I said. "You make me laugh."

On Day 31, Dr. Burroughs decided to fish for GVHD. Graft versus host disease could become a serious battle between the host cells and donor cells, and we wanted to catch it early before any serious complications could arise. Dr. Burroughs had ongoing concerns about Andrew's gut being affected by GVHD, and was eager to start treatment if tests confirmed her hunch. I was on parent duty the day of surgery to perform an endoscopy and colonoscopy. Early that morning, Andrew and I were escorted deep into the bowels of the hospital for the necessary paperwork and prep work before surgery.

"Not interested! I'm not going!" Andrew told the nurse as he was wheeled into the elevator.

She had been through this many times with him, and had no problem distracting him with personal questions. The first time we met, I had given her a cheat-sheet, telling her about his love of books, video games, and of course, chickens.

"What's your favorite book these days, Andrew?" she asked.

"*Super Fudge*. You know, Judy Blume," Andrew replied.

"Doesn't Fudge have a pet turtle?"

"Uh huh. But chickens are better. You can't ride a bike with a turtle."

He showed her Stuffed Frightful, squeezing the yellow felt beak between his fingers. In the next sentence, they were talking about their favorite movies. *Hunger Games* had just premiered in theaters and she had already seen it. He peppered her with questions about each detail he remembered from his reading sessions with Sue.

"Do you like any other action movies?" she asked as we rounded the corner in to day surgery.

"The best ever is *Bourne Identity*, with Matt Damon. He's cool," Andrew said.

"That's a favorite of mine, too!"

The discussion immediately took off on another tangent. Before Andrew realized it, his clever nurse had calmly prepped him for surgery. Minutes later, a young doctor walked in to review medical notes with Andrew. Since he had recently turned eighteen, we were running into HIPPA laws. We had obtained full guardianship a month before, but apparently the documents hadn't made it into this doctor's file.

Andrew interrupted. "I don't know what you're talking about, but we're talking about movies," he said as the doctor began to describe a colonoscopy.

"So, what's your favorite movie?" the doctor asked, setting down his clipboard.

Andrew clearly answered, "I like Bourne movies."

Neither the nurse nor I reacted until the doctor began sputtering and turning red. He glanced at me with a look inquiring what kind of mother I might be.

"Well, I guess you are eighteen now, so sure, I imagine some people might like those kind of movies. Why do you like those movies?"

"Because there's a lot of action in them," Andrew replied.

The doctor looked appalled.

The nurse had long since given me the wink, realizing the doctor thought Andrew said he liked *porn* movies. We let him squirm a little longer before pointing out his misunderstanding.

"Which is your favorite of the three movies?" I asked Andrew.

"I like the first one, *Bourne Identity*," he replied.

Quickly, the doctor looked at the nurse and realized his mistake. Just as quickly, he realized his embarrassment was not to be short-lived. I felt bad for him, knowing his mistake would surely become a staff favorite.

Jon and I were both at the hospital for rounds on Day 33. We expected the results from Andrew's first post-transplant bone marrow biopsy, as well as results from the scope.

Dr. Burroughs began the discussion. "Andrew's bone marrow results are back. He is what we call a 'mixed chimera,' which means he only engrafted part of Hannah's cells, and remains with part of his own cells."

I leaned back in my chair, trying to absorb another round of conflicting information.

"To greatly simplify it, there are four major building blocks in the marrow that we look for. As of Day 28, only three of Andrew's were measurable. That's normal, by the way," she added. "We don't expect to see the fourth one for a while yet."

"What do Andrew's particular numbers tell you?" Jon asked.

"Well, we always hope to see them closer to one hundred percent, but with Andrew's number's ranging from 9 percent to 90 percent, we don't know whether he will ultimately accept or reject the donor cells. I'm hopeful, but we will just have to wait and see."

Wait and see. I had been doing that my whole parenting career, yet this time, I was okay with the waiting. My son's pain had diminished, and it was thrilling to watch him come to life.

To add to the unexpected news, we were told that Andrew had GVHD in his gut. I was surprisingly calm and unworried about this new information.

"How do you treat it?" I asked.

"We will start a course of steroids today, then taper him off over the next several weeks," she said.

Prednisone. A drug we were all too familiar with. When Dr. Burroughs left, Jon and I walked back to the room and looked at our sleeping son. Jon reached out to smooth Andrew's bald head.

"He seems to be improving a little each day. Remember how desperate things felt a month ago?"

I nodded. Even with his body ravaged by the treatment, I could tell we were in a better place than we had been for the past decade. I also realized it was the first time in years that his mouth was clear of ulcers. They seemed to have vanished, leaving only a crisscross of white scars as a reminder of a lifetime of pain.

I nestled my head in the crook of Jon's shoulder, remembering our argument, his question, *"Will you be okay?"*

"I'm okay now," I said, pointing to my chest. "With this. With Andrew."

He squeezed me tight. "I can tell. I watched you when Dr. Burroughs was talking, and knew something had changed."

Jon returned to work and I walked down the hall to find the children's playroom empty. Huddling against the cold window to get cell reception, I dialed Julie's number. She picked up on the first ring.

"Hi! I was just thinking about you. Did you get the test results back?"

I told her about Andrew being a mixed chimera and what that meant. I also told her about the GVHD.

"Is that freaking you out?"

"Not really. I'm surprised he hasn't fully engrafted, but when Dr. Burroughs didn't seem too concerned, I relaxed. I'm actually okay with it."

"I don't believe for a minute that he will reject his sister's cells," she said confidently. "He's got better things to do than hanging around the hospital!"

I didn't want to be placated. She didn't know that I had flirted with despair. *It's not that easy,* I wanted to say, but instead, I remained quiet.

"Are you there?" she ventured.

"Yep."

"I'm sorry if I sounded uncaring. I know this is hard, but believe me when I tell you that I have this feeling he's going to amaze us all."

"I hope you're right," I said. "But it's pretty overwhelming."

We talked for a little while about nothing important and hung up, promising to talk again in a couple of days. I lingered in the playroom, watching an unexpected snow flurry frustrate the construction crew outside. I pressed my face to the window as the blue crane lowered two exterior wall segments into place. A crew of four people, suspended by ropes, hung from above to weld and bolt them into place. My view of the outside world was changing again.

I entered the room to find Andrew alert and ready for a walk. I noticed he had stirred the contents of his breakfast plate around, but it was clear he hadn't taken a bite. Daily visits with a nutritionist had been added to our schedule a few days before with little progress.

Robin, Andrew's nutritionist, was a sweet gal with smooth, perfectly tinted caramel-colored hair that skimmed her shoulders, and stylish glasses that framed her brown eyes perfectly. I patted my mouse-blonde hair, envisioning a color-job like that. Even with the fabulous hair, Robin oozed a PTA mom look about her and I could see she was no match for Andrew and his newfound teenage attitude. He called her Food Lady.

"How are you today, Andrew?" Robin greeted him for the first time.

Andrew jabbed a thumb in my direction. "Ask the Food Nazi here."

I raised my hand a little sheepishly. "That's me."

Robin was scanning the stack of papers I had filled out for her. Lists that included how much Andrew ate, drank, and what his poop looked like.

"Hmmm. Let's see. Can you point to the most accurate picture?" she asked Andrew, holding up a chart with six different textures of poop on it.

Andrew pulled the SpongeBob comforter over his head. "I'm not talking to you. Talk to the bird!" he said, thrusting Stuffed Frightful at her.

Food Lady ignored him. "Okay. Let's look at what you are eating... a cherry popsicle, four pretzels, a rainbow fruit strip, two grapes..." She turned the pages of my journal, looking for something. "Is this all you are eating, Andrew?"

"I like beef," he said.

Robin looked at me. "He likes beef," I said, suppressing a laugh.

"And A1 Sauce," Andrew said to clarify.

Now I was getting irritated. "Andrew, can you take that blanket off so she can hear you?"

Andrew pulled the blanket down and flipped his new medical bracelet around and around until the clink of chain settled back into place.

"Is he drinking enough fluids?" Robin asked me.

"We're working on that."

"But I'm not thirsty. *Ever,*" he told us.

Robin pulled out her calculator and started tapping at the numbers. "I'll be right back." Then she scooted from the room.

"I think we failed another test," Andrew told Stuffed Frightful.

She came back with six bottles of water and juice, which she set on the table in front of Andrew.

"It's pretty common for people to not feel thirsty after transplant. Maybe you can just drink one cup each hour you are awake, then you won't have to have any more for the rest of the hour?"

Andrew pulled the covers back over his head. Discussion over. Robin handed me a stack of papers, all entitled, "High Calorie Nutrition for the Undernourished." I looked at the list. I didn't find pretzels or popsicles.

Andrew continued to be underwhelmed by the food offered him, so when my mom visited the next day, we tried another tactic. "You know what Hannah told me this morning?" she said.

Andrew lay in bed, disinterested, toggling between Cartoon Network and the Cooking Channel.

"She said the chickens are laying like crazy now that it's spring. But there are no blue eggs in the laying boxes."

Andrew rolled over to face her. "But why? Frightful always lays, even in the winter."

My mom knew she had him hooked. "That's the funny thing. Hannah was in the garage and she saw Frightful sitting on an old sweatshirt on the bottom shelf of your Dad's workbench."

Andrew sat up in bed. "What was she doing there?"

"I guess she got all puffy and hissed at Hannah when she tried to put her in the coop," my mom said. "And she hasn't been eating."

"She's gone broody!!" Andrew yelped. "We have to call Hannah!"

My mom covered a smile as she dialed our home number in search of Hannah.

"She's screeched and pecked at me all afternoon," Hannah told her brother. "And she won't eat!"

Andrew looked panicked. "She thinks she gonna hatch chicks. Give her watermelon. She'll get off the nest for that!"

"Where are we going to get watermelon in March?" Hannah asked, baiting her brother. She was the one who had hatched the plan.

"I don't know, but she has to eat!"

My mom took the phone from Andrew. "I'll find some and bring it to the house. Don't worry."

When Jon returned to the hospital that night, he brought Andrew a small plate of sliced watermelon.

"From Frightful," he said.

Andrew ate the whole plate.

Chapter 30

On Day 38, Dr. Burroughs announced her plans to discharge Andrew by the end of the week. Although he was eating some, he was still on TPN for most of his nutritional needs, and many of his medications were still administered by IV. How they could possibly detach him from the rubber lines and poles in just a few short days, I didn't know.

I spent the next three days in class at the SCCA in downtown Seattle learning to care for someone on a neutropenic diet. It was designed for people with weakened immune systems, in order to protect them from bacteria and other harmful organisms that could wreak havoc in a fragile body. My head was spinning with the rigid requirements of food choice, purchasing, and preparation.

"I suggest you grocery shop with multiple carts so that meats don't touch vegetables or fruit. Dry goods should be in a third cart," droned our instructor.

Yeah right, like I was going to drag around a train of grocery carts behind me. Won't they all touch anyway when the checker gets her hands on them?

Purell was introduced as my new best friend. I stashed bottles in our van, our house, my coat pockets, and my purse. Anne called her housecleaner and requested a deep cleaning and disinfection of our entire house. Even with all the careful planning, I was scared to death. I wasn't ready for Andrew to re-enter our unsanitized world. Not yet.

"Andrew is able to take all of his medications now by mouth," Dr. Burroughs told me on Day 40. "And this morning I plan to take him off of his TPN. Let's see how he does with his eating. Does this sound like a good plan to you?"

Noooo! I screamed in my head. "Yes," I squeaked out.

"And I want him to start physical therapy to get his muscle tone back," she added. "I will arrange for that today."

Nancy, Andrew's new physical therapist, had him pegged before she walked in the door. "I'm hungry, Andrew. Are you?"

"Nope."

"You won't mind if I eat this cake here, will you?" she said, fishing a fork from her pocket.

Andrew looked over at the cake. "I like Red Velvet Cake. And I like beef."

"Mmmm. I like Red Velvet, too," Nancy said, stuffing another piece of fluffy cake in her mouth. "That reminds me, I'm supposed to make something for Volunteer Appreciation Day. Would you be interested in helping me?" She concentrated on her cake.

Andrew glanced at her as if it were a trick question. "I would if I weren't attached to these dumb poles. Plus, I can't leave this hallway. Too many germs," he grumbled.

Finishing the last bite of cake, Nancy stood up and stashed her fork back in her pocket. "That's not a problem. I'll see you later then." The session was over.

Andrew's eyes followed her out the door. After a few quiet moments, he looked over to me on the cot and said, "She's a strange one, Mom."

On Wednesday morning, there was a sticky note on our door that read, "Nancy will be here at 2:00 p.m."

Who's Nancy? I thought, before remembering the strange cake-eating woman. I couldn't imagine what the next physical therapy session would be like. At 2:00 p.m. sharp, a cart rumbled down the hall and stopped in front of our door. A persistent knock came from the other side.

"Andrew, can you open the door for me? My hands are full," a voice called from outside.

Grumbling, Andrew hoisted himself out of bed, unplugged the IV poles from the wall, and drug them to the door. With a quick thank you, Nancy moved in and began setting up a mock kitchen.

"We're making Red Velvet Cake today," she announced to her speechless patient.

She proceeded to pull measuring cups, bowls, utensils, baking pans and carefully packed ingredients from the bottom shelf of the cart—much like the Harry Potter character Hermione, pulling a full-sized tent out of her magical purse.

Within minutes, Nancy had transformed our room into a working kitchen. Handing Andrew a set of surgical gloves, she began her lesson.

"So I heard you want to be a chef. How about you show me your stuff?" she said.

"What do you want me to do?"

"Bake a cake."

For the next forty-five minutes, Nancy had Andrew reaching up high to retrieve measuring spoons she had set on top of cabinets, and squat down low to grapple with unruly bags of flour. She asked him to blend, sift, and finally mix 200 strokes with a wire whisk. His arms were sore and he was tired, but there was a smile lighting his face.

Nancy read from her recipe card. "The last step is to put red dye in the batter. It calls for two teaspoons."

"I like it *my* way," Andrew said, dumping the entire bottle of red food coloring into the golden batter.

A gleeful, impish grin spread across his face, and my heart melted. Nancy, like Sue, spoke a language Andrew could relate to. She was able to enter his world, see things the way he saw them, and make him feel capable of something he could never have done just weeks before.

I woke up Thursday morning to see someone had written, "FRIDAY: Discharge Day!" in big blue letters across the top of the white board.

"No! This is too fast. I'm not ready!" I cursed the unwanted message.

I couldn't imagine Andrew, minus two poles and four pumps full of IV medications grinding away twenty-four hours a day. Taped under the announcement was a list of back-to-back appointments scheduled for the next day. My throat tightened and I felt the tingle of tears. I didn't want to think about tomorrow. I wanted coffee.

Dr. Burroughs caught me in the hall as I was making my escape. "Let's talk," she said, leading me to the playroom.

Was it bad news? I couldn't handle any bad news. Dr. Burroughs studied me for a moment. "You've been here a very long time. It's a big deal to go back home."

Without realizing what was on my mind, I asked, "Will things ever get back to normal?"

She eyed me carefully, leaning forward in her chair. "Things will never be normal."

The words felt like a slap to my face and I shrunk back from the sting of it. Unconsciously, I raised my hands to rub at my reddened cheeks. Why would she say something like that? Hadn't I been laboring each day for two years in hopes of getting our lives back?

"I don't believe that," I said.

Dr. Burroughs's face softened. She picked up her chair and moved it next to mine. I stared out the window at the nearly complete hospital addition that soared four stories above the building we were in. The exterior trim and facade was complete, a breathtaking example of contemporary Northwest architecture. A new construction team was completing the internal workings of one of the most sophisticated medical buildings in the region. How I wished they could construct *my* internal workings.

"What I meant was, you can never go back to your old life the way it was. Everything has changed. Andrew has changed."

Tears spilled down my face, clear evidence of my silent grief. Dr. Burroughs turned to me, her hands on my knees.

I stared at her through my tears. "I'm scared to go home. I don't think I can take care of him."

Home was a thirty-minute drive across the Lake Washington floating bridge, but to me it felt light years away.

"We aren't just letting you go, you'll be on a very short leash," she said with a smile. "When you wake up each morning and Andrew is well, then know it's a *good* day. We don't know what will happen tomorrow, but we do know what is happening today. Live in the goodness of today."

I allowed the truth of her words to sink in. They reminded me of Becki's advice months before when she encouraged me to be present, to live in the moment.

"But I'm not sure how to do that."

"Expand your definition of normal," she said. "Make room for the unexpected — that will allow you to live your life."

Standing up to leave, she placed her hand on my shoulder in a parental gesture of encouragement. "You are brave. Your son is strong. You will be okay," she whispered into my ear.

After she left, I slipped into the community bathroom and bolted the door. Gripping both edges of the sink, I looked up and met myself in the mirror. Green eyes stared back at me, full of questions. Why am I so scared to go home? How do I re-enter my life? How can I care for an adult child that requires 24-hour nursing care? The medications, IV's, caring for the Hickman line — if I screwed up, it could mean the difference between life and death.

Stepping back from the sink, I considered the mother in the mirror without judgment. Was I the same woman who held a newborn baby on her chest one early July evening? The one who feared she wouldn't be able to raise a child she didn't know? Had I done a good job?

The green eyes in the mirror twinkled. *Are you ready to admit that you have done the very best you could?* they asked. *That you have loved this boy and raised him well? That you gave up your life to fight for his life?*

Sinking to the floor, I allowed the reality of those words to wash over me. I felt... relief. Jon was right. We left no stone unturned. We had done everything.

A moment later, I heard silent words speak to my soul, "You are not alone."

"I am not alone," my heart replied.

A flurry of activity descended on us Friday morning. Jon and I were anxious about taking home our fragile, skinny, and bald child. Newly untethered from the last of his poles, Andrew walked around the room — a free man. Clutching our coffee cups like a life preserver, we were whisked off to the first meeting of the day.

"You'll be administering Andrew's IV's at night until he doesn't need them anymore," a woman with frizzy yellow hair said. She recited the directions from a note card and demonstrated on a miniature Hickman line attached to an IV bag. She handed the apparatus to Jon. "Now repeat what I did."

I watched Jon as he first flushed the line with saline, then attached the bag like she demonstrated.

"Next, I will show you how to prime the line and prep the machine. You'll need a new set of batteries every night..."

I lost her after 'batteries' and began to daydream. What should I make for dinner tonight? I'm hungry for real food. Do we have any groceries in the fridge? I bet I'll have to get some. Hannah can help me... she loves to cook.

"Now it's your turn," Miss Yellow Hair said.

She took the bag and Hickman line from Jon and dropped it in my lap. I returned her look with a blank stare.

"I will probably be taking care of the IV's for a while," Jon said when I didn't reply.

"Nope. You gotta do it, too." She crossed her arms over her ample bosom.

I fumbled my way through it and must have passed, because the next thing I knew, she was packing up and handing us a packet of directions and the name of the company that would be shipping IV bags to us every two days.

Walking back down the hall in a daze, I saw that Anne had arrived and was packing up our room. She had volunteered to stay with Andrew while Jon and I attended our exit meetings.

"Andrew, can you help me with the books? Let's put them in the bag," I heard her say.

I saw Andrew clutching Stuffed Frightful and his Shadow action figure in one hand while grappling for his *Hunger Games* trilogy. "These go with me," he said, scooting around the other side of the room.

Such emotion was bottled up in that little room, and for some weird reason, I felt attached to it. Almost like I was leaving part of myself behind.

Andrew began talking to Shadow, contorting his arms and legs in every possible direction.

"Are you nervous about going home?" Anne asked him.

"I want to see my chickens. Grandma Cherry said they're laying eggs. Araucanas lay blue ones. Sometimes they're greenish, depending on their diet," he responded.

Jon and I left for our next appointment.

"I'll be going over Andrew's medication list with you," the pharmacist said. "I put them in a spreadsheet for you so you won't get them mixed up." He handed us a three-page chart.

I snorted. "Good Lord! Can a human swallow this many pills in one day?!"

I had an immediate flashback to my pre-transplant conference with Dr. Lewis, and the room began to swim. I let out a half giggle at the absurdity of it. Jon put his hand over mine. The quaking in my body slowed and I was able to listen as the pharmacist went over each medication and the time it was to be taken. Andrew's medication alone would be my full time job.

Our last meeting finished four hours later. We were both numb. We were reminded over and over that we were on a short leash and that Andrew would be required to remain in seclusion for a year. We were warned about keeping him away from any possible infection and to stay within a twenty-five minute driving radius of the hospital. We were shown how to administer medications, prepare food, and bathe him with the Hickman line.

"You will need to report to the SCCA outpatient clinic at 7:30 tomorrow morning," our nurse said as we were ready to leave.

Jon left to fill the prescriptions while Anne and I finished packing. Moments before we left, Dr. Burroughs poked her head in the door. "I know you feel overwhelmed today, but I want you to remember to take one day at a time. We will take care of tomorrow when it gets here." She hugged me. "As for today, it's a *very* good day!" she said, and left the room.

I looked around the empty room, at my son, and my friend who had organized my life for the past year. I thanked the nursing staff in the hallway, each of them I now knew by name. I stared out the window at the glassy façade of the new building next door and offered a silent prayer for all the children who would benefit from its being there.

And then I walked out the door for the last time.

Chapter 31

Jon chased his lawn mower around the lawn, eagerly cutting grass that seemed to have sprouted another two inches in only a few days. Hannah wandered aimlessly through the house while I sorted Andrew's daily medications. Without thinking, she picked up and set down artifacts around the kitchen that included a set of car keys, a receipt for the cleaners, and a dog leash left haphazardly on the counter next to the treat jar.

"What can I do? We can't go anywhere, and Andrew doesn't want to do anything. I'm so bored I could die!" she said.

I watched her throw her teenage self onto the sofa and flop backwards in exasperation. Too consumed and overwhelmed by my nursing duties, I didn't bother to answer.

"Mom, didn't you hear me?" she called from the couch.

Glancing in to the family room, I saw my daughter's legs pointing straight up, moving in an air ballet.

"I did. What do you want me to say? I can't get him interested in anything, either."

Andrew was under strict quarantine for a year. No visitors, no outings — except for the unauthorized kind, like our brief visit to the park on the way back from a medical appointment. He was not allowed contact with Frightful for at least six months, so when she caught sight of him downstairs, we all had to endure her constant tapping at the window — a beak-sized jack hammer.

I stepped over the cat and headed toward the playroom with Andrew's 11:00 a.m. assortment of meds. Our house had become a tomb filled with nothing but pills, medical supplies, X-Box, Netflix, and the Food Network channel. Andrew had been watching the same, ten-minute segment of *Dinner Impossible* over and over again until it was etched into his memory. Currently he was watching the episode, "Spring Training Triangle." No wonder Hannah was going crazy.

Hannah forcefully entered the room. "Can't you watch something else? Why do you keep rewinding it to the lamb shoulder? You've already seen it a billion times!"

"I like it. See how they make the marinade?" he paused the recording with the remote, "I think the truck in the background is from Sysco. They're a national restaurant supplier. I wonder if they will deliver here?" he rambled on without taking the time to look at her.

In a huff, Hannah left the room. I followed her, and saw Frightful sitting in the wicker chair on the porch. I knew the chicken was looking for her human friend.

I slipped out to join her. "Be patient, girl. You'll be together soon."

With the exception of watching Frightful roam the yard from his bedroom window, Andrew had only spoken to her using gestures through the playroom windows. Doctor's orders.

Frightful allowed me to scoop her into my lap, probably out of desperation for human contact. "How old are you?" I asked absently, calculating the years that had passed. It occurred to me that she had been a part of our family for what felt like a lifetime. She had outlived our original clutch of chicks and now queened over six new adolescents. "You're about nine, I think."

I continued talking to her, wondering if all chickens lived that long. Frightful paced my lap, leaving micro-showers of dust on my legs before finding a suitable spot to sit. She tucked her scaly dinosaur legs beneath her, easing her body into an egg shape of feathers. A comforting presence settled over me.

"Thank you for showing up when Andrew needed you most," I said. "Thank you for searching him out in the darkness, for singing to him, for being his hero, and leaving gifts in the form of beautiful sky-blue eggs. But most of all, sweet girl, thank you for loving him."

She regarded me with hooded eyes, and spoke, steady and even.

"Cluck-cluck-cluck-cluck."

It's easy to love him.

Sue arrived when Frightful and I were still on the porch. I watched her walk in through the garage, knowing Andrew would be thrilled to see her.

"The stories are in my head, Sue. I need you to read them to me just like that," I heard him say. Andrew was on the sofa, eyes closed, waiting for the words to drop out of the sky like manna. Two minutes into the story he opened one eye. "You forgot that Frightful has to carry Shadow. He's too weak to walk."

"You didn't tell me that," she said.

He let out a puff of air. "Well, he just is."

Looking back at the pages Andrew had asked her to read, Sue adjusted the story, and without missing a beat, the pages morphed into the pictures of Andrew's imagination. Characters floated in and out of his version of the *Hunger Games*, new districts were created, and hand-drawn maps were translated into words to soothe his mind and take him away from this feeling of the unfamiliar.

Andrew flashed his medical bracelet at Sue, begging her to ask him a question. He fingered the black caduceus on the front, two snakes intertwined around a short staff. "You know what this is?" he said. "It's my superhero signal."

Sue leaned in to get a closer look. "That's right, I forgot. It's pretty cool!"

He handed her a stack of tattered Judy Blume books, bracelet forgotten. "It's time for Fudge to meet Frightful."

While Sue thumbed through the old books, Andrew held out a folder of tissue paper drawings. "These are my drawings of Shadow. Thirty-two drawings, to be exact. They're all the same."

"I see Shadow has a new cape and an IV pole," Sue said.

"Yep. And a Hickman line. See?" He pointed to a squiggly black line dangling from Shadow's chest.

When Sue had finished looking through each one, he took the tissue drawings back, carefully sliding the stack between the pages of a *Calvin & Hobbes* comic book. "Let's read that one," he said, pointing to *Fudge-a-Mania*. He caught sight of me hovering in the doorway. "You can leave now, Mom. Sue and I are reading."

Hannah found me sorting pills again in the kitchen after Sue left. "Andrew won't do anything but study weird recipes on the Cooking Channel, and he still won't eat. I don't get it," she said.

I tucked a stray hair behind her ear as she practiced her scowl. I was always surprised at how much it bothered her when her brother didn't do things the way she would like. That was supposed to be my job.

Leaving to deliver the pills, I slipped into my studio to catch up on email. A half hour later, I smelled garlic and what I thought was rosemary wafting up the stairs. I realized I hadn't thought about dinner yet. Grocery shopping for the required neutropenic diet was a nightmare.

Andrew couldn't eat anything from the deli or bakery department, pickled or fermented foods, food that hadn't been cooked, or any fruit that could not be peeled. Every perishable item had to be bagged separately, boxed items and cans in the far side of the vegetable cart. Leftovers were sketchy. The process required for storage was so daunting that I usually tossed it.

Sitting in my studio, mentally scanning the pantry, I figured I had the fixings for spaghetti. That would have to do for tonight.

"Here, brother!" I heard Hannah say.

I wandered into the hallway to see that she had dropped a single plate on his lap, artfully arranged with long slices of sautéed zucchini.

"Now eat! I sautéed it in marinade like they used in 'Spring Training Triangle.'"

When he hesitated, she gave him the same scowl she had been practicing downstairs. "I'm not leaving until you eat it."

Andrew, who had only eaten SpongeBob mac and cheese for the last week, ate the entire plate of garlic zucchini without argument. Smiling, I headed back to my studio, knowing Hannah had found her role again.

At our next visit to the SCCA, Dr. Burroughs was thrilled to hear about Hannah's zucchini dish. "You've got to eat more of your sister's cooking," she said.

Andrew grunted. He still was barely eating, and despite his quick wit, he still experienced nausea, and exhaustion.

"I want to hold Frightful. What do you think of this Hazmat suit?" he said, thrusting a stack of papers at her. "There are eleven good ones on Amazon, but this one is the best."

Startled, I couldn't figure out what he was talking about, but then I figured this was his solution to the ban on bird-to-boy contact.

"You can also purchase gloves, an oxygen tank, and a fully equipped helmet with its own filtration system," he said expectantly.

I rubbed my hand across my eyes, trying to conceal my embarrassment.

Dr. Burroughs laughed, enjoying his perfectly logical solution. "Soon, buddy, I promise I'll let you know when you and Frightful can be reunited."

Our next appointment was with the endocrinologist. She asked me when Andrew had gone through puberty. "With such a long history of prednisone use, it can delay things. I want to get an accurate sense as to whether or not we can expect him to grow more."

I studied Andrew on the exam table, his long legs crisscrossed awkwardly underneath him. Kinky patches of red-gold hair stuck out from his newly fuzzed scalp, and his skin was a translucent shade of pink. He was wearing headphones, hunched over his iPhone laughing at something on YouTube.

"Put it away, Andrew," I said, irritated.

"I can hear everything you say. I just don't want to. Too boring for words," he replied.

"Andrew, have you shaved yet?" the pretty doctor asked him.

I figured she was barely thirty-five, yet already she was one of the most sought-after endocrinologists in the city.

"My dad did it once." He ran a finger across his upper lip, absently rubbing at a few downy hairs. "I think I might be sprouting some pinfeathers though."

I felt my cheeks redden, and stifled a laugh. I knew what he was proposing.

"You are *not* part-chicken, Andrew," I said.

"Hannah says I am!"

"Since when did you start believing what Hannah says?"

He squinted his eyes at me in a mock sneer. The doctor looked from me to Andrew. "Pinfeathers, huh?"

"Yep. My chicken gets new feathers after she molts. I think I molted."

"I'd say you're getting whiskers, buddy. That's pretty cool." Andrew scowled.

As we left the clinic, I could see him still rubbing at his lip from the corner of my eye.

"Pinfeathers?" I asked.

He refused to look at me. "You're both wrong."

* * *

On Day 54, Andrew was so bored he thought he might go berserk, so I decided to take him to the grocery store — incognito, at six o'clock in the morning. The grocery store is someplace you wouldn't think was very exciting until told you weren't allowed to go, and then it all becomes really interesting. It was our second unauthorized outing, and Andrew was dressed like he was planning to rob a bank. Except for a hospital facemask and blue latex gloves, he was wearing all black, including a stocking cap pulled down over his missing eyebrows and a worn pair of motorcycle boots. This was our attempt at keeping him protected from germs. I was in my uniform — a fleece pullover, yoga pants, flip-flops, sunglasses and one of Jon's baseball caps.

We stepped across the threshold into the kingdom of plenty, the sliding doors whooshing shut behind us. Shimmering, saturated colors filled our vision. Produce displays drew us in, begging us to pick up, smell, taste. I reveled in the vapor of an orange peel when I pushed my fingernail into its flesh and the hollow sounding and heavy watermelon that fell into the bottom of my cart with a clunk. I felt like we had entered Narnia for the first time. Under the excitement of color was the faint buzz of fluorescent lights and soothing music meant to encourage us to buy, buy, buy.

Our mission was to get all kinds of pseudo-junk food that was chock full of preservatives so it couldn't possibly have any contaminants in it, go bad, or need to be properly handled for an immune-compromised diet. I figured ice cream was a shoo-in, and cereal, chips and crackers were a close second. But Andrew had other plans. With an apple in one hand, he jerked his head to the side, extracted a handwritten list from his shirt pocket, and took off down the cereal aisle. With gleaming eyes, he grabbed a basket and headed straight for the meat section and didn't even slow when I waved a box of Reese's Puffs in his direction.

"I would like the rack of lamb in the case," I heard him say to the butcher.

Oh hell no! I started to jog down the aisle, slowing only to shove the Puffs on a shelf next to a box of gluten free granola.

"Thank you, but we can't buy that today," I told the butcher as he put the dinosaur-like carcass on the scale.

Andrew pointed to the back counter. "I sure like the brown paper you wrap it in," he said brightly.

I looked the butcher in the eye, shaking my head. "We're not buying it."

The butcher cocked his head in question, leaving the lamb ignored, its bony white fingers pointing to the ceiling. Red digital numbers flickered on the front of the scale as if unsure whether or not to land on the weight.

"I'm making dinner tonight," Andrew said, as if it were a fact I was unaware of. "Robert Irvine has some excellent ideas for lamb and roasted potatoes and asparagus because they make your brain smart."

I didn't give a damn what Robert Irvine thought, and I really hated the Cooking Channel. I glared back at my smiling bank robber. Then Andrew turned to me and did the most extraordinary thing. He kissed me. A quick press of his lips to my mouth, his breath steamy through the fabric of the mask. I raised my hand to my face as if to catch it. It was the single most affectionate thing he had done. Ever.

Without another word, the butcher wrapped the lamb, slapped a sticker on the front and handed it to Andrew. "I'm sure your mom will enjoy that dinner, young man," he said, winking at me.

We ate a fifty-five dollar dinosaur skeleton for dinner that night. In his own words, Andrew rocked it.

Chapter 32

We were still making three trips to the SCCA in Seattle each week as we neared Day 70. This was both a comfort and royal pain in the butt, as it took up most of the day. On this particular trip, Andrew was receiving an immunoglobulin (IVIG) infusion to boost his immune system, and we were expecting to hear the results of his latest chimerism tests. Jon was back at work and Hannah in school. Everyone was back to a normal routine except Andrew and me.

I was mid-way through my commute when I heard a voice from the passenger seat. "Uh, mom?"

"What?"

"You know the shoe I have on?"

"Yeah."

"Well, it's a little roomy."

"Like what? What do you mean?" I asked, impatient.

I glanced at the clock, calculating that we could make it in time if I managed to avoid every red light on Eastlake Avenue.

"I dunno," he said, squirming in his seat.

"What's wrong with the shoes?" I demanded, becoming more and more frustrated with his cryptic way of communicating.

"It seems something is missing."

"Like what?"

"Those inserty things."

"What?"

"And my socks."

"You don't have socks?"

"Well, I do. They're at home. And my other shoe."

I looked down into the passenger foot well. Sure enough, Andrew was only wearing a left shoe. The other foot was bare. I raked my fingers through my hair the way Jon did when he was exasperated with me. Was I this infuriating to him? I hoped not.

When we arrived, I knew they would never allow Andrew upstairs with bare feet. Leaving him alone in the car, I ran up to the gift shop and bought a pair of non-skid slipper socks with crimson and gold flowers on the top of each foot. Then I went up to the radiology lab on the second floor and hijacked some of those papery blue elastic footie cover-ups you find at the paint store.

With his makeshift shoes, Andrew and I carefully navigated the tightly packed parking garage. People emerged from their cars in all states of being to slowly make their way to the floors above. If you are unprepared for the reality of this secret world, it can be very overwhelming. Patients are in all stages of cancer treatment, bone marrow transplant preparation and recovery. The bulk of the population is bald and most are struggling to remain at an acceptable weight.

Perhaps the most disconcerting sight is the color of people's skin. After so many visits to this isolated world, it was easy for me to guess at the condition of people's bodies by looking into their faces. Some faces were grey — the color of ashes — some had a yellow hue, and others were as pale as a porcelain doll. Sometimes, I saw bright eyes shining out from drawn, angular faces, connecting with my own in a silent exchange of hope. Like so many others, Andrew was pale, bald, and weak, yet he possessed a burning sense of determination behind his eyes. He was fighting, finding his own way in this foreign world where we had landed.

As we were led to one of twenty-three infusion bays that day, I realized we had joined yet another tribe: The tribe of survivors. An incredible feeling of gratitude washed over me. I wanted to burst through the curtain of each bay, shake every patient's hand, thank them for being brave and for bringing us hope simply by just being there.

Dr. Burroughs stopped by in the middle of Andrew's infusion. "It's a good day, Andrew! Your numbers keep trending up. It seems you and your sister are getting along well!" She smiled and handed me a stack of papers with his most recent chimerism numbers.

Andrew grunted, barely tearing his eyes from his iPad.

"She bugs me. Hannah. She makes me eat zucchini and won't let me watch the Cooking Channel. She's worse than Food Nazi here," he said, jabbing a finger in my direction. Despite trying for an insult, a sheepish grin spread across his face.

Six hours later, we shuffled back down to the parking garage to head home. No one asked him about his shoes.

Day 100 came and went without much fanfare. Andrew continued to struggle with GVHD in his gut, but another slow taper of prednisone seemed to keep everything at a low simmer. There were days, and sometimes weeks, when I feared the worst, but like Dr. Burroughs had wisely counseled, we began to live for each day. And Day 115 was a good day.

"Andrew, would you please unload the dishwasher?" I asked, dropping two heavy grocery bags on the counter.

"You know I can't touch dishes. Germs," he said.

"Dirty dishes. These *clean* dishes have your name written all over them."

"Not interested," he said with a smirk.

"Well, I'm not either. That's why you're doing them," I replied, throwing a clean dishtowel in his general direction.

Andrew made a half-baked attempt at unloading the dishwasher before scrambling out the door and running across the yard to the hen house.

Shortly after our 'Hazmat' appointment with Dr. Burroughs, Andrew had fashioned his own Hazmat suit from an old pair of coveralls, rubber kitchen gloves, motorcycle boots and a full facemask helmet, which he wore all spring. He was recently freed of it after promising to change his clothes and wash his hands immediately following contact with any of the chickens. Since then, he and Frightful had been inseparable.

While I finished unloading groceries, I watched Hannah approach Andrew. He was sitting in the coop with Frightful, seemingly oblivious to brewing storm clouds that had kicked up a chilly wind. Four new adolescent chicks wandered the perimeter, keeping a wary eye on the queen of the hen house.

"Hey birdy-bird. I want a job like this!" He pointed to his iPad, where Alton Brown was hosting a current episode of *Cutthroat Kitchen*. "I want to be a chef in a kitchen that is huuuge! One that has a deep fryer like the ones I showed you. You know I have mad knife skills."

He pantomimed chopping motions on his lap, keeping his fingers straight to avoid contact with the imaginary blade. Frightful sat quietly, waiting for the rest of the story. Andrew absently patted her back. She clucked. A few feathers blew off and scattered in the wind. He shoved her inside his jacket.

"I don't know why you insist on molting this time of year. Don't you get cold?" he asked.

Andrew zipped his coat part way and leaned against the fence — two friends lounging in companionable silence.

Hannah and Sawyer joined him in the coop. "What are you two talking about?" she asked, chucking a tennis ball into the woods. Sawyer flew out of the coop, leaped over a glossy clump of salal, and was gone in an instant.

"That's classified information," Andrew said.

"Does Frightful know you want to be a chef?" she asked.

"Yep. She thinks it's cool."

Sawyer came back with his ball and a beard full of wet leaves. She threw the ball again, but this time he stayed, flopping down at her feet.

"Frightful missed you when you were in the hospital," Hannah said, twirling a feather between her fingers.

Andrew squeezed the chicken's beak and she let out a series of clucks in protest. "She talked to me. In my head," he said.

"When?"

"When I was sick."

Hannah stood there, pondering her brother's words.

"She loves you, you know."

"She's my birdy-bird," Andrew replied. He stood up and dusted off his pants before opening the door to the laying boxes. "Let's check for eggs, Frightful."

The rest of the chickens squeezed past his legs and scattered into the yard. Andrew put three eggs into the pocket of his silky basketball shorts and marched back in the kitchen.

"Got another green one!" he shouted above the vacuum cleaner, then hightailed outside again before I could call him back.

A minute later, I looked up to catch a glimpse of riotous red chemo-curls and a pair of hands pressing Frightful to the window. She looked like one of those Foster Farms chicken ads. The one where the plumped up 'imposter' chicken had smacked into a moving vehicle.

"Back-ACK!" I heard through the glass. Then there was a whole lot of chortling before the bird disappeared and a skinny boy took off across the lawn.

"Why does he keep bringing chickens in the house?" Hannah asked when I finished the vacuuming.

"I don't know. Maybe he thinks they're human?"

She rolled her eyes and mumbled something that sounded like, "That's really dumb."

I pretended I didn't hear her.

* * *

Eight months later, our family squeezed into one long row of the auditorium where Andrew would graduate from high school. His entire high school education had been compressed into ten short months. He took a cooking class and American history. The other classes were a crash course in growing up.

Sitting on the aisle was Sue. Andrew had invited her as his guest of honor, and when she arrived, he handed her a new tissue paper drawing of Shadow.

"For you to keep," he said, dropping it in her lap. "See? No more Hickman line. But he has a broken foot now. Jumped too high." He gave her a goofy smile and skipped to the front of the room to sit with his class.

Jon put an arm around Hannah's shoulders and reached for my hand. "I can't believe we're here," he spoke in my direction.

I squeezed his hand and nodded, tears welling at the back of my eyes before the ceremony had even begun. Introductions were made, and then Andrew stepped up to the microphone with his kinky crazy-hair and an untucked shirt.

I looked to Jon in surprise. "Did you know about this?"

"Nope."

Andrew began to read from a stack of notecards. "I owe my life to my sister, Hannah," he said.

Grandma Connie reached for the Kleenex at the end of the aisle and passed it down.

"She donated her bone marrow to me when I was sick so I could get my power back. She made me eat zucchini when I got home from the hospital. Now I am better and I plan to be a chef someday."

The audience clapped politely. Andrew waved his arm in a wide arc and pointed to the back of the room. "Lights! Camera! Action!"

A picture of Frightful popped onto the screen at the front of the auditorium. I stifled a giggle.

"I have a touch of autism," he said to his audience.

I snorted as laughter and tears warred for control. Jon dug an elbow into my ribs and someone from the row behind us passed me a tissue.

Andrew turned to look at the screen, then jabbed a finger in the air, "Next!"

An elaborate PowerPoint chart displayed a variety of chickens with bullet point lists beneath each one. To the right was a sketch of a skinny boy in pants with spiky red hair and a cape. The title on the screen read: *Why I Think Chickens Have Autism.*

Jon and I sat in stunned silence as Andrew listed the ways he thought chickens were similar to people with autism.

"Chickens look at you with their beak," he said, reading off a crinkled notecard. "They don't look you in the eye because their eyes are on the sides of their head." He gestured to the screen, where a giant picture of a chicken head loomed over the audience. "Chickens like to talk to themselves unless they are laying an egg, then they talk to everyone really loud. Buck-buck. Buck-ACKKK!"

A few snickers rippled through the room and I felt my face redden.

"They like to find quiet places to lay in the dirt where nobody will bother them," he said, reading by rote the words his teacher had typed for him.

How had my son made these connections? I reached for Jon's hand and squeezed, the heat in my face spreading to the rest of my body. I heard my mom rip a few Kleenex from the box and pass it back to Connie. The audience sat silently, enthralled.

"My chicken, Frightful, is most like me because she likes to be near other chickens, but nobody forces her to talk or play. She just likes to hang out."

An unfamiliar picture flashed on the screen — a grainy shot of Andrew and Frightful on the porch, presumably deep in conversation. I wondered if his teacher took it when he visited our house earlier in the year.

"But most of all, chickens are smart, even if the world thinks their brain is too small to understand things."

The snickers from moments before turned to sniffles as parents and friends of other autistic and special needs kids realized that my son had honed in on the truth. He *was* smart. He felt deeply, and he knew himself, perhaps more than most of us did.

The last photo appeared. "This is Frightful," Andrew said. "She is my secret-keeper."

I held my breath as I studied the photo he had chosen. It was my favorite. Taken when he was thirteen, while cradling Frightful in his arms, the photo showed a look of immense joy on his face. I remembered dressing him that day in a crisp white shirt and combing his hair back with Jon's hair gel. I had been determined to get the perfect family photo of the four of us. But after two hours, with little success by our hired photographer, Andrew had run to the coop in search of Frightful. On the way to her car, the photographer took a few quick shots of my son and his bird. That photo is still my favorite today.

The screen went black and Andrew quietly joined his classmates in the front row. The audience breathed — an almost imperceptible pause. Then they stood to applaud the autistic boy who had somehow articulated the truth.

Chapter 33

Of all the stories I have read about heroes, for one thing I am certain: We can all be heroes in our own lives, even with all our flaws, baggage, fears, and uniqueness. Not one of us is perfect. If I were to continue to strive for the perfect 'normal' life, I would be sadly disappointed. It doesn't exist. The grass is not greener on the other side. The next-door neighbor doesn't have a better life than I do. It's just different, with a different set of problems. Even Andrew's heroes have their own Kryptonite. And just like us, their story never really ends. There is always another chapter, a sequel, another movie. A hero goes through the same trials as us mere mortals, and the story still goes on.

When I ask myself when our story will be finished, I find I cannot answer. Will it be the day Andrew is set free from all the medications, infusions, and appointments? Will there come a day when I get a call saying, "Your son is well now, he has no sign of GVHD, no Trisomy 8 in his body?" Will I believe it? Will I lay my head down that night, allowing the fears and anxieties of the last two decades to melt away into the earth? Or do I sweep the nightmare under the carpet and pretend it never happened? Is it possible to feel whole again? Do I really *want* to be the person I once was? The truth is, I don't think I would fit in her skin.

All these questions were bombarding me as I set the table for dinner. I was adapting a favorite soup recipe to Andrew's dietary restrictions. 'Mommy Minestrone', my children called it when they were little, and they had asked for it by name today. As I pulled ingredients from the pantry, I heard Hannah and Andrew in the playroom down the hall, bickering over an X-Box game.

"Just play this one with me, then I will play HALO with you," Hannah pleaded.

"Noooo, Hannah!" he grumped, followed by the sound of video games being knocked over. I sucked in my breath, knowing how long Hannah had worked to stack and organize them. I peered around the corner to catch a shock of red hair exiting through the garage door. Hannah called out to her brother. Silence. A minute passed before the sound of the television floated into the kitchen, and the faint glow of the screen seeped into the dark at the end of the hall.

Gathering my stack of carrots, celery, onions, and a zucchini from the garden, I set about dicing them for my soup. Finn was at my feet, hoping for scraps to fall off the table and into his mouth. "It's not gonna happen," I told him, nudging a furry rump with my toe.

Dropping the veggies into a soup kettle hot with olive oil and freshly minced garlic, I slowly begin to stir. *Just until the onions become glassy,* I told myself.

Hannah's heated words drowned out the TV as she began arguing with Andrew again. When did they start arguing so much? What was the problem this time? I couldn't tell. As long as nobody was mortally wounded, I figured they could settle it on their own.

Without thinking, my hands chopped a bunch of fresh basil, then plucked tender leaves from the woody stems of an oregano plant. They would go into the soup after the tomatoes, beans, and chicken broth. And then, at the very end, when the flavors had time to meld, I would add salt and pepper and red pepper flakes for a little heat.

My little radio behind the kitchen sink crackled. Laura Story's comforting voice streamed into the kitchen in a staccato of static. Jon had offered to wire the kitchen for speakers, but I liked my scratchy little radio. Laura was singing "Blessings." I swayed to the music, singing:

'Cause what if your blessings come through raindrops?
What if your healing comes through tears?
What if a thousand sleepless nights are what it takes to know?
You're near

What if my greatest disappointments or the aching of this life?
Is the revealing of a greater thirst this world can't satisfy?
What if trials of this life?
The rain, the storms, the hardest nights
Are your mercies in disguise.

I continued to hum, reflecting on God and how my vision of Him had changed in the past years. I knew in the very deepest part of me that He was not only a man. He was the lake, the light, and the wise women who counseled me. God used the nurses and doctors who helped us—Julie, Sue, Becki, Anne, Diana, Leah—and everyone else who arrived when we needed them. God was the color of the Parisian sky in my oil pastels, and was in my fingers that created the picture of my flaming heart. God was the chicken that loved my son, who called for him at the gate every morning.

I thought about how we were all moving through our grief. How it was finding its place in our lives, shaping us, refining us, changing us. The great Alchemist had done his job, and somehow we had emerged through the fire, forged of stuff altogether stronger than the individual pieces that went into the making.

For me, acceptance of this life had been difficult. It wasn't until I was willing to live into the reality of our story that I was able to let go of the picture perfect plan I had counted on. Once I accepted our new way of being, I wondered why I hadn't done it sooner. It wasn't simple or easy, but it felt so natural, so right. I had finally made my peace with it.

My singing was interrupted by Andrew shouting from the hallway. "You still can't sing, Mom! You'd never make it on *American Idol!*"

I shouted back down the hall, "You're wrong! I'm sure I'll be in the top ten!"

The sound of a resumed video game floated into the kitchen. I breathed in deeply, then sighed, as the pleasure of preparing a meal for my family registered in my overtired brain.

When dinner was ready, I wandered down the hall to invite the kids to eat. Jon was due home any minute. I found Hannah sprawled across the day bed, her chin in her hands, feet up the back wall with her toes making circles around a long forgotten dinosaur poster. Andrew was sitting in a chair with Frightful in his lap, absently playing with her wing while talking to the television. Frightful looked up as I walked into the room, staring at me with her yellow eyes. "We're all good here," she seemed to say. I put my hand across my mouth to conceal a smile.

Hannah caught my eye with a look that said, "I *tried* to tell him!"

My first instinct was to admonish him, repeat exactly what Hannah's eyes had conveyed: *chickens don't come in the house,* but something held me back. It was like a set of arms wrapped themselves around me, held me in place and said, "Look! Look at what is here in front of you! What do you see?"

My mind worked slowly, assembling together the pieces of the picture. We were home. We were okay. My grown children were bickering like siblings do. Andrew was healthy, his face just now showing some color. After graduation, with the help of a job coach, he had landed a part-time job as a prep-chef in a local catering kitchen. In a few short weeks, Hannah would be starting her junior year in high school.

The playroom, now a media room, was a mess, littered with empty cups, plates of half eaten snacks, and piles of video games spilling from the shelves. It had been an unremarkable day — nothing special or out of the ordinary. We were simply living.

I heard Jon's car in the drive as an answer formed in my mind.

What did I see?

I saw that we were living out the answers to our agonizing prayers. We had been given a new life, one we were still learning to embrace. We discovered that a willingness to change was not only the secret to survival, but the secret to happiness. And out of that would come joy — someday.

I imagined Jon walking in to this scene. What would *he* see? Would he notice the mess, the unmade bed, and a dusty chicken sitting on our son's lap? Or would he sense the magic that lay beyond the mess? Would he understand the significance?

The door to the garage clicked shut and I felt Jon behind me, his hands dropping the usual stack of mail and bills at our feet. His arms wrapped around me tightly, replacing the invisible arms that held me back just moments before. He shifted his weight so his chin rested on the top of my head, and I felt him take in the scene before us: looking from Andrew, to his chicken, to Hannah sprawled on the bed with a smile. So ordinary, yet extraordinary. My hands reached up behind me, searching for Jon's face. He grasped them in his own hands, bringing my palms to the sides of his head, then sliding his hands down my shoulders, my arms, and finally to my waist where he pulled me in close.

"I'm home," he spoke into my hair.

As I stood there in that room, anchored to the earth by my husband's arms, I knew without a doubt that I lived in the company of heroes.

Epilogue

My twenty-year-old son was on the porch, perched in an ancient green wicker chair. He shifted his weight, paint flecked off, leaving a grassy-colored ring around the base of each leg. Frightful was on his lap, nesting in the space between his knees.

Andrew reached for her beak, pulling her head towards him. "So you can see me better," he said. He patted her silky feathers, mottled in blacks, caramel, and gold. A lone tail feather escaped, twirling to the ground. "Mom is telling our story tonight, Frightful. To a herd of people that are gonna be all dressed up like she is."

Frightful leaned forward, her beady bird-eyes blinking.

"I wonder what Mom will say? Will she tell them the important stuff? I told her to tell those people about you. You're the only one who knows what we've been through. Nobody else understands, except maybe Sue. I guess Mom does a little bit, too. But she wasn't there in our head. She doesn't know what it was like. She doesn't understand why we had to leave and go to a special place inside our head where nobody could touch us. You and me and Katniss and Iron Man and Shadow were there. Especially Shadow. He was there the whole time. He got sick, too, and we had to fix him. But he is better now. He is happy now."

Frightful pulled her beak free, craned her neck around and stood up, her scaly feet clutching Andrew's leg for balance. Then there was a fluffing of feathers, an arching of wings, and a full body shake before she sat down facing out toward the world. A low crooning, followed by a *chirp!* came from her chest—a song she sang only for Andrew.

"Coo-coorrr. Krrillll...Chirp. CHIRP!"

I was there all along, Andrew. I remember.

Andrew shifted again, this time tucking her under his arm.

I set my overnight bag in the hall and went in search of my purse. "Are you ready to come in, Andrew?" I called through the open door.

That night, I would be sharing our story at an annual fundraiser for Seattle Children's Hospital and the Children's Autism Center. Word of our journey had traveled to the right set of ears and it was determined we fit the theme of the event perfectly. We were their two-for-one deal.

It was my first time speaking in front of an audience and I was allotted nine minutes to sum up the last twenty years of our lives with Andrew. For days, a mixture of anticipation and terror plagued me. At night, I was haunted by visions of falling off the stage, becoming ill, or losing my voice. I knew I had only one chance to command the attention of an audience that had been guests at too many fundraisers, had heard too many compelling stories, and were always asked to dig deeply into their pockets. What would make my story any different?

The first draft of my speech filled thirteen pages. When I finally dared to speak the words aloud, I was home, alone. I set my iPhone on timer, perched it on the back of the bathroom sink, and closed the door. When I finished reading, it read twenty-three minutes.

"I can't seem to get my mind wrapped around the right words," I told Jon as we finished the dishes one night.

He gave me a pat answer. "I know whatever you say, it'll be great."

I wasn't as confident.

The next day I rewrote the speech. Then I cut and rewrote the speech again. The iPhone in my bathroom hideaway said twelve minutes when I read this time. A friend joined me at Starbucks later that day where she cut and rearranged my story even more.

"Speak only the words that matter to you most," she said, making the last edit. "Imagine you're telling your story to a stranger. Give them the highlights right away, give them a reason to listen to you," she said.

In the end, after the final edits, I was able to weave the fabric of our lives together as a family doing our best to raise a child who was autistic and critically ill.

Before leaving for the Gala, I went in search of Andrew. I found him at the kitchen table absorbed in his new *Calvin & Hobbes* book, surrounded by a bowl of grapes, a jug of Betty Crocker frosting, and a red velvet cake mix.

"We'll be home in the morning. Grandma Cherry will spend the night with you and Hannah," I told him. It felt like such a normal thing to say and do, that I almost giggled.

"You're talking about me tonight, aren't you?" he asked without looking up from his book.

Surprised by his sudden interest, I replied, "I am. I'm talking about our family, too."

I could see his mind making calculations, his face contorting as thoughts tumbled around. "Okay, but be sure to tell them about Frightful," he said, reaching for a handful of grapes.

While Jon loaded our car with our two overnight bags, I ran upstairs to deliver a gift to Hannah. She wasn't in her room, so I tucked the little box and a card into the folds of her quilt—the same one that traveled to the hospital with her. It read:

"My Dear Hannah,
I wouldn't have a story to tell,
were it not for you. You are my hero.
Love, Mom"

Jon and I joined the silent auction before dinner. Women in glittery gowns and cocktail dresses made their way through rows of auction items, while men in tuxedos clustered in groups enjoying samples of the Washington wines to be auctioned later that night. For a long time, I hovered at the far end of the Mezzanine, watching as people spilled from the elevators and melted into the crowd. It felt surreal, like I was stepping back into real time after having been away from the world for a lifetime.

After dinner was served, I caught sight of the event coordinator. She flashed her hand at me, "Five minutes," she mouthed.

I quickly took a few bites of my entrée and felt it lodge halfway down my throat. I guzzled water and dropped a handful of extra strength Tums into my mouth in an effort to abate the feeling that I might barf all over the microphone once I made it to the stage.

Minutes later, I was introduced to a noisy and festive audience. I stood on the podium, with Jon at my side, gazing into a sparkling crowd of four hundred. The Fairmont Olympic Hotel ballroom was crowded with an assortment of Seattle's elite — high tech executives, philanthropists, big money private donors, hospital guilds, and the best doctors in the medical community — people who expected to be entertained, to be moved, to be impressed. What qualified me to be the one to speak to their hearts tonight?

I thought of my friend coaching me the day before. "Stand tall, but not stiff. Don't lock your knees, don't grip the podium, don't wring your hands. Look at the crowd. Smile. Gesture. It's easy. Piece of cake."

My hands were shaking. I grabbed onto the podium. I felt like I might be sick. But then I paused, allowing the sounds of the dining room to slowly register in my ears. I heard the chime of forks hitting china, servers questioning, wine goblets filling, and the growing hum of festive conversation. Jon touched my shoulder, sending a wordless signal of confidence: *You can do this.*

I scanned the crowd until I met a solitary face of anticipation. Keeping hold of her eyes, I leaned into the microphone and told her my secret.

"My son's best friend is a chicken named Frightful. He taught her to ride in his arms while cruising the neighborhood on his electric bike."

The woman in the red ball gown put down her fork and smiled back at me. The room was silenced. Looking directly into the faces of the crowd, I knew my story would be heard by those that needed to hear a message of hope.

I continued. "The young man I've had the privilege to raise is an expert on World War II history, is obsessed with superheroes, and is an accomplished chef who hopes to own his own restaurant someday. He is quirky, kind, frustratingly rigid, strong, persistent, and one of the bravest young men I know. He is also autistic."

I looked out to the crowd. I could tell I had their attention— the leaning in, hands in their laps, a look of anticipation on their faces. I could do this. I had been waiting a lifetime to tell our story, and now I had an audience.

"But our story doesn't end there. When Andrew started school, a predictable pattern of high fevers and painful ulcerations would emerge for ten days of every month. And then I overheard Andrew tell Frightful he thought his body was trying to kill him..."

I told the audience about Dr. Torgerson, about the bone marrow transplant, about medical miracles, and what I was learning about faith. When I finished, I sought out the woman in red. From the center of the ballroom, she smiled, brought her hand to her mouth and pulled it away in the gesture of a kiss—a similar gesture I had seen my children do many times before. She smiled and nodded, then stood with the rest of the room in applause.

As I descended the podium, I caught sight of Dr. Torgerson, his bright smile, his unmistakable gold-rimmed spectacles and silk bowtie. He waved, a shy wave, and mouthed the words: *Well done.*

* * *

The sound of running feet reached my ears long before I was fully awake. Andrew had been waking up early for days, running through the pre-dawn light to fetch Frightful in the coop. Each morning, I found them on the porch wrapped in Jon's down jacket and a cozy fleece blanket.

"Frightful's voice sounds different," Andrew told me one morning. I had joined him on the porch, wrapped in my own blanket. I shivered as the December air pushed its way through the folds, forcing me to pull it tighter around my neck.

"How so?" I asked.

"It's lower. See?" He tapped the top of her beak with his finger and she clucked.

"She sounds fine to me," I said. I hadn't noticed anything different besides the fact that she always seemed to be in the process of molting.

"Her voice is different. She's quiet," he said, determined to make me understand.

Frightful started to coo deep in her chest. It sounded exactly like her familiar chicken song.

"How come you're out here so early?" I asked. "It's barely light."

"Frightful wants to talk, so we're talking," he replied.

Frightful nestled her body further into the folds of the blanket. One glassy eye stared at me through a half closed lid. I left the two of them on the porch and went in search of tea. Jon and Hannah would be up soon, and I wanted a few quiet moments to myself before I had to face the demands of my day.

When I wandered out to the coop that afternoon to gather eggs, I saw Frightful alone, sitting in a small patch of filtered sunshine.

"Craaww-cruk-cruk. Craaww."

I desperately wanted to know what she was trying to tell me.

"Craaww-cruk-cruk. Wraaawwwww."

My frustration mounted and I felt tears push at the back of my eyes.

"I don't know what you're trying to say, little bird."

I reached down to scoop her in my arms and she let out a weak *chirp* and pecked at my hand. I wondered if I had hurt her. I set her back down and the two of us sat in silence.

She didn't speak again.

Jon left for work early the next morning, leaving me the luxury of spreading out across the whole queen-sized bed. I scooted to the hump in the middle and immediately fell into a deep sleep.

Minutes later, Andrew came tearing into the room. "Something happened to Frightful!" he cried.

I sat bolt upright, shaking off the remnants of an early morning dream. Andrew stood at the foot of my bed, still as a statue made of stone.

"Something happened," he whispered this time. "She fell off the perch."

My heart sank. It was like hearing the voice of my eight-year-old boy, the one who told his pet chicken that his body was trying to kill him. I suddenly understood what Frightful was trying to tell me the day before. She was saying goodbye.

Andrew led me to the coop, his long, awkward strides slowing the closer we got. I knew what I would see when we opened the door. I knew I would be teaching my son about death—about grief and love and loss. I would tell him grief, love, and loss are woven tightly together, none fully experienced without the others.

I opened the door and saw Frightful's small body crumpled below the perch.

"We'll find a special place for her," I told him as I lifted her into my arms. She felt too light, like she had left only the shell of herself behind.

Andrew fisted both hands at his sides, then brought them to his face to hide his eyes. I recognized the gesture. It was similar to the one he used to show Frightful what pain felt like. He sniffed, tears leaked through his fists and dropped to the floor.

"Do you think she's sleeping?" he asked.

I didn't know how to answer. His mind knew she was gone, but his heart was in denial. That's the thing about letting go. We never know how long it will take. Sometimes it happens in a flash, and other times, we have to struggle through the hard work of grief.

"Frightful is not sleeping, Andrew," I said through my own tears. "She lived a long life and passed away. Let's find her a safe place to rest her body."

Andrew's face crumpled into an outward picture of grief, but he remained silent, standing behind me in the doorway. I wanted him to cry out, rage, beat the walls of the coop with his fists at the unfairness of life. That's what I wanted to do. Yet I wasn't surprised at his reaction; it was almost always counterintuitive. I knew his emotions would go deep, sinking into the depths of his soul to be processed in his own unique way.

"But where did she go?" he asked, his voice calm and curious. "I loved her."

He crossed both hands over his heart, and this time, I sobbed. I had no answer. How could I explain this mystery to my son who thinks in the literal? I was still absorbing the shock of it myself.

"She will be okay," he said, reaching out to pet my hands that cradled his best friend.

Was he talking about me? Himself? All of us who had grown to love her, too? I knew we would hear about Frightful's death for a long time. I knew he would make the symbol for bird when he was especially missing her comfort, or he would make a benign remark about her over a bowl of spaghetti that reminded him of the worms she dug up in Jon's garden. But the secrets she kept would be interjected into conversations with no obvious connection. Those, I would have to riddle out in order to discover what my son was really trying to say. When I unraveled those secrets, I would realize that my son's way of processing life was brilliant.

When Sue pulled into the driveway a week later, Andrew met her outside. "Follow me," he said.

He led her into the woods, past the huckleberry bush and to a depression at the base of a fir tree.

"Sit here," he told her, crouching on his knees next to his friend. He pointed to a stack of newly unearthed stones ringed around a rotting branch that stood on its end. Strips of moss draped across the tops of the rocks.

"Frightful is gone. Mom said she was a very old lady. I don't know where she went, but I think she's in heaven now," he said.

Sue put an arm around her friend and pulled him close. His body went rigid, then relaxed.

"I think you're right," she said after a while. "Frightful had to be strong for you, now it's time for you to be strong for her. She would want that."

Andrew picked up a stick and scraped an "F" in the dirt. He surrounded the letter in a diamond shape, like Superman.

"I miss her with my whole heart," he said.

Sue traced the superhero symbol with her finger. "She still lives in your heart, Andrew. She will always be there."

Andrew stared at the rocks, dry-eyed. "But she was my birdy-bird." he said. He pinched his thumb and first finger together and placed his hand on his chest.

Sue covered his hand with hers, her heart breaking for her young friend. "I wonder if Frightful knew she had to stay until you could hold her again?" she said. "I think she needed to make sure you were okay."

The tears finally came, and Andrew wiped his nose on his sleeve. A ruffle of leaves broke the tension as a buff-colored hen cut through the salal and made her way to the clearing where Andrew and Sue sat.

"What are you doing here, Daisy Duke?" Andrew asked.

The young hen scratched, pecked a few times, then settled under the green canopy to witness Sue and Andrew's tribute to Frightful.

"Would you like me to tell you a story?" Sue asked after a while.

Andrew placed his hand in his lap, his fingers still fanned out in Frightful's symbol.

"Yes. And make sure this time Frightful has a cape."

~

Frightful was with us for over ten years. To this day, the place
we buried her is a protected piece of our yard. I know chickens
can't talk, but Andrew and Frightful had a bond—a soul-
speak—that went far beyond words. With all that Andrew had
to endure, Frightful was his confidant, his strength, and his
emotional oasis. With his loving sister's genetic assistance,
amazing healthcare professionals were able to address his rare
physical condition. But it was Frightful, the chicken, who saved
my son.

~

~ Survival Guide ~

Tips and resources for parents, caregivers, friends, and family

So you've found yourself in the middle of a raging storm? What do you do next?

When BIG things go wrong in my life, my natural instinct is to search for a way out. I don't want to feel the pain. But sometimes pain, discomfort or even an earthquake in our lives is what makes life real. Tragedy demands us to stop and assess who we are, what we are doing, and what choices we are making every day. A crisis affords us a moment of stillness before we take action. There is an odd pause when the storm hits that forces us to take inventory and stop any pretending we formerly had the energy to live with. That pause — that moment — is the place where grace has the chance to enter and we have the chance to recognize it.

Here are some practical things I learned about staying healthy, happy, and raw enough to recognize grace (if only a little!):

Tip 1: Take care of yourself first. You will do no one any good if you crash and burn. Lock the bathroom door. Take a breath. Hide in the car with your favorite song and weep. Whatever you choose to do, take care of yourself. FIRST!

Tip 2: Become part of a 'tribe.' Find the 3:00am people (it can be as few as one or two) in your life who are truth-tellers — those who will be honest with you, support you, laugh with you, love you, and stick with you even when your life is a disaster.

Tip 3: Surround yourself with people who will listen to you rant and will trust you will take action when you need to. When my son was young, I found many of these people were within the special needs parenting community. The best supporters made me laugh in the middle of my tragedy. They were often older, wiser, and more experienced than I.

Tip 4: Nurture your marriage. Raising a special needs child, or any major life crisis can fracture a marriage. Regroup *every* day, even if it's a simple text that says, 'I love you.' Throw a frisbee, go for a walk, watch a favorite comedy, or do whatever you do to remember why you started this journey in the first place. Take turns to give each other the grace to have a bad day. Carve out time to listen to one another — really listen — with your eyes and ears and heart.

Tip 5: Don't be afraid to **ask for help**. I resisted for many years until I was ready to crumble. There are many resources at a hospital including social workers, palliative care, ombudsman, and a chaplain.

Tip 6: Find someone to be your representative or 'Life Coordinator,' so you can **concentrate on the crisis**. Let them interface with questions and offers from well-meaning people.

Tip 6: Start a **blog**, or have someone do it on your behalf. It can be a simple way to communicate with a large group of people who want to know what is going on and find out how they can help. One friend used takethemameal.com to create a customized online sign-up sheet that made it easy for people to bring us meals.

Tip 7: Sleep is the ticket to sanity when you are in the hospital. It strengthens your immune system and allows you to make sane decisions. Invest in noise cancelling headphones or use earplugs. I use a facemask to block out the light. I've tried them all, and in my opinion, the best one is Bucky Eye Mask. Find it on Amazon.

Tip 8: Beware of making on-line purchases when you are sleep deprived. I like to **virtual shop** and add multiple items to my cart, dream about it, then exit the site before I am tempted to dig out my credit card.

Tip 9: Get outside and move! **Exercise** releases all those good hormones that keep your mind and body happy. Many hospitals and community centers offer restorative yoga classes. If you don't have enough time for a class, put on a jacket and take a walk, even in the rain. You may never FEEL like doing it. Do it anyway.

Tip 10: I learned how to **meditate**, and I use *Insight Timer*, a mindfulness app. My daughter uses *Relax Melodies: Sleep Zen Sounds* to help fall asleep. You'll find both online.

Tip 11: I started using a mantra, repeating a phrase whenever my mind would race with worry. I change up my mantra as need be, but I find "All is well right now" helps me reframe my thoughts and **stay in the moment.** Find one that suits you.

Tip 12: Keep a stash of **healthy food** at the hospital with you. When I was there for weeks, and then months, it became my solace at 1:00 a.m. when I finally realized I hadn't eaten all day.

Tip 13: Institutional toilet paper is like sandpaper. In order to avoid itchy butt, bring your own 2-ply **toilet paper** when you check in to the hospital.

Tip 14: A **smile** and an approachable demeanor go a long way when dealing with a medical team. Be polite, even if you have to grit your teeth. Know when to follow the advice of the team, and when to advocate for your loved one. You're the one who knows them best!

Tip 15: Bring a friend to important medical appointments to **take notes.** Ask lots of questions. Don't be afraid to disagree or ask for a second opinion.

Tip 16: Give yourself permission to feel. **Cry.** Cry a lot. Alone. With other people. In the car. It just might be what the doctor ordered! Crying has been proven to release toxins, kill bacteria, improve mood, relieve stress and boost communication. So go ahead, reach for the Kleenex and let go of your sorrows!

Tip 17: If a friend or loved one is in crisis, do NOT ask them what you can do, and do NOT tell them you feel helpless. They may have no idea what to ask for, and *they* are the ones who feel helpless. **Take action.** Do something that others would never think to ask of you. Clean toilets. Do laundry. Fill the refrigerator. Bring by healthy snacks, soft socks, new underwear, and lip balm. My neighbor shoveled three weeks of dog poop off my front lawn and cleaned the chicken coop. The night I came home and discovered what he had done, I cried.

Tip 18: Bring meals to the hospital for the caregiver. One family friend brought me a picnic breakfast of steel cut oats, a fresh fruit salad, breakfast muffins, and stuffed the basket with an assortment of tea bags. It was the first real meal I had eaten in days!

Tip 19: Reading was nearly impossible in the hospital because I couldn't concentrate long enough to keep the story straight. I appreciated magazines with short articles and lots of pictures, Sudoku, knitting, scanning news on my iPad, and binge **watching shows on Netflix**. My favorite series was *Friday Night Lights*.

Tip 20: Don't believe everything you read on the Internet. Give yourself a **break from social media** so you won't be tempted to compare yourself to others that look like they have a perfect life.

Tip 21: When I was going through the darkest days with my son, I decided to write a **daily gratitude list** and email it to one friend, the same friend, and she sent me a list back. It began changing my outlook on life. Now on hard days, I send my friend many lists to help get me through those hard days.

Tip 22: Start a **journal**. It actually helps to get your feelings out of your head and onto paper. You might keep one at home, one in your car, or a small one tucked in your purse. In addition to purging angsty feelings, I make a point to write funny things that my kids say. Looking back later, I am reminded of all the reasons why I love them so much.

Tip 23: Stop to **pet a dog or cat**, or watch birds soar across the sky. Animals have a way of grounding us and reminding us to live in the moment.

Tip 24: Visualize a mini vacation. With your eyes closed, picture a place (real or imagined) where you feel safe and relaxed. Using all your senses, feel yourself in comfortable clothes, hear pleasant sounds, see beautiful colors, taste something delicious. Visit this spot whenever you need to relax and de-stress.

Tip 25: Give yourself a pep-talk by reading from a daily devotional or gratitude book. I love the devotional, *Jesus Calling*, by Sarah Young, and a little gratitude journal called, *Daily Gratitude: 365 Days of Reflection*, by National Geographic.

Tip 26: Laughter truly is the best medicine! A hearty **laugh** is contagious. It reduces the stress response, increases resilience, boosts immunity, combats depression and relieves pain. When I was stuck in the hospital, I found that witty banter back and forth with a friend over text would break my cycle of stress and help me cope.

Here's a short list of resources to help get you started:

AUTISM
The word 'autism' can strike terror in the hearts of parents, leaving them feeling confused and helpless. Fortunately, there are countless resources on the Internet for information about autism, and chances are, your community and local school district will be able to guide you to help.

If you are just learning about ASD, I like the groups, Autism Speaks (autismspeaks.org), Autism Now (autismnow.org), and the National Autism Association (nationalautismassociation.org.)

If you are in Washington State, these are excellent resources:

University of Washington Autism Center
depts.washington.edu/uwautism/

Seattle Children's Autism Center
seattlechildrens.org/clinics-programs/autism-center/

Washington Autism Alliance & Advocacy
washingtonautismadvocacy.org

SELF CARE
I am a big fan of MBSR (Mindfulness Based Stress Reduction) developed by Jon Kabat-Zinn, at the University of Massachusetts Medical Center. MBSR is a program designed to assist people with pain and a range of conditions and life issues that can be difficult to treat in a hospital setting. It uses a combination of meditation, body awareness, and yoga to help people become more mindful of living in the present moment.

You can find more information about MBSR here:
http://www.umassmed.edu/cfm/
  mindfulnessnorthwest.com

HEALTH & WELLNESS
Taking care of your mind and body is equally important for both
patient and caregiver. Surrounding yourself with a supportive
network of people will help you strike a healthy balance in your
life.

Identify your sources of stress and seek out ways to cope. Get
moving, engage socially, avoid unnecessary stress, accept the things
you can't change, and make time for fun—even in the middle of life's
raging storms. Try volunteering in your community. People who
spend time helping others, get as many benefits as those they help.

Get help when you need it. Consider finding a skilled listener to
help support you through difficult times. A great resource for
therapists nationwide is: psychologytoday.com.

Feed your body good food! Eating fresh, in season, whole foods
helps to fuel our bodies and keep our minds alert. I love grazing
through cookbooks that educate me about the food I am putting
in my body. A couple of my favorites are: *Eat, Taste, Heal: An
Ayurvedic Guidebook and Cookbook for Modern Living,* and *Giada's
Feel Good Food, by Giada De Laurentiis.*

FAITH
Nothing makes you question the existence of God like a personal
tragedy. Don't be afraid to face these hard questions. Make time to
look for a safe and healthy faith community. If you bring up death,
doubt, or heavy drinking, and they look at you like you have three
heads, keep looking. A healthy faith community is comfortable with
you wherever you are in your own faith journey, without expecting
you to be someone you are not.

Stephen Ministries was helpful for me. They provide confidential, one-to-one care to people experiencing a difficult time in life, such as grief, divorce, job loss, chronic or terminal illness, relocation, or transition. For information about Stephen Ministry, go to their website: stephenministries.org. To find a care ministry near you, call: 314-428-2600.

CHICKENS

Having backyard chickens is all the rage. Not only are they easy to raise, you will have fresh, organic eggs filling your refrigerator every day! For anything you ever wanted to know about raising and caring for chickens, check out Gail Damerow's books. My favorite is called, *Storey's Guide to Raising Chickens*.

Want a fun weekend project? Try building a chicken tractor. There are tons of free plans and tutorials on the Internet that will keep you and your family entertained, and the chickens contained!

HUMAN-ANIMAL BOND

The human-animal bond is a mutually beneficial and dynamic relationship between people and animals that positively influences the health and well-being of both. Research has shown that connecting with animals eases stress, pain, and improves overall functioning in adults and children alike. If you are considering a service animal for your child or loved one, these sites can help lead you in the right direction: cci.org, servicedogsforamerica.org, 4pawsforability.org.

* * *

For a comprehensive, up-to-date resource guide, including a list of books, websites, blogs, movies, recipes and smartphone apps that have to do with autism, self care, health and wellness, faith, chickens, human-animal bond and more, go to my website:
www.kristinjarvisadams.com

Acknowledgements

The best advice I received while writing this book came from my editor, Lynn Price at Behler Publications, and my agent, Roger Williams. After they read my initial manuscript, I received an editorial letter saying, "More chicken." *More chicken?* How would I get inside the mind of a backyard hen? With the gentle guidance of Roger, I was able to step inside the mind of the bird that had the most profound impact on my son's life. In the end, I discovered the voices of hope in our story came not only from our chicken, but also from our faithful village. Those who supported us, cheered for us, and cried with us during twenty years of searching for answers. They are the people who continue to walk with us today.

Thank you to Jennifer Seber and Paula Dobkins. I couldn't ask for better sisters; Pete and Lynn Baker who took care of our animals on the days we couldn't make it home; Paul Hogben, Jon's lifelong friend who snuck 'contraband' into the hospital to watch Seahawks games; my book club women who sent meals and love; Sammamish Presbyterian Church who supplied care in countless ways; the Palliative Care Team at Children's who arranged for a private showing of *The Hunger Games* for Andrew; Woodinville Rotary for delivering an abundance of Valentines on a very lonely day; our blog followers who sent kind words and prayers; and finally, the person who hung from a cable to spray paint a message of hope on a beam outside our window. You all made us feel loved. You are the village.

But I most want to thank the love of my life, Jon, who is not only an incredible husband and father, but has supported me in everything I have set my heart to. To my children, Andrew and Hannah, who allowed me to share their story—every detail of their brave journey—because I knew it was a story that needed to be told. An eternal thank you to my parents, Terry and Cherry Jarvis, and Jon's parents, Larry and Connie Adams who have been an incredible support to us since the day our children were born. To Julie Tisdale and Becki Barrett, my early readers and dear friends who challenged me to dive deeply into the story to dig out the truth. Corbin Lewars who first read a jumbled pile of writing and helped me to discover the story hidden inside. To Sue Erland, Andrew's friend, companion, and comrade in adventure, her gentle voice I still hear coming from a recording in my son's room at night. To my 'wise women' who guided me safely through the most difficult days of my life: Carol Simon, Jeanne Snook, Carol Elliot, and L.A. To Anne Holmdahl, Diana Sonnega, and my Wednesday morning writing group—a powerful group of truth-tellers.

To those who never stopped believing they could help my son: Dr. Troy Torgerson, Dr. Lauri Burroughs, Dr. Rob Nohle, Dr. Merrell Wiseman, and Joan Suver, PA-C.

My deepest gratitude goes to all of the unnamed doctors, nurses and advocates at Seattle Children's Hospital, Seattle Cancer Care Alliance, and Fred Hutchison Cancer Research Institute for their unsurpassed level of care and expertise.

In loving memory of Larry H. Adams
a.k.a. "Grandpa Man"

Printed in the USA
CPSIA information can be obtained
at www.ICGtesting.com
JSHW022209140824
68134JS00018B/957

9 781941 887004